W9-CCB-079

the LODGE
CAST IRON
cookbook

**A Treasury of Timeless,
Delicious Recipes**

the LODGE CAST IRON cookbook

A Treasury of Timeless, Delicious Recipes

**COMPILED AND EDITED BY
PAM HOENIG**

Oxmoor HOUSE®

ISBN-13: 978-0-8487-3434-3
Library of Congress Control Number: 2011936504

Printed in the United States of America
Eighth Printing 2017

Oxmoor House
VP, Publishing Director: Jim Childs
Editorial Director: Susan Payne Dobbs
Creative Director: Felicity Keane
Brand Manager: Vanessa Tiongson
Senior Editor: Heather Averett
Managing Editor: Laurie S. Herr

The Lodge Cast Iron Cookbook
Project Editor: Sarah H. Doss
Senior Designer: Melissa Clark
Assistant Designer: Allison Sperando Potter
Director, Test Kitchen: Elizabeth Tyler Austin
Assistant Directors, Test Kitchen: Julie Christopher, Julie Gunter
Test Kitchen Professionals: Wendy Ball, R.D.; Allison E. Cox;
    Victoria E. Cox; Margaret Monroe Dickey; Alyson Moreland
    Haynes; Stefanie Maloney; Callie Nash; Catherine Crowell Steele;
    Leah Van Deren
Photography Director: Jim Bathie
Senior Photo Stylist: Kay E. Clarke
Associate Photo Stylist: Katherine Eckert Coyne
Assistant Photo Stylist: Mary Louise Menendez
Production Managers: Theresa Beste-Farley, Tamara Nall Wilder

Contributors
Writer/Editor: Pam Hoenig
Editorial Consultant: Mark Kelly
Copy Editors: Donna Baldone, Norma Butterworth-McKittrick,
    Carmine Loper, Barry Smith
Indexer: Mary Ann Laurens
Interns: Erin Bishop, Christine Boatwright, Maribeth Browning,
    Laura Hoxworth, Alison Loughman, Mamie McIntosh,
    Lindsay A. Rozier
Test Kitchen Professional: Kathleen Royal Phillips
Photographer: Mary Britton Senseney
Photo Stylists: Missy Crawford, Mindi Shapiro Levine,
    Lydia DeGaris-Pursell

Time Home Entertainment Inc.
Publisher: Richard Fraiman
VP, Strategy & Business Development: Steven Sandonato
Executive Director, Marketing Services: Carol Pittard
Executive Director, Retail & Special Sales: Tom Mifsud
Executive Director, New Product Development: Peter Harper
Director, Bookazine Development & Marketing: Laura Adam
Publishing Director: Joy Butts
Finance Director: Glenn Buonocore
Assistant General Counsel: Helen Wan

To order additional publications, call
1-800-765-6400 or 1-800-491-0551.

For more books to enrich your life, visit
oxmoorhouse.com

To search, savor, and share thousands of recipes,
visit myrecipes.com

Cover: Cranberry Apple Pie (page 260)
Back Cover: Shirred Eggs with Ham and Tomato (page 22) and Iron Skillet Roasted Mussels (page 95)

NOTE TO READERS:

The publisher of this book has made every reasonable effort to ensure that the activities in this book are safe if conducted as instructed and performed with reasonable skill and care. However, the publisher cannot and does not assume any responsibility or liability whatsoever for any damage caused or injury sustained while performing any of the activities contained in this book. You are solely responsible for taking all reasonable and necessary safety precautions when performing any of the activities contained in this book.

CONTENTS

ACKNOWLEDGMENTS

First and foremost, we want to offer heartfelt thanks and gratitude to the contributors who made this book possible. They include chefs, cooking school teachers and culinary educators, cooking show hosts, food writers, culinary bloggers, cookbook authors, National Cornbread Cook-off winners, the International Dutch Oven Society, Terlingua chili cook-off participants, and home cooks (including Lodge family members and employees, past and present) from all over the country and even Australia. When we came calling, asking whether they might be interested in contributing a recipe to this project, almost without exception the response was a ringing "Yes!" That unhesitating generosity, coupled with the culinary creativity of the individual recipes and the personal connection many of these contributors have to cast iron (please be sure to read A Cast Iron Memory and Crazy for Cast Iron stories you'll find sprinkled throughout the book for their anecdotes), has made working on this book an unparalleled pleasure.

A great big shout-out needs to go to Carolyn Kellermann-Millhiser, a great-granddaughter of our company's founder, Joseph Lodge, and Barbara Clepper, who assisted us in the selection of recipes from *A Skillet Full of Traditional Southern Lodge Cast Iron Recipes & Memories* cookbook.

We'd also like to offer a heaping helping of thanks to our friends (more like cousins) at Martha White, who work with Lodge to make the National Cornbread Cook-off one of the premier contests in the country.

We also want to thank the team at Oxmoor House for making this project possible.

welcome to our family's table

My great-great-grandfather Joseph Lodge would have difficulty recognizing the company he founded in 1896, with the brand presence of Lodge Cast Iron having grown to world-wide stature. We proudly continue the tradition of being a family-owned cookware manufacturer in the tiny town of South Pittsburg, Tennessee. That tradition also extends to our employees, many of whom are descendants of the original employees at Lodge.

Emerging from that familial bond is an intrinsic belief that every skillet, Dutch oven, griddle, serving piece, and grill pan should be as welcome on your family's table as it is on ours.

Our family's table stretches across generations to parents preparing countless meals for their children, grandchildren, and great-grandchildren, ofttimes using the same handed-down skillet, a moving reminder of our cookware's legacy of versatility and durability.

The table includes hundreds of thousands of camp cooking devotees attending competitions and enjoying delicious recipes that defy the senses; Scout leaders assisting youngsters earning cooking merit badges; nine-year-old 4-H'ers toting skillets to the main stage to compete in a cornbread cook-off during South Pittsburg's annual National Cornbread Festival; Japanese cooks preparing fabulous cuisine; restaurant chefs the world over utilizing countless cooking techniques to prepare appetizers, entrées, and desserts; and cooking show hosts with the popularity of rock stars and Oscar winners crafting an endless array of recipes with Lodge Cast Iron.

The Lodge Cast Iron family knows no boundaries. Our table is as rich in heritage as it is in flavor, and you're as welcome to the table today as folks were at the turn of the nineteenth and twentieth centuries.

With great appreciation for friends and customers for more than a century, and from every member of our family table to yours, we say, bon appétit, y'all!

H. Lee Riddle

H. Lee Riddle, great-great-grandson of Joseph Lodge
New Product Development Manager for Lodge Cast Iron
February 2012

LODGE CAST IRON: A SONG FOR A COOK'S SOUL

Ask any devotee of Lodge about their favorite cookware, and you will hear a constant refrain: "Cookware fads may come and go, but cast iron cookware is forever."

There are countless verses to support their claim.

In 1896, Englishman Joseph Lodge selected the tiny town of South Pittsburg, Tennessee, to be home to his foundry, and today it continues to produce cast iron skillets, Dutch ovens, griddles, kettles, and grill pans. Cast iron pots and kettles became popular in the seventh and eighth centuries, with cooks the world over singing praises about their versatility and durability.

The primary quality that inspires the devotion of Lodge fans is the heat-seeking nature of cast iron, a fact known and appreciated by everyone from George Washington's mother, Mary Ball Washington, who valued her cast iron cookware so much that it's mentioned in her will; to Lewis and Clark, who brought the cookware with them on their expedition of discovery; to twenty-first-century cooks who use it to bake, sear, broil, sauté, fry, braise, and stir-fry meals on their stove-tops, in their ovens, and over campfires.

Joseph Lodge

Tennessee is known for many things: frontiersman Davy Crockett, the Jack Daniel's Distillery, Elvis Presley, and Nashville, America's Music City. As the sole domestic manufacturer of cast iron cookware and the oldest family-owned cookware company in the United States, Lodge shares the stage with many of our state's luminaries; however, the universal acclaim for our cast iron cookware and its historical connection with our nation's past arguably places us as the soul of American cooking ("Thank you, thank you very much").

As the sole domestic manufacturer of cast iron cookware and the oldest family-owned cookware company in the United States, Lodge shares the stage with many of our state's luminaries; however, the universal acclaim for our cast iron cookware and its historical connection with our nation's past arguably places us as the soul of American cooking ("Thank you, thank you very much").

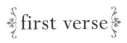
first verse
COMMITMENT TO QUALITY

Throughout the twentieth century, Lodge survived the development of numerous new metals for several enduring reasons: Cast iron is not only a superior conductor of heat, but it also heats slowly and evenly and retains heat longer than any other cookware. In addition, cast iron cookware resists scorching and burning, and it cooks food evenly—treasured attributes when frying or searing.

Not all cast iron cookware is created equal. In recent years, several brands of inferior imported cast iron cookware have entered the market. While the price might have initially been attractive, customers have come back to Lodge, their enthusiasm for our cookware backed by the stringent quality control of the Lodge foundry. Maintaining foundry traditions established centuries earlier and using a privately held metal formula that was developed just for cookware, each piece of Lodge Cast Iron is created by pouring molten iron into individual sand molds. Lodge metal chemistry is monitored with every pour, a standard not found in any other cast iron foundry in the world. Our exacting quality control produces cookware with legendary cooking performance that becomes better generation after generation.

﴾second verse﴿
COMMITMENT TO INNOVATION

Time moves forward. Technological advances bring about new products, and Lodge has kept apace with competition by updating, improving, and expanding the performance and use of its cast iron cookware.

For centuries, cast iron required a process called "seasoning" to create the much-revered easy-release, or natural nonstick, cooking surface. Early in this new century Lodge broke with cast iron cookware convention and introduced its Logic Series, with foundry seasoning, winning the *Good Housekeeping* "Good Buy Award" in 2003. Logic quickly transformed Lodge from a regional cookware manufacturer to a performer on the national stage, with cooks of all ages rediscovering the prized cooking principles of cast iron.

Lodge maintained the innovation trend in 2007 with the creation of the Signature Series: seasoned cast iron with stainless-steel handles. The series combines sophisticated styling with superior cooking performance, with the added benefit of handles that remain cool to the touch during stove-top cooking.

This innovation garnered first-place honors in the cookware category of the 2008 Housewares Association Design Award competition and the Best in Show award among 13 houseware categories (350 products), including lighting, kitchen electronics, home environment, and furniture.

Technological advances bring about new products, and Lodge has kept apace with competition by updating, improving, and expanding the performance and use of its cast iron cookware.

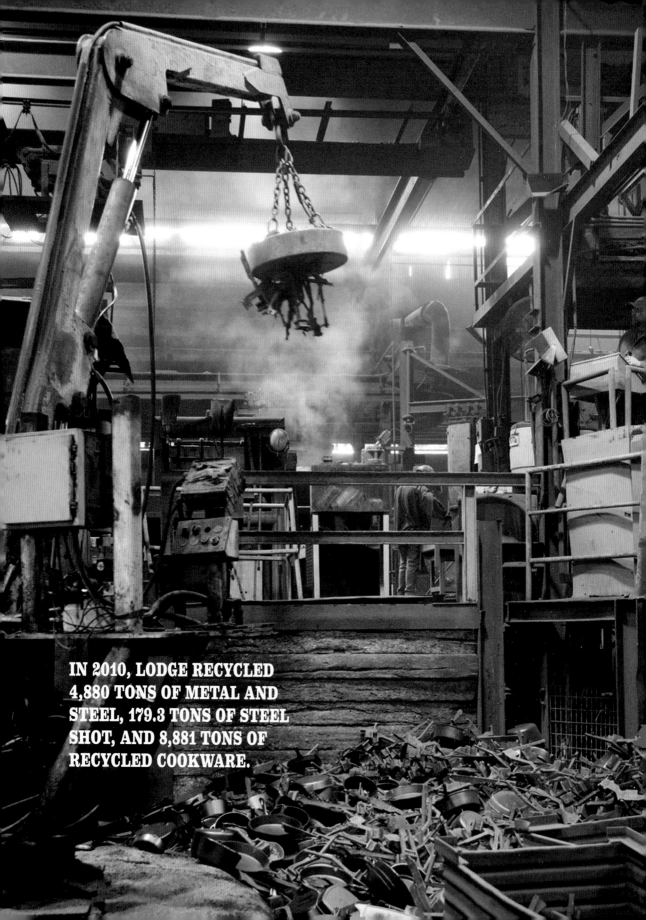

IN 2010, LODGE RECYCLED
4,880 TONS OF METAL AND
STEEL, 179.3 TONS OF STEEL
SHOT, AND 8,881 TONS OF
RECYCLED COOKWARE.

All accolades aside, superior cooking performance, product versatility, moderate prices, and depth of line are the foundation of Lodge's every success. Staying true to our founder's values, Lodge Skillets and Dutch Ovens are widely recognized as essential items in every kitchen. Lodge Grill Pans/Reversible Griddles take top honors in every product comparison test, and our Camp Dutch Ovens and Grills are "must haves" for campers.

third verse
GREEN IS MORE THAN FRIED TOMATOES

The longevity of cast iron cookware is a boon to sustainability. Indeed, many pieces of Lodge made in 1896 remain in use today.

But that's just one of our "green" initiatives. In 2010, Lodge recycled 4,880 tons of metal and steel, 179.3 tons of steel shot, and 8,881 tons of recycled cookware. We also donated 6,350 tons of foundry sand to fill a borrow pit in New Hope, Tennessee. Our sustainable practices extend to using paper inserts and corrugated materials for packing.

To add a purified dash of pride to our efforts, a stream flows from South Pittsburg Mountain through the Lodge foundry, with three settling ponds cleaning the water before it flows into the Tennessee River.

Some frogs in our ponds sing that it isn't easy being green. Our refrain is that they're all wet.

> The longevity of cast iron cookware is a boon to sustainability. Indeed, many pieces of Lodge made in 1896 remain in use today.

closing bow

Every family's song traces the history of relatives in times of toil and days of ease. For the Lodge-Kellermann family, the song centers around the vision Joseph Lodge established when he opened his foundry five generations ago and what his reaction to the company's twenty-first-century foundry might be.

For Lodge President Henry Lodge, the words were loud and clear during a 2010 interview: "I think he'd just say, 'Wow!' I don't see how it could not have exceeded all of his expectations. For longevity. For product quality. For the range of products we offer.

"I think he'd be amazed. Just amazed."

NATIONAL CORNBREAD FESTIVAL

Most cornbread recipes include cornmeal, buttermilk, eggs, and bacon grease or vegetable oil. But we're most proud of the recipe that has made the National Cornbread Festival (NCF), held in Lodge's hometown of South Pittsburg, Tennessee, every April a destination for folks from 28 states and seven foreign countries for the past 15 years. The secret is as basic as the Lodge cast iron skillets used to prepare countless varieties of cornbread.

"You could have 1,500 volunteers from another community, and it wouldn't be as successful," says culinary consultant Louis Hopkins of Richmond, Virginia. "The people of South Pittsburg are warm and caring; no other community I've been to is as welcoming."

In the mid-1990s South Pittsburg was in a quandary. Several industries had departed, and a bypass put salt on the economic wound by removing much-needed traffic from the town's commercial district. Community leaders realized its best assets were Lodge, makers of the world's best cast iron cookware, and area residents. Those two ingredients generated a recipe for success.

"We had talked about a festival, but we couldn't put a concept together," says Ed Fuller, NCF President. "But then someone said, 'Cornbread Festival.' What's more Southern than Lodge and cornbread?"

Very quickly, the festival grew from being a local event to one that turns the town of South Pittsburg (population 3,300) into a small city of 50,000.

Food, obviously, is the primary ingredient for the NCF's success. The National Cornbread Cook-off features main-dish cornbread meals, with the only requirements for a submission being that the ingredients include one package of Martha White Cornbread or Corn Meal Mix and that the dish be cooked in Lodge Cast Iron Cookware. We're delighted to include in this book (pages 234-250) the recipes from grand prize winners since the beginning of the cook-off in 1997.

Food, obviously, is the primary ingredient for the NCF's success. The National Cornbread Cook-off features main-dish cornbread meals, with the only requirements for a submission being that the ingredients include one package of Martha White Cornbread Mix and that the dish be cooked in Lodge Cast Iron Cookware.

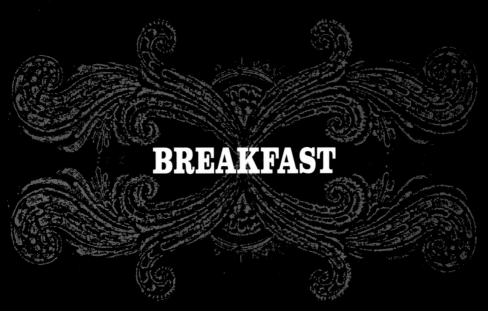

BREAKFAST

What says breakfast better than a cast iron skillet filled with crispy bacon? Well, we think breakfast is far more than bacon, and this chapter offers a wonderful selection of egg dishes, pancakes, and breakfast breads to start your day off right!

This easy-to-prepare dish has been a longtime breakfast favorite in the Ryder-Topalian household. Since the ingredients can be changed according to the season, it's always a snap to make with whatever you have in your fridge or whatever is ripe in your garden. "This is my go-to recipe for whenever we have houseguests. It's beautiful when it comes out of the oven, with its puffed-up golden brown top, and it provides everyone with a satisfying start to their day," says Tracey Ryder, cofounder of Edible Communities, a network of more than 65 regional food magazines across the United States and Canada devoted to the local foods movement.

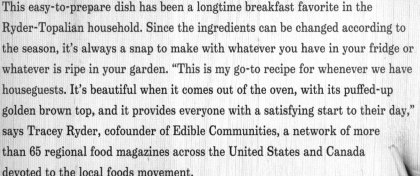

SEASONAL BREAKFAST FRITTATA

serves 8

¾ pound bulk mild Italian pork sausage or chorizo
6 large eggs
1 cup heavy cream
Salt, freshly ground black pepper, and red pepper flakes

2 large handfuls baby spinach, Swiss chard, or arugula, washed and spun dry
8 ounces feta cheese, crumbled
1 large ripe tomato, coarsely chopped (optional)

1. Preheat the oven to 375°.

2. Cook the sausage in a 10-inch cast iron skillet over medium heat, stirring often, until it crumbles and is no longer pink. Remove the sausage and drain on paper towels. Drain all the fat from the skillet, but do not wipe the skillet clean because you want some of the sausage flavor left behind.

3. Place the eggs, cream, and salt and black and red pepper to taste in a large bowl; whisk until the mixture is foamy. Add the sausage, spinach, feta, and, if desired, tomato and stir until all the ingredients are fully incorporated and coated with the egg mixture.

4. Pour the egg mixture into the skillet and cook over medium heat until it begins to set and hold together around the outside edge. Place the skillet in the oven and bake until the top of the frittata has puffed up and is golden brown, 25 to 35 minutes.

5. Slice the frittata into 8 wedges. Serve immediately.

This recipe, suitable for breakfast or a light lunch, is from chef David Waltuck of Chanterelle. Waltuck is best known for the innovative and elegant cuisine served at his groundbreaking restaurant, formerly in downtown New York City. Not as well known is the brief period when Chanterelle experimented with breakfast service. Simple yet luxurious, the dish epitomizes the Chanterelle approach. It makes one serving, so multiply amounts for additional servings desired. You'll need a mini 5-inch cast iron skillet for each serving.

SHIRRED EGGS WITH HAM AND TOMATO

serves 1; recipe may be multiplied

1 tablespoon unsalted butter

2 slices Black Forest or other cooked ham, trimmed to fit pan

2 tablespoons tomato sauce, homemade or good-quality jarred

2 extra-large eggs

1 tablespoon heavy cream

Salt and freshly ground black pepper

1 teaspoon coarsely chopped fresh herbs (tarragon, chervil, and/or chives—just one herb or a mixture)

1. Preheat the oven to 350°.

2. Melt the butter in a 5-inch cast iron skillet over low heat. Remove the skillet from the heat.

3. Place the ham in the bottom of the pan. Spread the tomato sauce evenly over the ham. Carefully break the eggs on top; drizzle the cream over the eggs. Season with salt and pepper to taste (go very light on the salt since the ham is salty).

4. Place the pan in the oven and bake for 5 to 6 minutes, checking occasionally. The whites should be set, but the yolks can still be runny.

5. Sprinkle the eggs with the herbs and serve in the skillet.

Susan Stockton, Senior Vice President of Culinary Production for the Food Network and Cooking Channel, generally cooks for two to four people, so her 12-inch skillet gets a workout. She loves using it for baking cornbread and finishing a seared steak in the oven, but she also has found that its heat retention makes it the perfect oven-to-table vessel for this skillet breakfast. Feel free to use any kind of leftover cooked potato—russet, red, sweet, new, or whatever you have on hand.

SKILLET BREAKFAST

serves 4

1 tablespoon olive oil	1 teaspoon white wine vinegar
1 small red onion, cut into thin half-moons	Salt and freshly ground black pepper
½ red bell pepper, cut into thin strips	4 large eggs
2 cooked potatoes, coarsely chopped	½ cup grated Monterey Jack cheese
1 garlic clove, minced	¼ cup grated Parmesan cheese
1 (10-ounce) package frozen spinach, thawed and squeezed dry	1 ripe tomato, chopped

1. Preheat the oven to 375°.

2. Heat a 12-inch cast iron skillet over medium-high heat for a few minutes. Add the oil, onion, pepper strips, and chopped potatoes; cook, stirring occasionally, until the onion is softened and the potatoes crisp slightly. Add the garlic and cook a few minutes more.

3. After you've squeeze-dried the spinach, sprinkle it with white wine vinegar and make 4 "nests" to hold the eggs. Place them into the potato mixture. Season with salt and pepper.

4. Crack 1 egg into each nest and place the skillet in the oven; bake until the eggs are set, about 10 minutes.

5. Sprinkle the cheeses over the top and bake a few minutes more, until the cheeses melt.

6. Add salt to taste to the chopped tomato and sprinkle the tomato over the eggs. Wrap the handle of the pan with a doubled-up kitchen towel, bring it to the table, and serve.

crazy for cast iron

A 30-year-old 12-inch cast iron skillet lives on my cooktop, ready to go. It's old enough to have developed a great nonstick patina. My husband brought it to our first home along with an Acme juicer and a few copper pots. I was doubly impressed by the fact that not only did Rick cook, but he also clearly knew the value of quality cookware. —Susan Stockton

CHARLIE'S SCRAMBLED EGGS

serves 4

6   large eggs
1   (14¾-ounce) can cream-style corn
½   pound bacon slices, cooked, drained, and crumbled

2   tablespoons butter or canola oil
¼   cup chopped onion
3   tablespoons chopped green bell pepper

1. Place the eggs in a large bowl and beat well. Stir in the corn and crumbled bacon.

2. Melt the butter in a 10-inch cast iron skillet over medium heat. Add the egg mixture and cook, stirring constantly. Add the onion and bell pepper just before the eggs are completely set.

All of Charlie Pickens's family loves to cook in cast iron. His dad drives to the Lodge Factory Store in South Pittsburg, Tennessee, from Birmingham, Alabama, several times a year to buy skillet sets to give as gifts to family and friends.

BOB'S SLOW EGGS

Bacon drippings or butter (2 to 3 tablespoons for a 10-inch skillet)
Eggs
Salt and freshly ground black pepper

Worcestershire sauce (2 dashes per egg)
Tabasco sauce (1 dash per egg)
Shredded sharp Cheddar cheese (about 1 cup per dozen eggs)
Paprika

1. Heat the bacon drippings in large cast iron skillet over low heat. Crack the eggs in the skillet, taking care not to break the yolks. Season to taste with salt and pepper, add the Worcestershire and Tabasco to each of the eggs, and sprinkle the cheese evenly over the top.

2. When the whites begin to cook, rake the bottom of the skillet with the edge of a fork, being careful not to break the yolks. Continue this process until the yolks start to cook; this folds the cheese into the softly cooked egg whites.

3. As the egg yolks begin to solidify, stir them into the other ingredients so you'll end up with yolk chunks that you wouldn't otherwise have.

4. Remove the skillet from the heat while the eggs are still too soft to serve; the heat from the skillet will continue to cook them. When the eggs have finished cooking (Bob likes them on the soft side), sprinkle them generously with paprika and serve them straight from the skillet.

Continuing his father's tradition, Robert Finch "Bob" Kellermann, CEO of Lodge, cooks the family breakfast on Sundays. Bob advises that the size of the skillet depends on how many eggs you'll be cooking—one dozen eggs will fit in a 10-inch skillet. He adds that it's important to cook the eggs over low heat, which means it will take time (typically 40 minutes to cook 18 eggs). If you're cooking a dozen or more eggs, you'll want to get them started before you fry the bacon or preheat the oven for biscuits, otherwise you'll be waiting on the eggs to finish when everything else is ready.

When her kids were growing up, weekend breakfast meant eating together for Jan Hazard, who is a cookbook author and one half of the Kitchen GadgetGals. No gulping down orange juice and grabbing a toasted bagel—Jan's family looked forward to leisurely breakfasts and gabfests. This is one of her family's favorites: ricotta pancakes flavored with citrus zest. Serve them up with real maple or berry syrup.

SUNDAY MORNING RICOTTA PANCAKES

makes about 12 pancakes

2 cups all-purpose flour	1½ cups milk
2 tablespoons sugar	½ cup ricotta cheese
2 teaspoons baking powder	Grated zest of 1 orange or
½ teaspoon baking soda	lemon
½ teaspoon salt	Light cooking oil
2 large eggs, separated	Maple or berry syrup

1. Combine the first 5 ingredients in a large bowl.

2. Beat the egg whites in a medium bowl with an electric mixer until soft peaks form; set aside. Combine the egg yolks, milk, and ricotta in another medium bowl and stir until smooth. Add the ricotta mixture to the flour mixture, stirring gently to combine. Fold in the beaten egg whites and zest with a rubber spatula just until there are no streaks of white left—the batter will be lumpy.

3. Heat a 10½-inch cast iron griddle over medium heat until hot. Grease with a light cooking oil. Pour a scant ½ cup of batter for each pancake onto the griddle and cook until bubbles form on the surface, about 2 minutes; turn and cook on the other side for 1 to 2 minutes, until lightly browned.

4. Serve immediately with maple or berry syrup or keep warm in a low-heat oven. Repeat with the remaining batter.

BUCKWHEAT PANCAKES

makes about 12 (4-inch) pancakes; serves 4

"Night Before" ingredients:

1¼ cups milk, warm but not hot

1   teaspoon active dry yeast
    (about half envelope)

1   cup buckwheat flour

½   cup unbleached all-purpose
    flour

2   tablespoons stone-ground
    cornmeal

2   teaspoons brown sugar

½   teaspoon salt

"Morning" ingredients:

1   large egg, separated

½   teaspoon baking soda

About ¼ cup water

1   tablespoon unsalted butter,
    melted

Vegetable oil

Unsalted butter, softened

Real maple syrup or sorghum
    syrup, warmed

1. Begin making the batter the night before you plan to serve the pancakes. Pour the warm milk into a medium bowl, preferably one with a spout for pouring. Stir in the yeast and set the bowl aside briefly until the mixture begins to bubble. Stir in both flours, the cornmeal, brown sugar, and salt. Cover the bowl with a clean dish towel and refrigerate overnight.

2. The next morning, let the batter sit at room temperature for 15 to 30 minutes. Beat the egg white in a small bowl with an electric mixer until soft peaks form; set aside.

3. Add the egg yolk and baking soda to the batter and stir well; stir in enough water to make the batter pourable. Add the melted butter and stir until the butter disappears. Fold the beaten egg white into the batter until no white streaks remain.

4. Heat a cast iron griddle or large skillet over medium heat. Pour a thin film of oil on the griddle or into the skillet. Pour or spoon the batter onto the hot surface, where it should sizzle and hiss; 2 to 3 tablespoons of batter will make a 3- to 4-inch pancake. Make as many pancakes as you can fit on the surface without crowding.

5. Flip the pancakes just once after 1 to 2 minutes when the top surface is covered with bubbles but before all of the bubbles pop. (The bubbles will be fewer and larger for buckwheat pancakes than for wheat flour pancakes; the surface will look like Swiss cheese.) The pancakes are done when the second side is golden brown, another 1 to 2 minutes. Repeat with the remaining batter, adding a bit more oil to the griddle or skillet as needed. Serve immediately with butter and syrup.

This recipe is from four-time James Beard-award-winning cookbook authors Bill Jamison and Cheryl Alters Jamison.

buckwheat

Probably brought to the American colonies by Dutch settlers, buckwheat pancakes became the most popular of all breakfast cakes in 19th-century America. They almost vanished in today's hyper-speed rush toward meals, but a renewed interest in grains has made them better known again. If buckwheat flour is not available at your grocery store, look for it at large supermarkets and natural food stores; coarser, grittier, and grayer than wheat flour, it is often sold in bulk. Buckwheat pancakes aren't complicated to make, but a good version demands overnight fermentation of the batter. The little extra time needed the evening before breakfast rewards you with a nutty, tangy, and toothsome pancake that is best prepared on a cast iron griddle or in a large shallow cast iron skillet.

If you want your pancake to be really full of fruit, use two apples (the sautéing will be a little awkward at first, but the slices eventually cook down), and adjust the amount of sugar and cinnamon to taste. Cookbook editor Pam Hoenig adapted the original recipe in *The Breakfast Book* by Marion Cunningham to make just a single serving for her daughter, Hannah.

HANNAH'S APPLE PANCAKE

serves 1 generously

¼ cup (½ stick) unsalted butter
¼ cup milk
1 apple (Hannah prefers Golden Delicious)
2 tablespoons sugar

½ teaspoon ground cinnamon
1 large egg
¼ cup all-purpose flour
Pinch of salt

1. Preheat the oven to 425°. Melt the butter in a 5-inch cast iron skillet over low heat.

2. While the butter melts, pour the milk into a 2-cup measuring cup. Peel the apple, then cut it off the core into 4 pieces. Cut each piece lengthwise into thin slices. In a small bowl, toss the apple slices with the sugar and cinnamon until well coated.

3. Pour half the melted butter into the milk and whisk well.

4. Add the apple slices and any loose sugar in the bowl to the hot butter in the skillet. Cook the apple slices over medium-low to low heat, turning them a few times, until softened; the sugar and butter will get nicely browned and bubbly. Remove the skillet from the heat.

5. Add the egg to the milk mixture and whisk to combine. Add the flour and salt and whisk until the batter is smooth. Pour the batter over the apples in the skillet, covering them.

6. Bake until the pancake puffs up and gets golden on top, with patches of brown, about 10 minutes. Enjoy the pancake straight from the skillet or invert it onto a serving plate.

a cast iron memory

When my mother-in-law, Constance Kingsley, passed away at the age of 88 and her household effects were being divided up, I made a beeline for her cast iron, which included 9- and 6½-inch skillets. I have fond memories of my father-in-law, George Kingsley, cooking bacon in the larger skillet when we came to visit, but I had never seen him use the smaller one. I soon discovered my own use for it—baking a single-serving German pancake, my daughter Hannah's favorite breakfast food. Her Mimi and Poppy would be delighted with its new use. —Pam Hoenig

Sarah Kirkwood "Pat" Lodge married the Rev. John Richard Lodge five years after they met at Auburn University during World War II. She enjoyed good food and exchanged recipes with many cooks in the parishes John served. Serve aebleskiver with maple syrup, jam, jelly or sprinkled with powdered sugar.

AEBLESKIVER

makes 30 aebleskiver

4 large eggs, separated
2 cups cake flour
1 tablespoon sugar
1 teaspoon baking powder
½ teaspoon salt

¼ cup vegetable shortening, melted
Scant 2 cups milk (2 cups less 2 tablespoons)

1. In a large bowl, beat the egg yolks with an electric mixer until thick and pale. Wash and dry the beaters. In a medium bowl, beat the egg whites with the mixer until stiff peaks form.

2. In another medium bowl, sift together the flour, sugar, baking powder, and salt. Add dry ingredients alternately with melted shortening and milk to the beaten egg yolks. Lightly mix in the beaten egg whites with a whisk.

3. Heat a Lodge Aebleskiver Pan over medium heat. Brush a small amount of shortening or oil in each well and fill almost full with batter. Cook over medium heat until bubbly; using knitting needles, wooden skewers, or a small fondue fork, turn each one over after 30 seconds and continue to turn them every 30 seconds until all the sides are cooked to form a ball. Continue to turn them until browned on all sides. Remove from the pan.

4. Repeat with the remaining batter, then serve as you like.

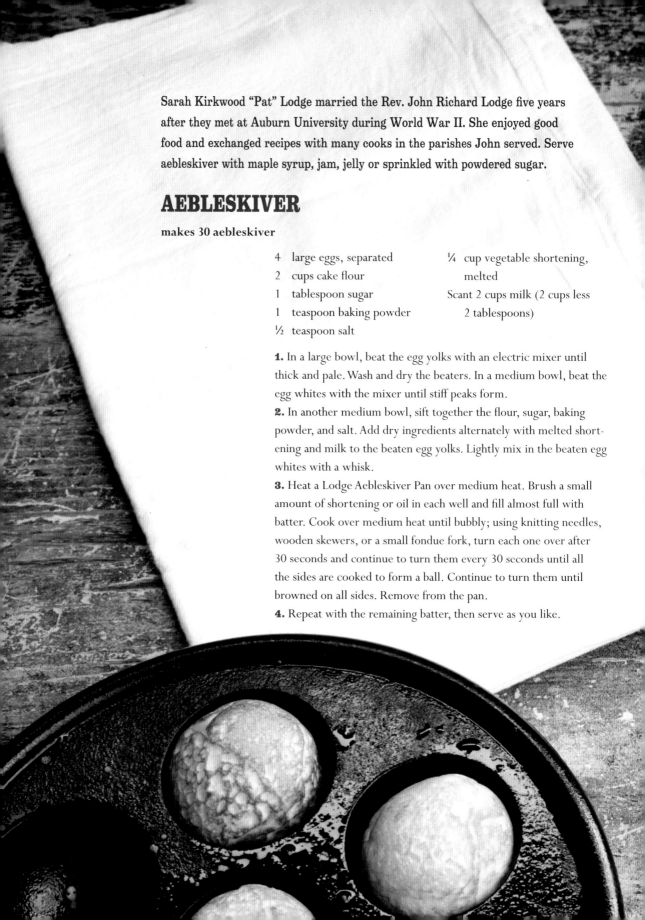

FRENCH TOAST AND FRIED GREEN TOMATOES

serves 4

4 large eggs	4 bread slices
¼ cup milk	¼ cup (½ stick) butter
¼ teaspoon salt	3 medium green tomatoes,
⅛ teaspoon freshly ground black pepper	sliced

1. Place the eggs, milk, salt, and pepper in a large baking dish and beat well. Add the bread and let it soak until the egg mixture is absorbed, about 5 minutes on each side.

2. Heat a greased 12-inch cast iron griddle over medium-low heat. Add the bread slices and cook until browned on both sides.

3. While the bread slices are cooking, melt the butter in a 10-inch cast iron skillet over medium heat. Add the tomato slices and fry 3 minutes on each side.

4. For each serving, serve slices of fried tomato over each piece of French toast.

Born on the Joseph Lodge Farm, Barbara Gonce Clepper developed a passion early in life for cooking in cast iron and collecting both recipes and cast iron cookware. This recipe comes in handy for an overabundance of garden-fresh tomatoes. "We plant more than 30 tomato plants every summer," explains Barbara, "and this helps use up some of the tomatoes."

BERTHA'S CARROT-ZUCCHINI MUFFINS

makes 24 muffins

1 cup all-purpose flour	¼ teaspoon ground allspice
1 cup whole wheat flour	1 large egg, beaten
¾ cup firmly packed light brown sugar	¾ cup orange juice
1 teaspoon baking powder	½ cup (1 stick) butter, melted
1 teaspoon ground cinnamon	2 medium carrots, finely shredded
½ teaspoon salt	1 medium zucchini, finely shredded
½ teaspoon baking soda	

1. Preheat the oven to 400°. Grease 2 (6-cup) cast iron muffin pans.

2. Combine both flours and the next 6 ingredients in a large bowl.

3. In a small bowl, stir together the egg, orange juice, and melted butter. Add to the dry ingredients, stirring just until moistened. Fold in the carrots and zucchini.

At 95 years old, Bertha Russell Gonce is still growing and picking her own zucchini. This recipe is a good way to use zucchini when it's quickly multiplying in your garden. These muffins are very good topped with cream cheese frosting.

4. Spoon the batter into the prepared muffin pans, filling each well three-fourths full. Bake for 22 minutes. Remove the muffins from the pan immediately and cool completely on a wire rack.

5. Repeat with the remaining batter.

These muffins from Martha Holland, who writes a weekly cooking column for her local paper, freeze very nicely. Let them cool completely, then freeze them in zip-top plastic freezer bags. To reheat, let the muffins thaw for about 15 minutes, wrap them tightly in aluminum foil, and place them in a preheated 400° oven for 15 minutes.

HAM AND SAUSAGE MUFFINS

makes 12 muffins *(pictured on page 18)*

1 tablespoon butter	½ teaspoon baking soda
¼ cup finely chopped green bell pepper	½ teaspoon salt
¼ cup finely chopped green onions	1 large egg
½ cup plus 2 tablespoons all-purpose flour	¾ cup buttermilk
½ cup yellow cornmeal	⅓ cup finely chopped ham
	⅓ cup finely chopped cooked sausage

1. Preheat the oven to 400°. Grease 2 (6-cup) cast iron muffin pans.

2. In a small cast iron skillet, melt the butter and cook the bell pepper and green onions over medium heat until softened but not browned, stirring constantly.

3. In a large bowl, sift together the flour, cornmeal, baking soda, and salt. In a medium bowl, beat the egg, then stir in the buttermilk. Add the egg mixture to the flour mixture all at once, stirring only until blended; do not overstir. Carefully fold in the ham, sausage, and bell pepper mixture, along with any butter left in the skillet.

4. Spoon the batter into the prepared muffin pans, filling each well full. Bake until nicely browned, about 20 minutes. Cool in pans 5 minutes. Remove the muffins from the pans and cool completely on a wire rack.

The cake is velvety, tender, and buttery, and the crumbs are big, dense, and sweet. It's an over-the-top rendition in the style David Bowers prefers in his cookbook *Bake It Like a Man: A Real Man's Cookbook*. With a layer of ripe peach slices (or plum, if you prefer) between the two layers, this is a real bakery-style coffee cake—the kind that makes you glad to face the morning. Served slightly warm with a scoop of vanilla ice cream, it also makes a fine dessert. For best results, remove any leftover cake from the skillet before storing.

FRESH PEACH CRUMB COFFEE CAKE

serves 8

Topping:
- 1½ cups all-purpose flour
- ½ cup firmly packed light brown sugar
- ½ cup granulated sugar
- 1½ teaspoons ground cinnamon
- ½ cup (1 stick) salted butter, melted

Cake:
- ½ cup (1 stick) salted butter, softened
- ½ cup granulated sugar
- ½ cup sour cream
- 2 large eggs
- 1½ teaspoons vanilla extract
- 1¼ cups all-purpose flour
- ½ teaspoon baking soda
- ½ teaspoon baking powder
- 1 pound ripe peaches (3 to 4 medium), peeled, pitted, and sliced

1. Preheat the oven to 350°. Liberally butter the bottom of a 10-inch cast iron skillet.

2. Place all the topping ingredients in a medium bowl and mix well to make a dense, smooth dough; set aside.

3. To make the cake batter, cream the butter and granulated sugar in a large bowl with an electric mixer until smooth. Add the sour cream, eggs, and vanilla and beat well. Place the flour, baking soda, and baking powder in a small bowl, stirring to combine; add to the batter all at once, stirring well to combine. The batter will be stiff.

4. Smooth the batter into the prepared skillet. Arrange the peach slices on top in a single layer. Crumble the topping mixture into big chunks and sprinkle on top of the peaches.

5. Bake until a toothpick inserted in the center comes out with crumbs clinging to it, about 45 minutes. (The cake will remain quite moist because of the peaches, but be sure you don't have streaks of raw batter on the toothpick.) Cool a little before cutting into wedges.

crazy for cast iron

Cast iron cookware is a treasured possession in my family. Many pieces were passed down from one generation to the next and became "family heirlooms." I'm not sure how long this tradition has been going on—at least five generations. I know that my mother, Almyra McDill Engelman, and my aunt, Wendell McDill Thomason, were given cast iron skillets from my great-grandmother when they were married. Today, I have one of my mother's wedding gift cast iron skillets. I enjoy collecting "aged" and antique cast iron cookware, too. I own several skillets, a Dutch oven, a griddle, and three cornstick pans. I have a cast iron skillet designated for "bread and vegetables" and one for "meats" because breads and vegetables tend to stick in skillets where meats have been cooked. I have found that nonstick cooking sprays do not add to the seasoning of the pan, so I use unsalted butter to grease my cookware and vegetable oil to season them. If you find that your prized cast iron piece has started to rust, just scrub off the rust with a dish scrubber and warm dish detergent, then reseason the pan with a generous coating of vegetable oil. —Cindy Schoeneck

In the South, grits are king. Cindy Schoeneck, who hails from Albertville, Alabama, says, "I recommend that 'newbies' try some type of cheese grits when you are first developing a taste for grits." This recipe is a variation of her cheese grits. "You can always omit the tomatoes if you want to try plain cheese grits. I also have added browned and crumbled sausage or bacon to make this more of a breakfast casserole."

TOMATO GRITS

serves 6 to 8

2   cups water
¼   cup milk
1   teaspoon salt
½   teaspoon freshly ground
    black pepper
1   cup quick-cooking grits
½   cup (1 stick) plus
    1 tablespoon butter
1   medium onion, chopped
3   garlic cloves, minced

1   (10-ounce) can diced
    tomatoes and green chiles
    (such as Ro-tel), undrained
1   pound breakfast sausage or
    bacon, cooked, crumbled,
    and drained on paper towels
    (optional)
1   cup (4 ounces) shredded
    cheese (Cindy prefers an
    aged Cheddar or fontina)

1. Preheat the oven to 350°.

2. Combine the water and milk in a large saucepan; bring to a boil. Add the salt and pepper; slowly add the grits, whisking vigorously until the mixture returns to a boil. Add ½ cup of the butter and continue to whisk constantly for 1 minute. Reduce the heat to low and simmer until the grits are thick and creamy, 3 to 5 minutes. Remove from the heat.

3. Melt the remaining 1 tablespoon butter in a deep 10½-inch cast iron skillet or Dutch oven over medium heat. Add the onion and garlic and cook, stirring occasionally, until softened. Add the onion mixture, tomatoes, sausage, if desired, and ¾ cup of the cheese to the grits; stir well. Pour the mixture back into the skillet or Dutch oven and sprinkle with the remaining ¼ cup cheese. Place the skillet in the oven and bake until the grits are hot and bubbly and the cheese on top has melted, about 30 minutes.

GRANNY'S SAUSAGE AND GRAVY

serves 6

1 pound bulk pork breakfast
  sausage
1 tablespoon canola oil
3 tablespoons all-purpose flour

1½ cups milk (or more as needed)
Salt and freshly ground black
  pepper

1. Cook the sausage in a large, deep cast iron skillet or in the bottom of a Lodge Combo Cooker over medium-high heat, stirring until it crumbles and is no longer pink. Remove the sausage and drain on paper towels, leaving 1 to 1½ tablespoons of drippings in the skillet. Add oil to pan.

2. Sprinkle the flour over the drippings and oil in the pan and cook over medium heat, stirring constantly, until the flour is browned. Add the milk, ½ cup at a time, and cook until the gravy has the consistency you prefer. Stir in the sausage, season with salt and pepper to taste, and serve.

This gravy is sometimes called country gravy or milk gravy. In the early 1900s, it was the usual breakfast food served at logging camps, where they started calling it sawmill gravy. Today it's popular poured over big, hot biscuits and served for breakfast, lunch, or dinner. This version is from Vickie Davenport. If you make the gravy in a Lodge Combo Cooker, use the lid to bake your biscuits.

TOMATO GRAVY

serves 4

Drippings from 2 cooked bacon
  slices
2 large ripe tomatoes, finely
  chopped
1 large Vidalia onion, chopped
Dash of Tabasco sauce

½ teaspoon salt
¼ teaspoon freshly ground
  black pepper
¼ cup all-purpose flour
1 cup leftover coffee

1. Heat bacon drippings in a well-seasoned 12-inch cast iron skillet over medium-high heat. Add the tomatoes and onion, stirring until the onion is softened, about 5 minutes. Add the Tabasco, salt, and pepper. Add the flour and cook, stirring constantly, until the mixture thickens.

2. Gradually add the coffee and bring the mixture to a boil, stirring constantly. Reduce the heat to medium-low and cook until thickened, about 5 minutes, stirring constantly. Serve as desired.

There are many different recipes for tomato gravy, or "mater gravy" as it is often called. It is good over biscuits for breakfast, lunch, or dinner. The secret is to constantly stir it—if you leave it for a second, it will lump up.

SOUP, STEW, GUMBO & CHILI

Nothing says comfort like a pot of soup or chili simmering away on the back burner of your stove. This chapter offers a wonderful collection of regional specialties that extend the length and breadth of the United States.

SOUTHERN GREENS SOUP

serves 4

This recipe is from Louise S. "Lou" Fuller, wife of Ed Fuller, president of the National Cornbread Festival, which is held each year in Lodge's hometown, South Pittsburg, Tennessee. Of course, Lou likes to serve this soup with hot cornbread!

2 tablespoons canola oil
1 medium onion, chopped
4 cups water
1 envelope dry vegetable soup mix (such as Knorr's)
2 pounds fresh turnip greens, washed, drained, and chopped
1 (20-ounce) can white beans, drained
1 (14- to 16-ounce) package Polish sausage, sliced
Hot water (optional)

1. Heat the oil in a 7-quart cast iron Dutch oven over medium-high heat; add the onion and cook until softened, stirring occasionally. Add the water and soup mix, stirring to combine. Bring to a boil and simmer 5 minutes.

2. Add the turnip greens and simmer 10 minutes.

3. Add the beans and sausage; simmer until the greens are tender, about 15 minutes. If you want the soup more "soupy," add hot water a little at a time until desired consistency.

TEX-MEX MINESTRONE

serves 6 to 8

This quick and hearty one-dish meal was contributed by International Dutch Oven Society member Debbie Hair.

1 pound lean ground beef
3 cups water
1 (28-ounce) can crushed tomatoes
1 (15-ounce) can black beans, drained and rinsed
1½ cups frozen or canned corn, thawed and drained
1 (14½-ounce) can beef broth
½ cup zesty Italian dressing
1 teaspoon ground cumin
1 cup small pasta shells
1 cup shredded Colby-Jack cheese

1. Brown the beef in a 12-inch cast iron Dutch oven over high heat, stirring often, until the meat crumbles and is no longer pink; drain.

2. Add the water and the next 6 ingredients; stir to combine. Bring to a boil; add the pasta, reduce the heat to medium, and simmer until pasta is just tender, about 8 minutes.

3. Sprinkle cheese over the top of each serving.

Southern Greens Soup

Allison Fishman, founder of The Wooden Spoon cooking school and former co-host of Lifetime's *Cook Yourself Thin*, offers this recipe, which was adapted from her cookbook, *You Can Trust a Skinny Cook*. If you don't live in an area where it's easy to purchase fresh clams, canned clams are the way to go. And don't ever throw out the liquid that comes in the can! "While I was making this chowder, I got to thinking about that 'clam liquor'; I wasn't sure if I should use it or throw it out (like you do with the liquid that comes with canned tuna), so I took a little sip," explains Allison. "It was *deee-licious*. Use it in Bloody Marys, chowders, and linguine with clam sauce. It's so flavorful that you can omit the bottle of clam juice in most of those recipes."

NEW ENGLAND CLAM CHOWDER

serves 5

2 bacon slices, cut into ¼-inch pieces
1 medium onion, chopped
3 celery ribs, chopped
1 bay leaf
½ teaspoon fresh thyme leaves
1 teaspoon kosher salt
½ cup white wine or beer
2 medium russet potatoes, peeled and cut into ⅓-inch cubes
2 cups fat-free milk
2 (6½-ounce) cans chopped clams, undrained
¼ cup chopped fresh parsley, plus more for garnish
Freshly ground black pepper (optional)

1. Cook the bacon in a large cast iron Dutch oven over medium heat, stirring occasionally, until crisp, 3 to 4 minutes. Using a slotted spoon, transfer the bacon to a paper towel-lined plate to drain, reserving drippings in skillet.

2. Add the onion, celery, bay leaf, and thyme to the bacon drippings. Add ½ teaspoon salt, cover, and sweat the vegetables over medium-low heat, stirring occasionally, until softened, about 4 minutes. Remove lid, add wine and cook, uncovered, until reduced by half, about 2 minutes.

3. Add the potatoes, milk, and juice from the canned clams to the pot. Bring to a simmer and cook, reducing the heat if necessary, until the potatoes soften, 8 to 10 minutes.

4. Transfer 2 cups of mostly solids from the pot to a blender or food processor and process until smooth, adding small amounts of liquid as needed to aid in processing. Return puréed mixture to the pan; add the clams and bring to a simmer. Stir in parsley, remaining ½ teaspoon salt, and, if desired, pepper to taste. Garnish with reserved bacon and more chopped parsley. Discard bay leaf before serving.

Manhattan's got that red clam chowder and New England has the creamy white one. Most people have a preference—but Long Islanders are the kind of people who think they don't have to choose. When you live on Long Island, you can be in New York City in half an hour or at the beach in 20 minutes. Why choose favorites when you can have it all? That way of thinking helps explain Long Island's namesake clam chowder, contributed by Allison Fishman. A little bit city, a little bit beachy, this chowder combines your favorite creamy tomato soup with fresh local clams.

LONG ISLAND CLAM CHOWDER

serves 8

1   tablespoon butter
1   tablespoon olive oil
1   medium onion, finely chopped (about 1 cup)
2   shallots, finely chopped
Kosher salt
15 to 20 cherrystone clams in shells (4 to 5 pounds), scrubbed
1   (28-ounce) can crushed tomatoes

1   (10-ounce) package frozen baby corn or 2 cups fresh corn kernels
1   cup half-and-half
⅔   cup chopped fresh basil
Pinch of red pepper flakes or to taste
1   baguette, sliced and toasted

1. Place the butter and oil in a 6-quart cast iron Dutch oven over medium heat. When the butter melts, add the onion, shallots, and generous pinch of salt; stir to combine. Cover and reduce heat to medium-low. Cook until the onions begin to soften, about 5 minutes.
2. Add the clams and cook until they begin to open, about 15 minutes. Remove the clams as soon as they open and separate the clam meat from the shells; discard the shells and set aside the clam meat. Discard any unopened clams. Chop the clam meat.
3. When the clams are removed, add the tomatoes to the pan and bring to a simmer over medium heat. Simmer 10 minutes, then add the corn. Cook until the chowder returns to a simmer, about 3 minutes (less if using fresh corn). Add the clam meat; return to a simmer.
4. Remove the pan from the heat and stir in the half-and-half, basil, and red pepper flakes. Serve the soup warm with plenty of toasted bread.

❧ chowder clams ❧

Although this recipe calls for cherrystone clams, Allison says to ask your fishmonger for whatever "chowder" clams he has. In New England, the quahog ("cohog") is the oversized granddaddy of the chowder clams. Littlenecks, topnecks, and cherrystones are simply smaller quahogs. Long Island fishmongers line up their quahogs from little to big, like they're the von Trapp family, so you can choose the size that fits your needs. Once you get to cherrystone size, you'll want to chop these puppies before you throw them into a chowder.

This easy-to-make chowder comes from Mary Karlin's book *Wood-Fired Cooking: Techniques and Recipes for the Grill, Backyard Oven, Fireplace, and Campfire*, which includes a chapter dedicated to cast iron and clay pot cookery. Mary adapted this popular chowder for stove-top preparation, but you can also cook it over indirect heat on a grill or a campfire. For a smokier flavor, roast the ears of corn in their husks over a direct fire before removing the kernels. If you don't have fresh clams, you can replace them and the sausage with fresh skinless salmon fillets or smoked salmon. If you use smoked salmon, cut back on the amount of salt you add for seasoning.

CLAM, SAUSAGE, AND CORN CHOWDER

serves 6

3 tablespoons olive oil

2 large celery ribs, cut into ½-inch-thick slices

½ pound bulk sweet Italian sausage

1 teaspoon kosher salt, plus more to taste

1¼ teaspoons freshly ground white pepper, plus more to taste

1 bunch green onions (white part and half of the greens), coarsely chopped

Kernels cut from 2 ears of corn or 1½ cups frozen corn kernels

4 cups fish or chicken stock

1 cup crème fraîche

2 dozen clams in shells, scrubbed

1 tablespoon fennel seeds

2 tablespoons chopped fresh dill fronds, plus more for garnish

Grated zest of 1 lemon

Juice of 1 lemon (optional)

1. Heat the oil in a 3-quart cast iron Dutch oven over medium heat; add the celery and cook 3 minutes, stirring occasionally. Add the sausage, salt, and pepper; cook, stirring occasionally, until the sausage crumbles and is no longer pink, about 5 minutes. Stir in the green onions and corn and add 2 cups stock. Bring to a boil; reduce the heat and simmer for about 15 minutes.

2. Stir in the crème fraîche and simmer 5 to 7 minutes. Stir in the clams, fennel seeds, dill, and lemon zest; cover and simmer gently until the clams open, 5 to 6 minutes. Discard any unopened clams. Add as much of the remaining 2 cups stock as needed to achieve the desired consistency; add lemon juice to taste, if desired. Add additional salt and pepper, if desired. Serve in warm bowls and top with more chopped dill.

crazy for cast iron

Cooking any chowder in my family's hand-me-down cast iron Dutch oven makes me nostalgic for camping trips with my folks and Girl Scout overnighters in the woods. That pot has enjoyed many a fun fireside gathering and heard loads of stories reminiscing about "the good ol' days."

—Mary Karlin

MCNEW'S OKRA STEW

serves 4

3 tablespoons canola oil

1 pound fresh okra, trimmed and sliced

½ pound smoked sausage, sliced

1 cup chopped onion

½ cup chopped green bell pepper

½ cup chopped green onions

2 garlic cloves, minced

¼ teaspoon salt

½ teaspoon freshly ground black pepper

½ pound shrimp, peeled and deveined

1 (15-ounce) can whole tomatoes, undrained, chopped

1 (10-ounce) package frozen baby lima beans, cooked until tender and drained

Hot cooked rice

1. Heat the oil in a cast iron chicken fryer or large Dutch oven. Add the okra and the next 7 ingredients; cook, stirring, until the okra is crisp-tender.

2. Add the shrimp, reduce the heat to low, and cook until they turn pink, about 5 minutes. Add the tomatoes with juice and cook 10 minutes. Add the lima beans and simmer 15 minutes.

3. Serve the stew over hot rice.

Alex McGregor, the owner of Walden Farm in Signal Mountain, Tennessee, brings fresh okra and other produce to Chattanooga's Brainerd Farmers' Market weekly during the summer. This is his recipe.

okra

Most Southerners love okra. This hot-weather crop is best picked small, while it's still tender.

Maybe twice a year, cookbook author James Villas loves nothing more than to throw a special Brunswick stew party for eight or ten fellow stewheads. "I don't think I've ever used the exact same recipe—which is one reason cooking Brunswick stew is so much fun," Jim says. Typically, Jim makes the stew a day in advance. For optimum flavor, he uses a hefty stewing hen, but if that's not available, he suggests using two ordinary 3-pound chickens. He serves the stew with country ham biscuits, coleslaw, homemade pickled peaches, and, for dessert, a hot berry cobbler with scoops of vanilla ice cream on top. "Rarely is there a cup of stew left in the pot or a morsel of food left on the table!"

SOUTHERN BRUNSWICK STEW

serves 8 to 10

4   bacon slices
¼   cup vegetable oil
1   (6-pound) chicken, cut
    into 8 pieces
2   medium onions, chopped
2   celery ribs (with leaves),
    chopped
1   carrot, chopped
1   medium smoked ham
    hock, trimmed
3   large ripe tomatoes, chopped
    and juices reserved
1   small dried red chile,
    seeded and minced

1   tablespoon Worcestershire
    sauce
1   teaspoon paprika
Salt and freshly ground black
    pepper
1½ cups fresh or frozen corn
    kernels
1½ cups fresh or frozen sliced
    okra
1½ cups fresh or frozen baby
    lima beans
1½ cups mashed cooked potatoes
    (optional)

1. Place a large cast iron Dutch oven over medium-high heat. Add the bacon and cook until crisp. Remove to paper towels to drain, reserving drippings in skillet; crumble the bacon and set aside.

2. Add the oil to the bacon drippings in the pan and heat over medium-high heat. Add the chicken, brown on all sides and transfer to a platter. Reduce the heat to medium and add the onions, celery, and carrot; cook 5 to 8 minutes, stirring occasionally.

3. Return the chicken to the pan and add the ham hock, tomatoes with juices, chile, Worcestershire, paprika, and salt and pepper to taste. Add enough water to cover the ingredients by 1 inch and stir. Bring to a steady simmer, skimming any scum off the surface; cover and cook slowly until the chicken is very tender, 2½ to 3 hours. Skim any excess fat from top.

4. Using a slotted spoon, transfer the chicken and ham hock to the platter; when cool enough to handle, remove and discard the bones and any skin. Shred the meats and return to the pan. Add the corn, okra, lima beans, and reserved bacon. Simmer, uncovered, about 1 hour, stirring every 10 minutes for the first half-hour and then frequently, to prevent the ingredients from scorching on the bottom of the pan.

5. Add the mashed potatoes, if desired, and cook, stirring, until the stew is thickened, about 15 minutes. Taste and, if necessary, adjust the seasoning. Ladle the stew into large soup bowls.

crazy for cast iron

Traditionally cooked in huge cast iron cauldrons at lavish church barbecues, fish fries, political rallies, civic fundraisers, tobacco curings, family reunions, and other such communal gatherings that involve feeding large numbers of people, Brunswick stew is a quintessential Southern creation that dates back centuries. There's almost as much debate over its origins—Virginia? North Carolina? Georgia?—as over the correct ingredients, but since this versatile meat-and-vegetable stew must simmer a long time over low, even heat, everybody agrees that the only acceptable vessel is a heavy cast iron pot.

It's also common knowledge that, even over the lowest heat, Brunswick stew must be stirred repeatedly to prevent scorching and that the texture should be such that the stew can be eaten as easily with a fork as with a spoon. —James Villas

a cast iron memory

Growing up in Dublin, Ireland, I often spent summers on Inisheer, the smallest of the three Aran Islands off the coast of Galway. This counted as summer camp for Irish kids. We were distributed, several teenagers to a house, among the island residents, and we spent our days roaming the island, practicing our Irish vocabulary, and listening to local musicians at night. But one of the things I remember most vividly is how the *Bean an Tí* (BAHN AHN tee—literally "woman of the house," and the sole name we all used to address our hostesses) cooked.

In the cottage where I stayed, the *Bean an Tí* had two cast iron kettles in her kitchen and not much more. The small cast iron kettle, known as a bastible, had legs to stand in the fire and a close-fitting lid. She'd put it in the fireplace and heap coals on the lid to bake the soda bread. The larger kettle served to boil the mountains of potatoes that, along with fish, made up our diet.

She boiled that larger kettle on the stove-top, except when the *Fear an Tí* (FAR AHN tee, "the man of the house") came home from fishing. We teenage boys would have already eaten by then and we'd watch while she'd boil his potatoes in the large kettle over a peat fire. She mostly cooked for us on the stove-top, but the man of the house preferred the taste of potatoes cooked in cast iron over peat. And after his day's labors on the waves, the woman of the house lugged that heavy kettle over to the fire to provide it for him.   —David Bowers

In his cookbook *Bake It Like a Man: A Real Man's Cookbook*, David Bowers offers this oversize recipe for a stew that's ideal for getting together with friends on a cold winter's night. It cries out for a Dutch oven that can simmer over a burner or, just as happily, on top of a woodstove. The chunks of beef cook in a thick, brown gravy enriched with two bottles of Guinness. If you use an American stout, which tends to be sweeter, leave out the brown sugar. Serve this stew with mounds of mashed potatoes—it tastes even better when reheated the next day.

BEEF IN GUINNESS

serves 8 to 10

5 pounds beef stew meat, such as chuck, cut into 1½-inch cubes
½ cup all-purpose flour
Salt and freshly ground black pepper
5 tablespoons vegetable oil
3 large onions, coarsely chopped

1 pound mushrooms, halved
2 (12-ounce) bottles Guinness Extra Stout
2 cups beef stock
1 teaspoon brown sugar
1 teaspoon dried thyme
Generous pinch of ground nutmeg
4 bay leaves

1. Combine the meat, flour, and salt and pepper to taste in a large bowl; toss until the meat is coated. Heat the oil in a large cast iron Dutch oven over high heat. When the oil is very hot, add the meat all at once and cook until it is well browned on all sides, about 10 minutes. Remove the meat from the pan; set aside.

2. Add the onions to the pan; reduce the heat to medium and cook, stirring occasionally, until the onions just start to soften, 3 to 4 minutes. Return the beef to pan and add the mushrooms, stout, stock, brown sugar, thyme, nutmeg, bay leaves, 2 teaspoons salt, and 1 teaspoon pepper.

3. Bring to a boil; cover, reduce the heat to low, and simmer gently, stirring occasionally, just until beef is nearly falling apart and easily pierced through with a fork, about 2 hours. Discard the bay leaves before serving.

OVEN BEEF STEW

serves 6 to 8

This stew was a meal that allowed Sarah Kirkwood "Pat" Lodge the time for her many volunteer activities, in addition to being the wife of a priest and the mother of four. Her daughter remembers Pat would frequently make this dish when the children (and later the grandchildren) came to visit. That way Pat could spend time with her family instead of at the stove.

2½ pounds beef stew meat
6 carrots, chopped
3 medium onions, quartered
5 medium potatoes, quartered
1 (10-ounce) package frozen green peas
2 bay leaves
2 beef bouillon cubes
1 tablespoon sugar
1 tablespoon salt
Dash of dried thyme
Freshly ground black pepper
2 (28-ounce) cans whole tomatoes, drained (reserving juice)
1 cup high-quality red wine or water
¼ cup cornstarch

1. Preheat the oven to 275°. (If you want to cut down the cooking time a bit, increase the oven temperature to 300°.)

2. Layer the first 13 ingredients (except the reserved tomato juice) in a well-seasoned 5-quart cast iron Dutch oven in the order listed. Combine reserved tomato juice and the cornstarch and pour over the top.

3. Cover and bake until the beef is fork-tender, 4 to 5 hours, stirring once or twice. Discard the bay leaves before serving.

CHICKEN STEW WITH FLUFFY DUMPLINGS

serves 6 to 8

1	plain or salt-and-pepper rotisserie chicken
4	cups chicken broth
4	cups cold water
1	tablespoon olive oil
1	cup chopped onion
¾	cup sliced celery
1½	cups sliced carrots
2	teaspoons chopped fresh thyme or ½ teaspoon dried thyme

	Kosher salt
½	teaspoon freshly ground black pepper or to taste
2	cups self-rising flour
¼	cup (½ stick) butter, cut into small cubes and chilled
2	tablespoons vegetable shortening
¼	cup half-and-half or cream

For chicken-and-dumpling devotees like food writer and cooking teacher Sheri Castle, the proof is in the dumplings. These are tender, fluffy pillows, rather like biscuits sitting atop the gravy of the delicious stew. Quick and easy, this stew begins with well-seasoned meat from a rotisserie chicken. The meat goes into the stew, and the trimmings enrich store-bought broth, yielding a full-bodied, rich, flavorful broth in only an hour instead of an afternoon. These old-fashioned chicken dumplings make a delectable, comforting meal that will please the whole family.

1. Pull the meat from the chicken; refrigerate, covered, until needed. Place the bones and skin in a large saucepan or small stockpot; add the broth and water. Bring to a boil; reduce the heat and simmer until the carcass falls apart and the liquid reduces to about 6 cups, about 1 hour. Strain the broth and set aside; discard solids.

2. Heat the oil in a 6-quart cast iron Dutch oven over medium heat. Add the onion, celery, carrots, thyme, and a pinch of salt; stir to coat. Cook, stirring often, until the vegetables soften, about 8 minutes. Add the reserved broth, 1 teaspoon salt, the pepper, and reserved chicken. Simmer until the vegetables are tender, about 10 minutes.

3. Place the flour in a medium bowl. Cut the butter and shortening into the flour with a pastry blender or your fingertips until crumbly. Stir in the half-and-half. The dough should be soft and sticky, but firm enough to hold together on a spoon.

4. Bring the stew to a low boil over medium-high heat.

5. Using a 1-ounce scoop or spoon, drop golf-ball-size dumplings evenly over the surface of the stew. Cover and cook until the dumplings are firm and look dry on top, about 20 minutes. If the dumplings are firm and fluffy but still wet on top, baste them with some of the hot liquid. Serve the stew and dumplings immediately.

POLISH PORK AND CABBAGE STEW *(Bigos)*

serves 6

There are many versions of this stew—some that include game, beef, and veal, along with the slowly cooked pork and cabbage that make this dish so beloved. This rendition comes from Joanna Pruess' *Cast Iron Cookbook: Delicious and Simple Comfort Food.* Serve it with boiled potatoes, sour cream, and rye or pumpernickel bread. The rich taste improves as the stew is reheated.

❧ bigos ❧

Bigos, the national dish of Poland, is typically made with sauerkraut and fresh cabbage, a variety of pork products (including ham, kielbasa, and fresh pork), and either apples or prunes to balance the tangy flavors. It was originally eaten by Polish aristocrats, who were the only people allowed to hunt game on their estates.

1   ounce dried porcini mushrooms
1   cup warm water
2   tablespoons canola or vegetable oil
5   ounces thick bacon slices, diced (about 1 cup)
1   pound lean boneless pork stew meat, cut into 1-inch cubes and patted dry
3   large yellow onions, coarsely chopped
1   small or ½ medium head green cabbage, cored and shredded
3   garlic cloves, minced
2   cups beef stock
1   cup Cabernet Sauvignon or other dry red wine

2   cups canned whole tomatoes, undrained, chopped
1   pound sauerkraut, rinsed under cold water and squeezed dry
1   cup pitted prunes, chopped
12 juniper berries, bruised
2   bay leaves
¼   pound cooked ham, diced
½   pound kielbasa, cut into ½-inch-thick rounds
Salt and freshly ground black pepper
Sour cream (optional)
1½ to 2 pounds small red potatoes, boiled, peeled, and cut into chunks (optional)

1. Soak the mushrooms in the warm water until softened, about 20 minutes. Drain the liquid through 2 layers of dampened paper towels into a container and set the liquid aside; rinse any grit from the mushrooms and set the mushrooms aside.

2. Heat a 10-inch cast iron Dutch oven over medium heat until just hot, about 3 minutes. Add the oil and bacon, and cook until the fat is rendered from the bacon. With a slotted spoon, remove the bacon to paper towels to drain, reserving the drippings in the pan.

3. Increase the heat to medium-high. Add the stew meat to the drippings and cook until browned on all sides, 8 to 10 minutes; using a slotted spoon, transfer the meat to a bowl, reserving the drippings in pan. Reduce the heat to medium; add the onions and cabbage, and cook, stirring often, until the onions are softened, 6 to 8 minutes.

4. Add the garlic and cook 30 seconds. Stir in the stock, reserved mushrooms and liquid, wine, tomatoes, sauerkraut, prunes, juniper berries, and bay leaves; bring to a boil, scraping the pan to loosen any browned bits. Cover, reduce heat to low, and simmer 2 hours.

5. Uncover, stir in the ham and kielbasa and cook 30 minutes. Add salt and pepper to taste; remove and discard the bay leaves. Serve the stew in soup bowls with a dollop of sour cream, if desired, and a little bacon sprinkled on top. If you like, serve with boiled potatoes.

This recipe comes from award-winning restaurateur and chef John Currence of Oxford, Mississippi. "Courtbouillon was one of the first things I watched my dad cook," recalls John, who grew up in New Orleans. "He loves to fish and loves to take over the kitchen and do his magic. I was amazed at the precision and care he took with cutting the huge pile of peppers and onions that it took to make the stew. I am convinced the anticipation made the final product that much better—that and the just-caught Louisiana redfish he used to make it."

CATFISH COURTBOUILLON

serves 8 to 10

2½ pounds catfish fillets
Salt and freshly ground black
  pepper
2½ tablespoons Creole seasoning
3 cups buttermilk
Tabasco sauce
½ cup (1 stick) unsalted butter
½ cup all-purpose flour
2 cups minced yellow onions
1½ cups minced celery
1 cup minced green bell pepper
⅔ cup minced canned roasted
   mild green chiles
2 tablespoons minced garlic
2 bay leaves
3 cups seeded and chopped
   ripe tomato (you can
   substitute chopped canned
   tomatoes, but only in a
   pinch)

4 cups canned crushed
   tomatoes
1½ tablespoons dried thyme
1 tablespoon dried tarragon
1 tablespoon cayenne pepper
4 cups simple shrimp stock
   (see note, page 55) or
   chicken stock
1 cup all-purpose flour,
   lightly seasoned with salt,
   freshly ground black pepper,
   and cayenne pepper
½ cup (1 stick) cold unsalted
   butter, cubed
4 cups cooked white rice
2 cups chopped green onions
½ cup chopped fresh parsley

1. Place the catfish fillets in a large baking dish and season to taste on both sides with salt and black pepper, and a little of the Creole seasoning. Cover with plastic wrap and refrigerate 30 to 60 minutes.

2. Pour the buttermilk over the catfish and add Tabasco to taste. Cover and marinate in the refrigerator at least 2 hours or overnight.

3. Remove the catfish from the buttermilk marinade, cut into 1-inch strips, and sprinkle with salt and a little more of the Creole seasoning. Refrigerate until needed.

4. Place a 7-quart cast iron Dutch oven over medium heat; add the butter. When it melts, whisk in the ½ cup flour and stir until smooth. Cook over medium heat, stirring constantly, until you have a deep brown roux (slightly darker than the color of milk chocolate), 20 to 30 minutes.

5. Stir in the onions, celery, bell pepper, and chiles and cook, stirring, until tender. Add the garlic and bay leaves and cook briefly, stirring. Stir in the chopped and crushed tomatoes, the remaining Creole seasoning, the thyme, tarragon, cayenne, and 3 cups stock. Bring to a simmer; continue to simmer 45 minutes, stirring regularly (the courtbouillon will thicken and scorch if it isn't watched carefully). Season with salt, black pepper, and Tabasco to taste.

6. When you're ready to serve, dredge the catfish in the seasoned flour, shaking off any excess. Melt 3 tablespoons cubed butter in a 10-inch cast iron skillet over medium heat. Add the catfish pieces in batches, taking care not to crowd the pan; cook until lightly browned on both sides. Transfer to paper towels to drain.

7. Add the catfish and remaining 1 cup stock to the simmering courtbouillon. Simmer until slightly thickened. Add the remaining cubed butter and stir just until incorporated. Discard the bay leaves before serving.

8. Place a small mound of rice into each serving bowl; ladle the courtbouillon over the rice and garnish with green onions and parsley.

note

To make a simple shrimp stock, heat *3 tablespoons olive oil* in a large cast iron Dutch oven over medium heat. Add the *shells and heads (if available) from 3 to 5 pounds of shrimp* (you can accumulate these in your freezer until you need them) and sear until they turn pink. Add *1 medium onion,* coarsely chopped; *2 celery ribs,* coarsely chopped; and *4 garlic cloves*, sliced. Stir until softened. Add *3 cups white wine, 4 bay leaves,* and *2 tablespoons black peppercorns.* Cover and bring to a simmer. Add *water to cover* the shells and simmer 15 to 20 minutes. Strain the stock through a fine mesh strainer; discard the solids.

CIOPPINO
(San Francisco Italian Fish Stew)

serves 6 to 8

Cioppino is a classic San Francisco seafood stew thought to have originated when fishermen would "chip in" whatever they had to a common pot. This recipe for cioppino from Al Hernandez, the food and wine editor of *The Vine Times*, brings the flavorful treat home to you. The recipe includes recommended seafood, but feel free to experiment and "chip in" whatever seafood you have available or prefer.

¼ cup olive oil
1 large yellow onion, chopped
½ teaspoon salt, plus more to taste
6 garlic cloves, finely chopped
1 teaspoon dried oregano
1 teaspoon dried basil
1 teaspoon red pepper flakes
¼ cup tomato paste
1 cup dry white wine
1 cup chicken stock
1 cup seafood stock or clam juice
1 (28-ounce) can peeled whole tomatoes, undrained

1 pound shrimp (16-20 count preferred)
1 pound scallops, preferably bay
1 pound mussels
1 pound clams
1 whole cleaned cooked Dungeness crab (about 2 pounds) or 2 pounds king crab legs, thawed if necessary
1 pound firm white fish fillets (such as cod, catfish, or halibut)
Freshly ground black pepper
1 loaf sourdough bread, sliced and toasted

1. Heat the oil in a large Dutch oven over medium heat. Add the onion and salt and cook, stirring occasionally, until softened, about 10 minutes. Add the garlic, oregano, basil, and red pepper. Stir in the tomato paste, wine, and chicken and seafood stock. Crush the tomatoes; pick out any tomato skins, then add the tomatoes and juice to the pan. Reduce the heat to low and simmer 30 minutes.

2. While the tomato mixture simmers, peel and devein the shrimp. Remove the tough crescent-shaped muscle from each scallop, if it's still attached. Scrub the mussels and clams and debeard the mussels, if necessary. Discard any mussels or clams that won't close.

3. Add the shrimp, scallops, crab, and fish to the pan. Cover and cook 10 minutes. Add the mussels and clams; cover and cook until they open, another 5 to 8 minutes (discard any that won't open). Season with salt and pepper to taste.

4. Serve the cioppino in bowls topped with a slice of toasted sourdough bread.

This recipe comes from the maternal grandmother of Gene Gautro, better known as Gumbo Man and the passionate force behind the Web site *gumbocooking.com.* Use meaty, bone-in chicken pieces, such as legs, thighs, and/or breasts, to extract the most flavor.

Even though this recipe is his grandmother's, Gene says that "it makes me think of my father, too, as he always kept a bottle of ground sassafras leaves on the table." If you are serving the entire pot of gumbo in one sitting, you can stir in the filé powder when you add the oysters. Otherwise, have diners add it to their own bowl. Boiling filé powder decreases its thickening power and causes it to lose flavor. Serve this gumbo with toasted French bread.

CHICKEN FILÉ GUMBO

serves 10

3 pounds meaty chicken pieces	3 garlic cloves, diced
1 cup sliced andouille sausage or any lean smoked sausage	2 teaspoons Creole seasoning (such as Tony Chachere's) or 1¼ teaspoons salt, ½ teaspoon freshly ground black pepper, and ¼ teaspoon cayenne pepper
1 cup bite-size pieces smoked ham	
2 large onions, chopped	
1 cup chopped celery	2 bay leaves
1 cup chopped green bell pepper	8 cups water
2 cups fresh okra, cut into ⅜-inch-thick rounds (fresh is best, but frozen works fine)	½ cup all-purpose flour
	⅓ cup bacon drippings or vegetable oil
1 (14½-ounce) can diced tomatoes, undrained	2 dozen oysters, shucked
	Hot rice
1 (10-ounce) can diced tomatoes and green chiles (such as Ro-tel), undrained	½ teaspoon filé powder per serving
	Tabasco sauce

1. Place the first 13 ingredients in a large cast iron Dutch oven and bring to a boil over medium-high heat. Reduce the heat to low and simmer 2 hours to extract the maximum flavor from the chicken bones. Using a slotted spoon, transfer the chicken to a large bowl. When cool enough to handle, remove the meat from the bones; discard the bones, skin, and cartilage and return the meat to the pan.
2. While the chicken cools, heat a large cast iron skillet over high heat. Add the flour and bacon drippings to make a roux (see *How to*

Make a Roux, below). Cook, stirring constantly, 5 minutes. Reduce the heat to medium and cook, stirring constantly, until the mixture begins to brown. Reduce the heat to medium-low and continue cooking, stirring constantly, until the roux browns to a milk chocolate color. Stir the roux into the chicken mixture in the Dutch oven and cook over low heat 45 minutes.

3. Add the oysters and cook over low heat just until the edges of the oysters curl, 5 to 6 minutes. Discard the bay leaves before serving.

4. Place a small mound of rice in each serving bowl; ladle the gumbo over the rice. Sprinkle with filé and stir to blend. Add a few drops of Tabasco to taste.

how to make a roux

Roux is the traditional foundation of flavor and thickening in making gumbo. Here, Gumbo Man Gene Gautro takes us through the steps of making a proper roux.

1. Start with a cast iron Dutch oven or deep skillet. You will need a spatula or wire whisk and a large spoon. Measure your oil (or bacon drippings) and flour, and have that ready. Turn the heat on high, place your pot on the burner, and put in the fat and flour. Stir with a rubber spatula or whisk until the mixture is well blended. When the mixture starts to bubble, stir constantly for 5 minutes, then turn the heat down to medium. Keep stirring.

2. In a few minutes, the mixture will start to darken. When you see a caramel color developing, turn the heat down to medium-low. Keep stirring, using your spatula or whisk. Don't stop. Relax—a traditional roux takes some time.

3. After a little more stirring, you will see the mixture getting browner. Keep stirring over medium-low heat—anything higher, and your roux is going to burn. Your goal is to get the roux browned to the color of milk chocolate or an old copper penny. When the roux reaches the color of peanut butter, it's about halfway there.

4. As your roux darkens and approaches the milk chocolate stage, turn your heat down to low. This allows you to maintain control of the darkening process without the risk of burning. You will probably see a slight amount of smoke rising from the pan; this is normal. Just turn on your vent to remove the smoke and keep stirring.

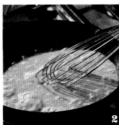

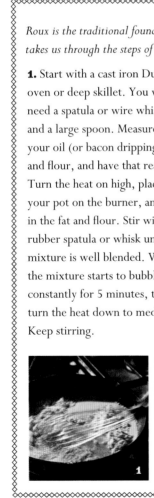

a cast iron memory

My father, Marcel "Blackie" Bienvenu, loved to fish, hunt, and cook—and he did all these things when he wasn't editing and publishing the local St. Martinville, Louisiana, weekly newspaper, *The Teche News*.

As long as I can remember, we had a camp on Catahoula Lake near the great Atchafalaya Basin, the largest swamp in the United States. Throughout the year, we spent long weekends enjoying the great outdoors. For many years, Papa was a Boy Scout leader and over time had accumulated a grand collection of cast iron pots in which to cook stews, gumbos, and jambalaya, fry seafood, and even bake cornbread and biscuits over a wood fire.

I was often at his elbow, and I learned firsthand how to make many of the Cajun dishes in Papa's repertoire. My older brother and I were in charge of cleaning the pots after the meals

were served. Under Papa's direction, we wiped them out once they had cooled with the Spanish moss that was readily at hand on the years-old, stately live oak trees on the camp property. The pots were given a quick rinse with hot water, and then were set on a grill in the wood fire to dry. With a wad of crushed newspapers, we gave the pots a wipe of oil, both inside and out, and then the pots were wrapped securely in newspaper or brown paper sacks.

Those pots were revered, and I often thought of them as the family's treasures. When Papa passed away, my siblings and I laughed when we learned that his cast iron pots were in his will! My two brothers, my sister, and I were the proud recipients of the pots he had loved and cooked in all his life.

Every time I use those pots, I repeat the cleaning process just as Papa had directed, and when I don't have a wood fire, they either go into a hot oven or on the grill of the barbecue pit. Then, I store them, carefully wrapped, in a special cabinet until the next time.

—Marcelle Bienvenu

This recipe is from noted cookbook author and educator Marcelle Bienvenu from St. Martinville, Louisiana. Marcelle's father, an avid sportsman and bon vivant, made this favorite of his when he returned from a hunt with his limit of mallard ducks.

DUCK, OYSTER, AND ANDOUILLE GUMBO

serves 6 to 8

4   mallard ducks, dressed and
    cut into serving pieces
Salt, freshly ground black
    pepper, and cayenne pepper
1¼ cups vegetable oil
1   cup all-purpose flour
3   medium yellow onions,
    chopped
2   medium green bell peppers,
    seeded and chopped

2   celery ribs, chopped
About 8 cups warm water or
    chicken stock
2   pounds andouille sausage, cut
    into ¼-inch-thick rounds
2   dozen oysters, shucked, with
    liquor reserved
¼   cup chopped green onions
Hot cooked rice

1. Season the duck generously with salt, black pepper, and cayenne. Set aside.

2. Heat ¼ cup oil in a large cast iron Dutch oven over medium-high heat. Brown the duck pieces evenly in the oil; remove the duck and set aside. Drain off the oil in the pan.

3. Heat the remaining 1 cup oil in the pan over medium heat; add the flour and cook, stirring slowly and constantly, to make a dark brown roux the color of milk chocolate. Add the onions, bell peppers, and celery. Cook, stirring occasionally, until the vegetables are softened and golden, 8 to 10 minutes.

4. Return the duck meat to the pan and slowly add enough warm water or stock to cover the duck completely. Add the sausage and reduce the heat to medium-low. Simmer, uncovered, just until the duck pieces are tender, about 2 hours.

5. Add the oysters, oyster liquor, and green onions; cook just until the edges of the oysters curl, 3 to 5 minutes. Add additional salt, black pepper, and cayenne to taste, if desired, and serve over hot rice.

gumbo

Gumbo, one of those iconic Acadian/Creole dishes of South Louisiana, can be made with just about anything on hand, such as seafood of all kinds and poultry, including wild duck or goose. Andouille, a smoky, coarse-ground pork sausage, gives this gumbo an intense flavor, and the addition of freshly shucked oysters and their liquor makes it a hearty meal to enjoy on a cold, wet, Louisiana winter night. Gumbo is traditionally served in deep bowls over rice and accompanied with crusty hot French bread. Acadians (Cajuns) sometimes like to serve it with yet another starch—baked sweet potatoes or potato salad!

Also known as green gumbo or gumbo aux herbes, this dish, without the chicken stock, andouille sausage, and bacon fat, is traditionally prepared on Holy Thursday for eating on Good Friday. This version is from Oxford, Mississippi-based restaurateur and chef John Currence.

GUMBO Z'HERBES

makes about 3 quarts; serves 12

½ cup (1 stick) unsalted butter
½ cup all-purpose flour
1 medium yellow onion, diced
1½ cups diced celery
¼ cup minced garlic
6 tablespoons bacon drippings
4 cups diced andouille or any kind of smoked sausage
1 bunch collard greens, washed, trimmed, and chopped
1 bunch mustard or turnip greens, washed, trimmed, and chopped

4 cups firmly packed fresh spinach, washed, trimmed, and chopped
3 cups chopped green cabbage
8 cups chicken stock
1½ teaspoons dried thyme
1½ teaspoons dried tarragon
1 teaspoon cayenne pepper
3 bay leaves
1 tablespoon filé powder
Salt and freshly ground black pepper

1. Melt the butter in a 12-inch cast iron skillet over medium-low heat; sprinkle the flour over the melted butter and stir until smooth. Cook the mixture over medium-low heat, stirring constantly, until you have a roux the color of milk chocolate, 20 to 30 minutes.

2. Stir in the onion, celery, and garlic; increase the heat to medium and cook, stirring, until softened, taking care not to burn the mixture. Remove from the heat.

3. Heat 2 tablespoons of the bacon drippings in a 7-quart cast iron Dutch oven over medium heat. Add the sausage and cook, turning occasionally, until well browned. Transfer the sausage to a medium bowl.

4. Heat the remaining 4 tablespoons bacon drippings in the pan over medium heat. Add the greens, spinach, and cabbage. Once they have completely wilted, add the stock and bring to a boil; reduce the heat to low and simmer until the greens are completely tender, about 12 minutes.

One of my favorite New Orleans holiday traditions is Holy Thursday lunch with Leah Chase at her restaurant, Dooky Chase. Ms. Leah always serves gumbo z'herbes on that Thursday, and there is something profoundly comforting about that meal service with Leah and the 150 or so folks lucky enough to spend the meal in her dining room on Orleans Boulevard. It just makes me feel centered, as if my soul has been cleansed.

I love to serve this with a dollop of potato salad. It works perfectly with the traditional rice, but the potato salad is an interesting twist you rarely see outside of South Louisiana. —John Currence

5. Purée the greens using an immersion blender. Add about 1 cup of the greens mixture to the roux mixture in the skillet and stir until smooth. Add the roux mixture to the puréed greens and stir until smooth. Bring to a simmer; stir in the sausage, thyme, tarragon, cayenne, and bay leaves and simmer 20 minutes.

6. Place the filé in a small bowl; add about 1 tablespoon of the gumbo broth and stir until smooth. Stir the filé mixture into the gumbo and simmer 20 minutes. Season with salt and black pepper to taste. Discard the bay leaves before serving.

VEGGIE CHILI IN CAST IRON

makes 8 cups; serves about 6

1	cup dried red beans	2	teaspoons chili powder
1	small canned chipotle chile in adobo sauce, chopped	½	teaspoon dried oregano
1	medium yellow onion, diced	½	teaspoon salt
1	large carrot, sliced	1	(14½-ounce) can diced tomatoes, undrained
2	celery ribs, thinly sliced	4	cups firmly packed fresh spinach, washed, trimmed, and chopped
2	cups mushrooms, diced		
1	garlic clove, minced		
1	tablespoon ground cumin		

1. Rinse and sort the beans and place them in a cast iron Dutch oven. Add water to cover 2 inches above the beans. Soak beans overnight, or use the quick-soak method: Cover the beans with 2 inches of water; bring to a boil. Boil 1 minute; cover, remove from the heat, and let them stand for 1 hour. Drain.

2. Add fresh water to 1 inch above the beans and bring to a boil. Reduce the heat to a simmer and add the chipotle, onion, carrot, celery, and mushrooms. Cover and cook until the beans are almost tender, about 30 minutes, adding more water as needed to keep the beans submerged in liquid.

3. Add the garlic, cumin, chili powder, oregano, salt, and tomatoes. Simmer about 20 minutes.

4. Add the spinach and simmer 5 minutes. Adjust seasonings to taste, if desired.

This recipe from cookbook author Robin Asbell is great for vegetarians, with the beans and mushrooms supplying protein and the spinach providing iron. Cooking the chili in cast iron gives the dish an additional boost of iron. For an even bigger hit of iron, soak the beans overnight in the Dutch oven. Serve this chili with cornbread, brown rice, or a peanut butter sandwich. It freezes well, so make extra to reheat later.

"Double the recipe, invite friends to bring the beer and lawn chairs, make a couple of skillets full of cornbread, and have a good time!" says Mike Gonce. If you do double the recipe, use a 7-quart Dutch oven.

TENNESSEE WHITE CHILI

serves 6

1 tablespoon canola oil
1 cup chopped onion
1 teaspoon minced garlic
1½ pounds chopped cooked
   chicken breasts, cut into
   small cubes
3 (15-ounce) cans Great
   Northern beans, drained
2 tablespoons chopped fresh
   cilantro or 2 teaspoons dried
   cilantro

2 teaspoons ground cumin
¼ teaspoon salt
¼ teaspoon cayenne pepper
Chicken broth (optional)
Shredded Monterey Jack cheese
   and crushed tortilla chips
   (optional)

1. Heat the oil in a 5-quart cast iron Dutch oven over medium heat. Add the onion and garlic and cook, stirring occasionally, until tender.

2. Stir in the chicken, beans, cilantro, cumin, salt, and cayenne and simmer 30 minutes. If you like, you can add chicken broth as you prefer.

3. Ladle the chili into bowls and sprinkle each serving with cheese and crushed tortilla chips, if desired.

Bob Hall of Taylorville, Illinois, won the 2009 International Chili Society World Championship with this recipe. Bob advises that every time you add green chiles to chili, the salt level will drop—so be sure to check the seasonings, and add salt to taste.

CHEF BOY-R-BOB'S CHILI VERDE

serves 8

2 tablespoons bacon drippings

2½ pounds pork tenderloin, trimmed and cut into ⅜- to ½-inch cubes

1 cup diced onion

4 garlic cloves, pressed

4 serrano chiles, thinly sliced

4 jalapeño chiles, seeded and chopped

2 green chiles, seeded and chopped

1 pound canned or frozen (thawed) green chiles

1 (14½-ounce) can chicken broth

1 (14-ounce) can green enchilada sauce

1 (7-ounce) can salsa verde

1 tablespoon ground cumin

1 tablespoon green jalapeño powder

2 teaspoons green chile powder

Salt

2 teaspoons cornstarch

Tabasco green jalapeño pepper sauce

1. Place the bacon drippings in a 6-quart cast iron Dutch oven over medium-high heat. Add the pork and brown on all sides. Add the onion, garlic, serranos, jalapeños, green chiles, half of the canned or frozen (thawed) chiles, the broth, enchilada sauce, salsa verde, cumin, jalapeño powder, green chile powder, and salt to taste. Cover and simmer 2 hours, adding water as needed during cooking to keep the mixture covered.

2. Thirty to 40 minutes before the end of the cooking time, add the remaining canned or frozen chiles and additional salt to taste; cover and cook 20 minutes.

3. Ten minutes before the end of cooking, adjust the thickness of the chili, if desired. Combine the cornstarch with just enough water to make a paste. Stir the cornstarch mixture in, a little at a time, until you have the desired consistency. Season with salt to taste and adjust the heat level to taste with the Tabasco.

This big and beefy chili, contributed by International Dutch Oven Society member Scott Clawson, has layers of flavor provided by a host of warming spices. Chocolate adds depth, and a final spritz of fresh lime juice gives it a vivid kick.

FLAT-IRON CHERRY-BOMB CHILI TEXAS-STYLE RED

serves 6 to 8

1 pound breakfast sausage

3 pounds flat-iron beef steaks, chopped

1 (8-ounce) can tomato sauce

1 to 2 (14½-ounce) cans chicken broth

5 hot cherry peppers, chopped

3 tablespoons ground cumin

3 tablespoons California chile powder

3 tablespoons New Mexico chile powder

1 tablespoon onion powder

1 tablespoon garlic powder

1 teaspoon ground cinnamon

¼ teaspoon freshly ground black pepper

¼ teaspoon cayenne pepper

Salt

Tabasco green jalapeño pepper sauce

1 cup semisweet chocolate chips

Juice of 1 lime

Sour cream (optional)

1. In a hot large cast iron skillet over high heat, brown the sausage and beef about 1 pound at a time. Transfer the browned meat to a large cast iron Dutch oven.

2. After all of the meat has been browned, add the tomato sauce, 1 can of the broth, and the cherry peppers to the Dutch oven. Stir in 1½ tablespoons each of the cumin and both chile powders, and add the onion powder, garlic powder, cinnamon, black pepper, and cayenne. Cover and cook over low heat 1 hour.

3. Stir in the remaining 1½ tablespoons each cumin and chile powders. Add additional broth, as needed, to achieve the desired consistency. Cover and simmer until the meat is tender, another 1 to 2 hours.

4. Season with salt and Tabasco to taste. Add the chocolate and stir until melted and well blended. Stir in the lime juice just before serving. Serve with a dollop of sour cream, if desired.

Cindy Reed of Houston, Texas, is the only competitor to have won back-to-back championships (1992 and 1993) at the Terlingua International Chili Cook-off.

"CIN-CHILI" CHILI

serves 4 to 6

1 teaspoon cooking oil

2 pounds beef chuck, trimmed and cut into ⅜-inch cubes

1 tablespoon dark chili powder

2 teaspoons granulated garlic

1 (14½-ounce) can beef broth

1 (8-ounce) can tomato sauce

Seasoning Packet #1:

1 tablespoon onion powder

1 tablespoon dark chili powder

2 teaspoons garlic powder

1 teaspoon chicken bouillon granules

1 teaspoon red jalapeño powder

1 teaspoon white pepper

½ teaspoon cayenne pepper

½ teaspoon salt

Seasoning Packet #2:

5 tablespoons chili powder

1 tablespoon paprika

1 teaspoon onion powder

1 teaspoon garlic powder

½ teaspoon white pepper

1 package Sazón seasoning (such as Goya)

2 serrano chiles

Seasoning Packet #3:

2 teaspoons ground cumin

⅛ teaspoon salt

1. Heat the oil in a 3-quart cast iron Dutch oven over medium-high heat. Add the beef and brown on all sides. Stir in the chili powder and granulated garlic when the browning is almost completed.

2. When the beef is browned, stir in the broth, tomato sauce, and Seasoning Packet #1. Bring to a boil; cover, reduce the heat, and simmer 1½ hours.

3. Stir in Seasoning Packet #2, floating the chiles on top. Bring to a boil; cover, reduce the heat, and simmer 20 minutes, adding additional broth or water as needed to get the desired consistency. Remove the chiles when they become soft.

4. Stir in Seasoning Packet #3 and simmer 10 minutes.

Dana Plocheck of Houston, Texas, won the 2006 Terlingua International Chili Cook-off with this recipe.

LADY BUG CHILI

serves 4 to 6

2 pounds coarsely ground beef (chili grind)
1 (14½-ounce) can beef broth
1 (8-ounce) can no-salt-added tomato sauce
1 jalapeño chile
1 serrano chile

Seasoning Packet #1:

1 rounded tablespoon onion powder
2 teaspoons garlic powder
1 tablespoon chili powder (such as Mexene)

Seasoning Packet #2:

2½ tablespoons light chili powder
2½ tablespoons dark chili powder
2 teaspoons ground cumin

¼ teaspoon freshly ground black pepper
¼ teaspoon white pepper
¼ teaspoon cayenne pepper
½ cube beef bouillon (such as Knorr's)
½ cube chicken bouillon (such as Knorr's)
¼ teaspoon brown sugar
1 package Sazón seasoning (such as Goya)

Seasoning Packet #3:

2 teaspoons chili powder (such as Mexene)
1 teaspoon ground cumin
½ teaspoon salt

1. Cook the beef in a 4-quart cast iron Dutch oven over medium-high heat, stirring until the meat crumbles and is no longer pink. Drain all the drippings from the pan. Add the broth and tomato sauce, stirring until blended. Float the jalapeño and serrano chiles on top and bring to a boil. Stir in Seasoning Packet #1. Cover, return to a medium boil, and cook 1 hour.

2. Remove the chiles and set them aside to cool. Cover the pan, return to a medium boil, and cook 15 minutes. When the chiles are cool, squeeze the juice into a small bowl and set aside.

3. Stir in Seasoning Packet #2. Cover and cook at a medium boil for 30 minutes.

4. Stir in the reserved chile juice and Seasoning Packet #3. Cover, reduce heat, and simmer 15 minutes.

Jim Maturo won first place in the People's Choice category in the Florida state chili cook-off in 2001 with this recipe. If you like beans in your chili, use pinto beans and cook them separately.

JIM MATURO'S CHILI

serves 4 to 6

1 tablespoon vegetable shortening

2 pounds beef chuck fillet steak, sirloin tip roast, or chuck, trimmed and cut into ½-inch cubes (or 2 pounds hamburger meat)

2 cups beef broth

2 cups chicken broth

1 (15-ounce) can tomato sauce or diced tomatoes

2 medium onions, diced

3 tablespoons pure ground red chiles (or substitute chili powder)

1 teaspoon cayenne pepper

1 tablespoon salt (2 teaspoons if you substitute chili powder for the ground red chiles)

3 tablespoons chili powder

1½ teaspoons ground cumin (1 tablespoon if you substitute chili powder for the ground red chiles)

2½ teaspoons minced garlic

1 teaspoon freshly ground black pepper

Toppings: grated Cheddar or Parmesan cheese, chopped onions, and sliced jalapeño chiles (optional)

1. Heat the shortening in a 4-quart cast iron Dutch oven over medium heat. Add the beef and brown on all sides.

2. Add the broths, tomato sauce, onions, ground red chiles, cayenne, and salt. Bring to a boil, then cover and continue to boil until the meat is almost tender, about 45 minutes.

3. Stir in the chili powder, cumin, garlic, and black pepper. Reduce the heat to low and cook 30 minutes. Adjust the consistency with more beef broth, if desired.

4. Serve with cheese, onions, and jalapeños for each diner to add to his or her bowl.

THE MAIN COURSE

Cook up dinner any way you like it—pan-sear it on a griddle,

braise it in a Dutch oven, or roast it in a skillet. Whether

you've got a taste for poultry, steak, ribs, or fish, or you're in

the mood to go meatless—you're going to eat well tonight!

If you haven't made pizza with cauliflower, prepare to fall in love. Minneapolis-based cookbook author and culinary instructor Robin Asbell created this hefty pie to show off the sweet flavor of roasted cauliflower, accented with piquant feta and Asiago cheeses. Baking the pizza in cast iron makes the crust crisp while it cradles all the goodies.

SKILLET CAULIFLOWER-FETA PIZZA

serves 2 to 3

1½ cups white whole wheat flour, plus more as needed

1 teaspoon rapid-rise yeast

¼ teaspoon salt

1 teaspoon honey

¾ cup warm water (110° to 115°)

2 tablespoons extra-virgin olive oil

3½ cups cauliflower florets (8 ounces)

½ cup chopped onion

½ small red bell pepper, seeded and chopped

2 garlic cloves, sliced

Canola oil

1 tablespoon sesame seeds

3 ounces feta cheese, crumbled

2 ounces Asiago cheese, shredded

½ cup chopped fresh parsley or basil

1. Preheat the oven to 425°.

2. Combine the flour, yeast, and salt in a large bowl or stand mixer fitted with the dough hook. Stir in the honey, warm water, and 1 tablespoon olive oil. Knead or mix in the bowl, kneading in extra flour if needed to make a soft, barely sticky dough. Place the dough in a well-greased bowl, turning to grease the top. Let rise in a warm spot until it is doubled in volume.

3. Toss together the cauliflower, onion, bell pepper, garlic, and remaining 1 tablespoon olive oil in a large roasting pan. Bake, uncovered, for 20 minutes. The cauliflower should be soft and partially golden brown. Allow vegetables to cool slightly.

4. Lightly grease a 12-inch cast iron skillet with canola oil and sprinkle the bottom with the sesame seeds. Punch down the dough. Turn dough out onto a lightly floured surface. Shape dough into a large round. Press the dough into the bottom of the skillet and up the side about 1 inch. Top with the roasted vegetables, cheeses, and parsley. Bake until the crust is crisp in the center of the pizza and the cheeses are melted and golden, about 30 minutes.

5. Tilt the pan and use a metal spatula to transfer the pizza onto a cutting board. Cut it into 6 wedges and serve.

a cast iron memory

Cooking is tightly woven into the fabric of my life. In many ways, it is who I am, and cooking in cast iron is the whole cloth for me. The iron got into my blood in the halcyon days of my early childhood in a place that now only lives in my memories, my grandmother's kitchen. In it sat a wood-burning stove, a magical place where Mamaw seemed to always be hovering, that is when she wasn't working the farm or policing us young'uns. Everything cooked on that stove was prepared in a pot or pan as black as it was. It was a blessing to have experienced food harvested and prepared at its source—all cooked in cast iron cookware.

My mom and dad before he was shipped out during WWII

In my early teens, I became a vegetarian, starting my own unique journey in cooking. I had to learn a whole new approach to food. Knowing that our cast iron pans were seasoned with animal fat, I stopped using mom's pans. When I moved off to college, I began acquiring my own cast iron, seasoned with vegetable oils. With mom's help, I learned to care for those pans, an art in itself, handed down from generation to generation. Many years later when my mom passed, I gathered with her sisters around mom's kitchen table to break bread one last time before her kitchen passed into memory. I asked if they wished a keepsake, and each requested one of her cast iron pans. I picked the one that she used the most. Of the things I kept from her home, that cast iron skillet is most cherished.

Recently, my Aunt Devota died; she was my mother's closest sister, in both age and life's journey. After the funeral, Joyce, my last remaining aunt, and I returned to Aunt Devota's apartment to spend a little time before parting. When Joyce asked if I wished a keepsake, it was Devota's cast iron pans that I chose. After all, it is elemental for me to hold the remembrance of my family in the enduring warmth of these heirlooms, to celebrate life and find inspiration creating eatable love in these beloved cast iron pans. From a simple cast iron skillet sprang many of my explorations in cooking and my life's work. —Biker Billy Hufnagle

This quick and easy one-pan rendition of quiche is bursting with fresh garden flavors and a decidedly Italian flair, yet the warm glow of the chipotle peppers adds a hint of south of the border. This quiche is perfect for brunch, but Harley-riding cookbook author Biker Billy Hufnagle also likes to serve it for dinner with a salad and a side of angel hair pasta topped with marinara sauce.

CRUSTLESS QUICHE CHIPOTLE

serves 6 to 8

2 tablespoons salted butter
1 medium onion, thinly sliced into half moons and the strips pulled apart
1 cup (¼-inch-thick) sliced carrots
1 medium zucchini, trimmed and cut into ¼-inch-thick slices
1 medium yellow squash, trimmed and cut into ¼-inch-thick slices
¼ cup sun-dried tomatoes in olive oil, drained and minced

2 chipotle chiles in adobo sauce, minced
4 extra-large eggs
1½ cups milk
3 cups (12 ounces) shredded mozzarella cheese
1 teaspoon dried oregano
1 teaspoon dried basil
½ teaspoon salt
½ teaspoon freshly ground black pepper

1. Preheat the oven to 400°.

2. Melt the butter in a large (7-cup) cast iron skillet over medium-high heat. Add the onion and carrots and cook, stirring often, until the onion begins to brown, about 3 minutes. Add both squash, sun-dried tomatoes, and chipotles; cook, stirring often, until the squash are tender, about 5 minutes.

3. While the vegetables are sautéing, combine the eggs and milk in a large bowl and beat until blended. Add 1 cup cheese, the oregano, basil, salt, and black pepper; stir well.

4. Pour the egg mixture over the vegetables in the skillet and stir just enough to combine. Sprinkle the remaining 2 cups cheese on top and bake until the top is browned and a fork inserted in the center comes out clean, about 30 minutes. Let cool for a few minutes before slicing into wedges to serve.

FRENCH CASSOULET, VEGETARIAN STYLE

serves 6 to 8

This recipe is from Brother Victor-Antoine d'Avila-Latourrette, a resident monk who lives under the Rule of St. Benedict at Our Lady of the Resurrection Monastery outside Millbrook, New York. Brother Victor-Antoine cooks and tends the gardens and monastery farm, supplying produce for both the monastery table and the local farmers' market. He has also written numerous books, including *Twelve Months of Monastery Soups*.

When the weather turns cold, Brother Victor-Antoine likes to serve this cassoulet accompanied by a loaf of good crusty bread and a green salad dressed simply with oil and vinegar. This stew reheats well, so you can have leftovers for the following day.

5　tablespoons olive oil
8　garlic cloves, minced
2　large onions, chopped
1　teaspoon fresh or dried rosemary
½　teaspoon dried thyme
½　teaspoon dried oregano
2　bay leaves
3　cups dry white wine, plus more if needed
2　medium carrots, diced
2　celery ribs, thinly sliced
2　medium potatoes, peeled and diced
2　cups diced tomatoes
Salt and freshly ground black pepper
1　large garlic clove, peeled
Butter or olive oil
2　(15-ounce) cans navy beans, drained and rinsed
1　cup tomato sauce
1　cup fine, dry breadcrumbs

1. Preheat the oven to 350°.

2. Heat the oil in a large, deep cast iron skillet over medium-low heat. Add the minced garlic and the next 5 ingredients and cook, stirring often, 2 minutes. Increase the heat to medium and add the wine; cover and simmer until the onions are softened, about 5 minutes. Stir in the carrots, celery, potatoes, and tomatoes; cover and simmer 10 minutes. Season with salt and pepper to taste.

3. Rub the large garlic clove over the bottom and side of a large cast iron Dutch oven, then rub the pan with butter.

4. Pour one-third of the vegetable mixture into the Dutch oven and sprinkle one-third of the navy beans over the top. Repeat the layers twice. Pour the tomato sauce over the top and sprinkle with the breadcrumbs.

5. Cover the pan and bake for 1½ hours. Check occasionally to be sure there is enough liquid; add more wine if the mixture seems to be getting dry. Discard bay leaves before serving.

In this recipe, Indian food authority Julie Sahni, whose School of Indian Cooking in New York City is renowned as one of the nation's best, adds flavor and texture to green beans with cashew nuts and spices, making it a delicious entrée accompanied with a bowl of plain-cooked brown rice. For a spicier version, increase the red pepper flakes to 1 teaspoon.

SPICY PAN-ROASTED GREEN BEANS *(Sem Masala)*

serves 6

1½ pounds fresh green beans	3 garlic cloves, thinly sliced
1 medium carrot	1 teaspoon kosher salt
2 teaspoons ground coriander	¼ cup water
1 teaspoon ground cumin	2 teaspoons fresh lime juice
½ teaspoon red pepper flakes	¼ cup roasted cashews
¼ teaspoon turmeric	2 tablespoons finely chopped
2 tablespoons light vegetable oil	fresh cilantro
1½ teaspoons cumin seeds	

1. Trim the ends of the green beans. Peel the carrot, cut into 3-inch-long, ¼-inch-thick matchsticks. Combine the coriander, cumin, red pepper, and turmeric in a small bowl. Set aside.

2. Place a Lodge Pro-Logic Wok over high heat until it is very hot, about 3 minutes. Add the oil and cumin seeds. When the cumin exudes aroma and turns several shades darker, add the garlic and let it sizzle until it turns light golden, 15 seconds. Add the green beans, carrot, spice mixture, and salt. Stir well and sauté until lightly seared, about 5 minutes. Pour the water over the vegetables and cover; reduce the heat to medium-low and cook until the green beans are tender, about 5 minutes.

3. Uncover the wok and cook until the excess moisture evaporates and the vegetables are pan-roasted and caramelized, about 6 minutes. Sprinkle the lime juice, cashews, and cilantro over the top, stir and serve hot, at room temperature or cold.

This tofu dish from cookbook author and *Bon Appétit* contributing editor Dede Wilson features a rich, savory flavor and comes together very quickly in a large cast iron wok. Serve it with rice.

TOFU-BOK CHOY STIR-FRY WITH OYSTER MUSHROOMS

serves 2

½ cup plus 1½ teaspoons water

2 tablespoons black bean paste with garlic

2 teaspoons soy sauce

2 tablespoons peanut oil

1 pound extra-firm tofu, drained and cut into 1-inch cubes

2 garlic cloves, minced

4 bunches baby bok choy (6 ounces total), root end removed and cut crosswise into ½-inch-wide strips

3 ounces oyster mushroom caps, stems trimmed and cut into ¼-inch-thick slices

1½ teaspoons cornstarch

Hot cooked rice

1 green onion, thinly sliced

1. Combine ½ cup water, the black bean paste, and soy sauce in a small bowl and stir well; set aside.

2. Heat the oil in a cast iron wok over high heat until hot. Add the tofu and cook, tossing once or twice, until the cubes just turn golden, about 5 minutes. Add the garlic and cook 1 minute.

3. Add the bok choy and mushrooms and cook 1 minute. Add the black bean paste mixture and toss well; cook until the sauce boils, about 1 minute.

4. Whisk together the cornstarch and remaining 1½ teaspoons water in a small bowl until smooth. Add to the wok and cook until the sauce thickens slightly, about 1 minute.

5. Serve the stir-fry immediately over rice; top with the green onions.

Cookbook author Biker Billy Hufnagle has been making this casserole for Thanksgiving for several years. It is a vegetarian protein dish with gravy that evokes the aromas and flavors of a traditional stuffed turkey dinner, and it's now a Hufnagle family tradition in its own right. It provides the added benefit of being cooked and baked in a single cast iron skillet, which saves on cleanup.

THANKSGIVING DAY VEGETARIAN CASSEROLE

serves 6 to 8

¼ cup canola oil

1 (8-ounce) package tempeh, cut into ½-inch-thick strips

1 (14-ounce) package extra-firm tofu, drained and cut into 1-inch cubes

2 tablespoons salted butter

1 medium onion, chopped

1 (8-ounce) package sliced baby bella mushrooms

1 (2.75-ounce) package peppered gravy mix (such as Southeastern Mills)

1½ teaspoons dried chervil

½ teaspoon ground savory

½ teaspoon ground sage

½ teaspoon dried thyme

½ teaspoon dried basil

¼ teaspoon dried oregano

¾ teaspoon salt

¼ teaspoon freshly ground black pepper

1. Preheat the oven to 350°.

2. Heat the oil in a large (7-cup) cast iron skillet over medium-high heat. When hot, add the tempeh and cook until golden brown on all sides, about 5 minutes. Remove the tempeh to paper towels to drain, reserving the oil in the pan.

3. Add the tofu to the pan and stir-fry until lightly browned. Remove the tofu to paper towels to drain.

4. Melt the butter in the skillet. Add the onion and mushrooms and cook, stirring often, until the onion begins to brown, about 5 minutes.

5. While the onion and mushrooms cook, prepare the gravy according to the package directions.

6. Return the tempeh and tofu to the skillet and stir to combine. Add the dried herbs, salt, and pepper and stir well. Pour the gravy into the pan and stir well. Transfer the skillet to the oven and bake until the top begins to brown, about 30 minutes. Serve hot from the pan.

Fish tacos, which originated in Mexico's Baja region, traveled up the coast to California, and now have gone national. They are traditionally made with fish that has been beer-battered and fried. This version, from Jennifer Chandler's cookbook *Simply Suppers*, uses marinated fish that is pan-seared in cast iron.

FISH TACOS WITH MANGO SLAW AND AVOCADO CREMA

serves 4 (2 tacos per person)

Mango Slaw:

2 cups finely shredded green cabbage

1½ cups finely shredded red cabbage

1 cup diced mango

¼ cup thinly sliced red onion (about half a small onion)

2 tablespoons seeded and finely chopped jalapeño chile

3 tablespoons fresh lime juice

2 tablespoons olive oil

Kosher salt and freshly ground black pepper

2 tablespoons coarsely chopped fresh cilantro

Avocado Crema:

2 large ripe avocados, peeled, pitted, and coarsely chopped

2 tablespoons fresh lime juice

¼ cup sour cream

Kosher salt and freshly ground black pepper

Fish Tacos:

¼ cup plus 1 tablespoon olive oil

2 tablespoons fresh lime juice

1 garlic clove, minced

½ teaspoon chili powder

4 (6-ounce) tilapia fillets

Kosher salt and freshly ground black pepper

8 small (4-inch) flour tortillas, warmed

1. Make the mango slaw: Combine both cabbages, mango, onion, and jalapeño in a large bowl. Add the lime juice and oil and toss until well combined. Season with salt and pepper to taste. Refrigerate until ready to serve or for up to 2 hours. Fold in the cilantro just before serving.

2. Make the avocado crema: Process the avocado and lime juice in a blender or food processor until smooth. Blend in the sour cream. Place the crema in a bowl and season with salt and pepper to taste.

3. Make the fish tacos: Whisk together ¼ cup oil, the lime juice, garlic, and chili powder in a small bowl until well blended. Place the tilapia in a shallow dish and pour the marinade over the fish. Cover and refrigerate for at least 30 minutes or up to 1 hour. Remove the fish from the marinade, drain off any excess, and discard the marinade. Season both sides of the fish with salt and pepper to taste.

4. Heat the remaining 1 tablespoon oil in a large cast iron skillet over medium-high heat until hot. Sear the fish fillets until they are well browned and release easily from the pan, about 4 minutes. Turn and cook until the fillets are cooked through, 5 minutes. Transfer to a plate and break into large pieces.

5. Assemble the tacos by placing the fish (approximately half a fillet per taco) in the center of each tortilla. Top with desired amounts of the slaw and crema. Serve warm.

Elizabeth Heiskell, the lead culinary instructor at the Viking Cooking School in Greenwood, Mississippi, contributed this dish. She and her fellow instructors served it to renowned chef, restaurateur, and educator Alice Waters when she visited the school.

CORNMEAL FRIED CATFISH OVER BLACK-EYED PEA SALAD WITH PICKLED JALAPEÑO RELISH

serves 6

6 catfish fillets
Hot sauce
Salt and freshly ground black
  pepper
3 cups plain white cornmeal
3 cups masa harina

3 tablespoons Cajun seasoning
1 tablespoon seasoned salt
Peanut oil
Black-eyed Pea Salad (see recipe)
Pickled Jalapeño Relish (see
  recipe)

1. Rub the catfish fillets on both sides sparingly with hot sauce and salt and pepper to taste; set aside. Combine the cornmeal, masa harina, Cajun seasoning, and seasoned salt in a large shallow bowl.
2. Pour oil to a depth of 4 to 5 inches in a 12-inch cast iron Dutch oven; heat over high heat to 375°.
3. While the oil is heating, dredge the catfish in the cornmeal mixture, tapping off any excess. Fry the catfish, in 2 batches, until golden brown on both sides, about 4 minutes per batch. Drain on a paper bag.
4. To serve, place desired amount of the Black-eyed Pea Salad on each of 4 plates and top with a catfish fillet and a dollop of the Pickled Jalapeño Relish.

BLACK-EYED PEA SALAD

serves 6

2 (15½-ounce) cans black-eyed
   peas, drained and rinsed
1 (14-ounce) can artichoke
   hearts, drained and coarsely
   chopped
½ red bell pepper, seeded and
   diced

1 (18-ounce) jar pepper relish
   or sauce (Elizabeth prefers
   Braswell's; it's sort of like a
   chowchow)
Salt and freshly ground black
   pepper

1. Combine first 4 ingredients in a medium bowl and mix well.
Season with salt and black pepper to taste. Cover with plastic wrap
and refrigerate overnight to let the flavors develop.

This makes more relish than you'll need for the recipe, but that's fine. Try it on
hamburgers or hot dogs, spooned over cream cheese as a tasty spread for crackers,
or served on the side with cooked greens of all kinds.

PICKLED JALAPEÑO RELISH

makes about 4 cups

2½ pounds jalapeño chiles,
   stemmed and chopped in a
   food processor with ¼ cup salt
2 cups thinly sliced onion
1 cup sugar

1 cup cider vinegar
1 tablespoon celery salt
1 tablespoon mustard seeds
½ teaspoon turmeric

1. Combine the jalapeño-salt mixture with the onion in a large bowl
and let stand 3 hours. Drain well.
2. Combine the sugar, vinegar, celery salt, mustard seeds, and turmeric in a small saucepan and bring to a boil. Reduce the heat, add
the jalapeño mixture, and simmer 5 minutes.
3. Let the relish cool to room temperature. Pour into Mason jars,
cover tightly and keep refrigerated up to 3 months.

In this recipe, food historian Jessica B. Harris gives Porgies the traditional South-ern treatment and fries them to a golden brown in a cast iron skillet. A twist that Jessica's mother learned from a fisherman is that instead of just dredging the fish, add a slathering of mayonnaise first to help the flavored cornmeal and flour adhere.

SKILLET-FRIED PORGIES

serves 6 to 8

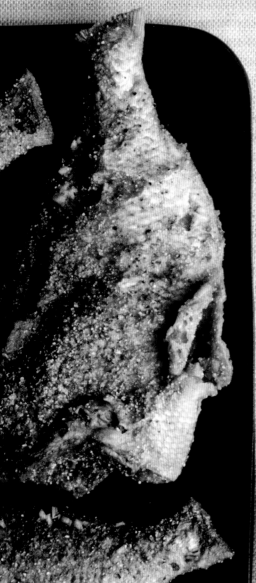

12 medium porgy fish
⅓ cup fresh lemon juice
Canola oil
1 tablespoon Seafood Boil (see
   recipe) or Creole seasoning
   (such as Zatarain's)

¼ cup plain yellow cornmeal
¼ cup all-purpose flour
Salt and freshly ground black
   pepper
½ cup mayonnaise

1. Have the fishmonger clean the porgies and remove the heads and fins.
2. Place the fish in a large bowl and sprinkle them with the lemon juice. Cover and set aside. Pour oil to a depth of 2 inches in a large cast iron skillet; heat over high heat to 350°.
3. While the oil is heating, grind the Seafood Boil into a fine powder in a spice grinder and combine it with the cornmeal, flour, and salt and pepper to taste in a paper bag. Brush the mayonnaise on both sides of the fish, then place a few fish at a time in the bag with the cornmeal mixture; shake to ensure that they are well coated.
4. Place the fish in the hot oil, being careful not to crowd the pan, and fry, in batches, until golden brown, 2 minutes per side. Drain on paper towels and place on a warm platter while repeating the procedure with the remaining fish. Serve immediately.

This is an all-purpose seafood boil that can be used for everything from cooking crabs to crawfish or to add a bit of seasoning, in this case to the coating for fried fish. It will keep for an entire summer in an airtight container.

SEAFOOD BOIL

makes about 1 cup

- ¼ cup commercial pickling spice
- 3 tablespoons coarse sea salt
- 2 tablespoons brown mustard seeds
- 2 tablespoons black peppercorns
- 1 tablespoon celery seeds
- 1 tablespoon freeze-dried chives
- 2 teaspoons red pepper flakes, or to taste
- 2 teaspoons dried oregano
- 1 teaspoon ground ginger
- 4 bay leaves

1. Place all the ingredients in a spice grinder and grind until you have a coarse powder. Stir well and make sure that there are no large unprocessed pieces. Pour the mixture into a glass jar. Close tightly and store in a cool, dark place.

Elizabeth Heiskell, lead culinary instructor at the Viking Cooking School in Greenwood, Mississippi, contributed this recipe on behalf of her good friend Nan. "Only she could turn leftover fried catfish into pure genius," says Elizabeth.

NANNIE'S CATFISH CAKES

serves 4; makes 8 (2½-inch) cakes

1 sleeve premium saltine crackers	4 large eggs, lightly beaten
2 tablespoons butter	4 teaspoons Tabasco sauce
¼ cup finely diced onion	4 teaspoons Worcestershire sauce
¼ cup finely diced yellow bell pepper	Salt and freshly ground black pepper
¼ cup chopped green onions	¼ cup olive oil
8 fried catfish fillets	Come Back Sauce (see recipe)

1. Place the crackers in a food processor and grind to crumbs; pour crumbs into a shallow bowl.

2. Melt the butter in a medium cast iron skillet over medium heat. Add the onion, bell pepper, and green onions; cook, stirring often, until tender.

3. Place the catfish fillets in a medium bowl and use your fingers or the back of a fork to mash them into bits. Add the beaten eggs, Tabasco, and Worcestershire; season with salt and pepper to taste. Add the onion mixture and stir well. Pat the catfish mixture into 8 cakes about 2½ inches wide and 1½ inches thick. Gently dredge the cakes in the cracker crumbs, coating well on both sides.

4. Heat a 12-inch cast iron skillet over medium-high heat and add the oil. Gently place the catfish cakes in the hot skillet and cook, in batches, until golden brown on both sides. Drain on a paper bag and serve with Come Back Sauce.

This sauce originated at the Mayflower Cafe in Jackson, Mississippi, where it was the house salad dressing. It got its name because diners kept "coming back" for it. (Except, so the story goes in her family, Elizabeth Heiskell's cousin, who, after enjoying his salad with Come Back Sauce and one too many glasses of wine, was very politely asked not to come back.) Come Back Sauce pairs well with any kind of fried food (try fried green tomatoes) and also makes a tasty dip for cold boiled shrimp.

COME BACK SAUCE

makes about 1¼ cups

- 1 tablespoon grated onion (using the large holes of a box grater)
- 1 cup mayonnaise
- 3 tablespoons fresh lemon juice
- 1 tablespoon vegetable oil
- 1 tablespoon prepared chili sauce
- 1 tablespoon Worcestershire sauce
- 1 teaspoon dry mustard
- 1 teaspoon salt
- 1 teaspoon freshly ground black pepper

1. Combine all the ingredients in a medium bowl and stir well. If the sauce is too thick to drizzle, add 1 tablespoon water to thin. Refrigerate in an airtight container for up to 2 weeks.

a cast iron memory

As a child growing up in Rosedale, Mississippi, on the Mississippi River, I always assumed I'd marry a Delta boy. After my parents' divorce and a move to Memphis, I often went back to visit the Delta. However, most of my time was spent in the "North." After dating a string of adorable Memphis boys, I realized something was always missing. When I met my future husband, Luke, it all clicked.

On our first date we were getting to know each other over dinner and discussing our families. Luke mentioned that he was gravely concerned about his sister's boyfriend. I was thinking drug addict, homeless, a guest of the state of Tennessee? What could it be? Luke slowly began to tell me a story about his visit to his sister's apartment. He noticed their father's Lodge skillet coated in rust. When Luke confronted his sister, she nervously explained that the boyfriend had cooked supper and put the treasured skillet in the dishwasher. Luke shook his head in utter disgust—how could she stay with someone like this? I wasn't sure either, but I was sure about one thing—I had finally found the Delta boy I had been looking for. —Elizabeth Heiskell

"I still remember eating my first trout," recalls Christy Rost, cookbook author and host of the public television series *A Home for Christy Rost*. "I was a teenager on vacation with my family in Colorado, and we stopped in a restaurant near Colorado Springs. When the trout was served, it filled the entire platter! I consumed every morsel. And years later, my husband, Randy, taught me to fish for trout in Colorado's lakes and streams." For Christy, there are few meals more satisfying than pan-fried trout, fresh from the Rocky Mountains. In this recipe, she dresses them with toasted hazelnuts, which provide a sweet, almost floral, nuance to the dish.

PAN-FRIED ROCKY MOUNTAIN TROUT WITH TOASTED HAZELNUTS

serves 2

2 (½-pound) rainbow or
   brown trout, cleaned
½ cup all-purpose flour
½ teaspoon kosher salt
¼ teaspoon freshly ground
   pepper mélange

2 tablespoons unsalted butter
½ cup chopped hazelnuts
2 lemon slices

1. Wash the fish under cold water and pat dry with paper towels.

2. Stir together the flour, salt, and pepper in a large, shallow bowl. Coat the fish lightly on both sides with the seasoned flour.

3. Heat a large cast iron skillet over medium heat. Melt the butter in the hot skillet, swirling to coat the bottom of the pan. Add the fish and cook until the skin is golden brown, about 5 minutes. Turn the fish over and add the hazelnuts to the pan; cook just until the fish flakes with a fork, about 5 minutes, stirring the nuts frequently to toast them evenly.

4. When the fish is golden brown on both sides and the meat is tender and just beginning to flake, carefully transfer the trout to plates. Top each fish with some of the toasted hazelnuts and a slice of lemon.

Cookbook author Jennifer Chandler loves to pan-roast fish. For fish that stays moist and flaky, she first sears it on the stove-top until it has a nice golden crust, and then she finishes cooking it in the oven. Jennifer uses this same technique with all types of fish. In this recipe, from her book *Simply Suppers*, she tops the fish with a flavored butter for an instant sauce.

PAN-ROASTED SEA BASS WITH CHIVE-GARLIC COMPOUND BUTTER

serves 4

Chive-Garlic Compound Butter:
1 cup (2 sticks) unsalted butter, at room temperature
2 tablespoons finely minced fresh chives
1 garlic clove, minced
Pinch of kosher salt

Pan-Roasted Sea Bass:
4 (4- to 6-ounce) sea bass fillets
Kosher salt and freshly ground black pepper
2 tablespoons olive oil
Chopped fresh chives for garnish

1. Beat the butter in a medium bowl with an electric mixer until light and fluffy. Add the chives, garlic, and salt and beat until thoroughly combined. Spoon the mixture in the shape of a log onto a piece of wax or parchment paper. Fold the paper over itself. Using your hands, shape the butter into a cylinder about 1½ inches wide (almost like making a Tootsie Roll). Once it is shaped, twist the ends to seal it. Place it in the freezer for 20 minutes to set, then refrigerate until ready to serve or for up to 1 month. When ready to serve, slice the roll into ¼-inch-thick rounds and remove the wax or parchment paper.

2. Preheat the oven to 375°.

3. Generously season both sides of each fish fillet with salt and pepper to taste. Heat the oil in a large cast iron skillet over medium heat until hot. Sear the fillets, skin side up, until they are well browned and release easily from pan, about 4 minutes. Turn and cook 1 minute, until seared. Transfer the pan to the oven and bake just until fish flakes with a fork, about 5 minutes.

4. Serve each fillet topped with a slice of Chive-Garlic Compound Butter. (Only 4 slices of the butter are needed for this recipe.) Garnish with chopped fresh chives.

This simple recipe comes from the mother-daughter team of cookbook authors and cast iron aficionados Sharon Kramis and Julie Kramis Hearne. Mussels should be cooked until their shells open up, and they are plump and juicy; if they don't open, don't eat them. Serve this delicious dish with a crusty loaf of your favorite bread to sop up all the tasty juices!

IRON SKILLET ROASTED MUSSELS

serves 6

½ cup white wine

¼ cup (½ stick) unsalted butter

1 leek (white part only), rinsed well and chopped

¼ teaspoon red pepper flakes

2 pounds mussels, scrubbed and debearded (discard any that don't close)

3 tablespoons chopped fresh parsley

Salt and freshly ground black pepper

1. Combine the wine, butter, leek, and red pepper in a 10- to 12-inch cast iron skillet or 5-quart Dutch oven and bring to a boil over medium-high heat.

2. Reduce the heat to medium; add the mussels and cover. Cook until the shells open and the mussels are plump, about 8 minutes. Discard any mussels that don't open.

3. Sprinkle the parsley over the top and season with salt and pepper to taste. Serve right from the skillet or Dutch oven with sliced bread.

This stir-fry comes from Asian cooking expert and cookbook author Nancie McDermott. She based it on the Thai dish chicken with holy basil (*gai paht bai graprao*), substituting shrimp—which, though not typical, is delicious and gorgeous—adding more onion and less chile heat, and using sweet Thai basil. It's wonderful served over rice, orzo, or couscous, or offered up with a salad or garlicky sautéed greens and good crusty bread and butter.

SHRIMP WITH FRESH BASIL, THAI STYLE

serves 3 to 4

2 tablespoons Asian fish sauce
2 tablespoons water
1 teaspoon soy sauce
½ teaspoon sugar
2 tablespoons vegetable oil
1 pound medium shrimp, peeled and deveined
1 cup thinly sliced onion (sliced into half moons and pulled apart into strips)

1 tablespoon chopped garlic
¼ cup finely chopped green onions
2 tablespoons coarsely chopped fresh cilantro
1 tablespoon seeded and chopped jalapeño, serrano, or other green chile
¾ cup loosely packed fresh Thai or other basil leaves

1. Stir together the fish sauce, water, soy sauce, and sugar in a small bowl and set aside. Prep the remaining ingredients, so you can add them quickly when they are needed.

2. Place a 10- or 12-inch cast iron skillet over medium-high heat until it becomes very hot, about 30 seconds.

3. Add the oil and turn to coat the pan evenly. Add the shrimp in a single layer and leave them to cook on one side, undisturbed, until their edges turn bright pink. Toss well and turn all the shrimp cooked side up so the other side can cook, undisturbed, for 15 seconds.

4. Add the onion and garlic and toss well. Cook 1 minute, tossing occasionally, until the onion softens and becomes fragrant and shiny; continue tossing so it wilts and softens but doesn't brown.

5. Stir the fish sauce mixture to make sure the sugar is dissolved and pour it around the edge of the pan. Toss well to season the shrimp with the sauce, then let cook, undisturbed, just until the shrimp are cooked through and the sauce is bubbling. (The sauce will not be thick; it will have the consistency of thin pan juices.)

6. Add the green onions, cilantro, and chile and toss well. Tear any big basil leaves into 2 or 3 pieces each (you want to tear the basil at the very last minute, otherwise it will darken). Add all of the basil to the pan over the shrimp and toss well. Cook 10 seconds and pour onto a serving platter deep enough to hold a little sauce. Serve hot.

In this recipe from Julie Sahni, author of the acclaimed *Classic Indian Cooking* and *Classic Indian Vegetarian and Grain Cooking*, shrimp are seared with ginger and black peppercorns. Julie suggests serving it with a green salad and sweet dinner rolls "to mop up those spicy juices" or with a fragrant rice pilaf studded with raisins.

BLACK PEPPER SKILLET SHRIMP
(Meen Varuval)

serves 4

1 pound large shrimp	½ teaspoon sugar
2 tablespoons vegetable oil	Juice of ½ lime
2 tablespoons shredded peeled fresh ginger	½ teaspoon kosher salt or to taste
2 teaspoons ground coriander	2 tablespoons thinly sliced green onions (green part only)
1½ teaspoons cracked black peppercorns	

1. Peel and devein the shrimp, leaving the last shell segment and tail intact.

2. Heat the oil in a 9-inch cast iron skillet over high heat until very hot, about 3 minutes. Add the ginger and cook, stirring, until it turns light brown and is caramelized, about 2 minutes. Stir in the coriander, cracked peppercorns, and sugar and let heat for 15 seconds.

3. Add the shrimp and cook, shaking and tossing, until they turn pink and curl up, about 2 minutes. Sprinkle with the lime juice, salt, and green onions. Stir gently and serve from the skillet.

This version of the classic rice dish (which is a Southern coastal interpretation of paella) is from Steven Satterfield, executive chef/owner of Miller Union in Atlanta. A few things are crucial to the final flavor of the dish. The first is using Carolina Gold rice, an heirloom variety of long-grain rice that is hand-harvested by its producer Anson Mills (buy it online at *ansonmills.com*). Sautéing the rice in fat for a good 5 minutes helps to infuse flavor into the individual grains. Lastly, no peeking while the rice is cooking—the covered cast iron pot is key to the development of the crust on the bottom. Steven likes to serve this with a green salad and roasted okra.

SAVANNAH RED RICE

serves 6 *(pictured on page 72)*

4 tablespoons bacon drippings

5 tablespoons butter

1 small yellow onion, diced

1 cup diced celery (inner leaves included)

2 garlic cloves, minced

2 tablespoons plus 1 teaspoon kosher salt or more to taste

2 cups canned organic whole plum tomatoes, undrained, chopped

2 cups chicken stock

2 tablespoons pepper vinegar or cider vinegar (if you use cider vinegar, add a pinch of red pepper flakes)

1¼ teaspoons freshly ground black pepper

¾ teaspoon dried thyme

2 bay leaves

2 dried chiles de arbol, chopped, or a pinch of red pepper flakes

2 cups long-grain rice (such as Carolina Gold)

½ pound andouille or chorizo sausage, grilled and sliced ½ inch thick

1 pound shrimp, peeled, deveined, and cut into bite-size pieces

1. Heat 2 tablespoons bacon drippings and 2 tablespoons butter in a medium saucepan over medium heat until melted. Add the onion, celery, garlic, and 1 tablespoon salt; cook, stirring often, until the onion and garlic are tender. Add the tomatoes, stock, vinegar, 1 tablespoon salt, 1 teaspoon black pepper, the thyme, bay leaves, and chiles; simmer 15 to 20 minutes, tasting for seasoning.

2. Heat the remaining 2 tablespoons bacon drippings and 2 tablespoons butter in a large cast iron skillet over medium heat until foamy. Add the rice and cook, stirring frequently, until it is opaque, about 5 minutes. This step is very important to the final flavor of the dish, so don't skimp on the time—but also don't let the rice burn.

3. Add 4 cups of the tomato mixture to the rice; stir to combine, and cover. Set a timer and cook the rice for 25 minutes over very low heat. DO NOT LIFT THE LID. After 25 minutes, turn off the heat and let the rice stand for 5 more minutes. AGAIN, DO NOT LIFT THE LID. While the rice cooks, add the sausage to the remaining tomato mixture in the pan; cover and keep warm over very low heat.

4. While the rice is standing, melt the remaining 1 tablespoon butter in a medium sauté pan over medium-high heat until foamy. Add the shrimp and cook, stirring just until cooked through; add the remaining 1 teaspoon salt and ¼ teaspoon black pepper. Add the shrimp to the sausage and tomato mixture, and stir well.

5. Pour the shrimp and sausage mixture over the rice. Remove and discard bay leaves. Gently fluff the rice (you don't want to break the grains) to combine. Serve immediately.

It's risky to use the word "barbecue" in the South because it means a wide range of things overall, and yet a very specific thing to each individual. In this recipe, from Sheri Castle, a food writer and cooking teacher in Chapel Hill, North Carolina, succulent shrimp are seared in a sensational barbecue sauce in a hot cast iron skillet. The high heat quickly cooks the shrimp and produces a spicy, buttery, lemony sauce to spoon over hot rice. The ingredient list looks long, but the recipe comes together quickly and relies mostly on pantry staples. Be sure to use jumbo or extra-large shrimp that will not overcook and turn rubbery.

BARBECUE SHRIMP OVER RICE

serves 8

⅔ cup tomato sauce

⅔ cup ketchup

⅓ cup unfiltered cider vinegar

¼ cup firmly packed light brown sugar

2 tablespoons Worcestershire sauce

1 teaspoon garlic powder

1 teaspoon onion powder

2 teaspoons cracked or coarsely ground black pepper

1 teaspoon salt

1 teaspoon sweet paprika

1 teaspoon smoked paprika

1 teaspoon dried basil

1 teaspoon dried oregano

1 teaspoon dried thyme

¼ teaspoon cayenne pepper or to taste

2½ to 3 pounds extra-jumbo shrimp (16 to 20), peeled and deveined

½ cup fresh lemon juice

½ cup (1 stick) butter, cut into small pieces

Hot cooked long-grain rice

1. Stir together the first 15 ingredients in a large bowl. Add the shrimp and toss to coat.

2. Heat a large cast iron skillet (preferably large enough to hold the shrimp in a single layer) over high heat until very hot. Carefully pour in the shrimp and sauce. (Watch out for spatters!) The liquid should boil and hiss.

3. Cook, stirring well and scraping the sauce from the bottom of the skillet, until the shrimp begin to turn pink and the sauce thickens, depending on size of the shrimp, about 2 minutes. Remove the skillet from the heat and add the lemon juice and butter. Stir until the butter melts and the shrimp are cooked through.

4. Serve immediately over plenty of hot rice to soak up the delicious sauce.

Janene White of Sacramento, California, offers this rich and creamy traditional Irish meal to fellow scallop lovers. Enjoy it as a main dish served with some astringent field greens or asparagus as a counterpoint. Or for the ultimate decadent surf-and-turf, serve it with your favorite steak dinner.

SCALLOP PIE

serves 2 to 4

½ cup milk	4 tablespoons butter
1 bay leaf	2 tablespoons all-purpose flour
1 pound scallops	1 garlic clove, crushed into a paste
Salt and freshly ground black pepper	½ tablespoon Irish whiskey
½ cup heavy cream	4 ounces mushrooms, sliced
2 cups finely chopped yellow onion	½ cup fine, dry breadcrumbs

1. Bring the milk and bay leaf to a simmer in a 10-inch cast iron skillet over medium heat. Add the scallops and season with salt and pepper to taste. Cook the scallops until they are opaque all the way through, about 5 minutes; remove them from the pan with a slotted spoon. If you're using sea scallops, cut each one into quarters when they're cool enough to handle. Pour the cream into a small bowl; pour the milk mixture through a fine wire-mesh strainer into the cream, discard the solids, and set aside. Wipe the skillet clean.

2. Preheat the broiler.

3. Add the onion to the skillet and cook over medium heat, stirring occasionally, until just softened. Add 2 tablespoons butter, stirring to melt, then sprinkle in the flour; stir continually for about 1 minute. (Don't overstir or the mixture will become pasty.) Slowly pour in the milk and cream mixture, stirring constantly. Continue to stir until sauce is smooth. Stir in the garlic and whiskey and simmer 5 minutes. Stir in the scallops and mushrooms.

4. Sprinkle the top with the breadcrumbs. Cut the remaining 2 tablespoons butter into small pieces and sprinkle over the crumbs. Place under the broiler until the top is browned.

Variation: Instead of breadcrumbs, you can spread mashed potatoes over the top. Sprinkle with the butter and bake at 350° until the top browns, about 20 minutes.

CASSEROLE OF SCALLOPS, CHESTNUT FARRO, AND HEN OF THE WOODS MUSHROOMS WITH SORGHUM VEAL GLACÉ

serves 4

This recipe comes from Linton Hopkins, chef/owner of Restaurant Eugene and Holeman & Finch Public House in Atlanta.

Chestnut Farro:

½ cup farro (Linton uses Anson Mills brand)

2½ cups chicken stock

1 bay leaf

1 teaspoon salt, plus more to taste

2 tablespoons unsalted butter

1 tablespoon minced jarred chestnuts

3 tablespoons minced shallots

1 tablespoon minced celery

½ teaspoon minced garlic

1 tablespoon minced fresh flat-leaf parsley

Grated zest and juice of 1 lemon

Freshly ground black pepper

Mushrooms:

1 pound hen of the woods (maitake) or shiitake mushrooms

3 tablespoons extra-virgin olive oil

Salt

1 cup chicken stock

1 teaspoon chopped fresh flat-leaf parsley

1 teaspoon unsalted butter

Freshly ground black pepper

Bacon:

2 ounces smoked slab bacon (Linton prefers Benton's)

Sorghum Veal Glacé:

4 teaspoons reduced veal stock or store-bought veal demi-glacé

1 teaspoon sorghum syrup

Scallops:

8 jumbo sea scallops

Salt

2 tablespoons peanut oil

1. Make the farro: Combine the farro, chicken stock, bay leaf, and salt in a medium saucepan; bring to a boil, reduce the heat, and simmer until farro is tender, about 2 hours. Remove from the heat.

2. Melt the butter in a medium cast iron skillet over medium heat until foamy. Add the chestnuts and toast. Add the shallots, celery, and garlic and cook, stirring occasionally, until the shallots are translucent. Add the farro to the skillet along with any liquid still in the saucepan. Stir in the parsley and lemon zest and juice; season with salt and pepper to taste; cover and keep warm.

3. Prepare the mushrooms: Preheat the oven to 350°. Break the mushrooms into smaller pieces (if using shiitakes, discard the stems). Place the mushrooms, olive oil, and salt to taste in a large cast iron

skillet. Place the skillet in the oven and roast until the mushrooms
are browned and tender, about 7 minutes.

4. Place the skillet over high heat. Add the chicken stock to the skillet and bring to a boil; reduce the stock to a glaze. Add the parsley
and butter; stir until the butter melts. Season with salt and pepper to
taste; cover and keep warm.

5. Cut the bacon into 4 cubes. Place the cubes in a small cast iron
skillet over medium heat and cook until golden brown on all sides.
Remove to a paper towel to drain.

6. Make the sorghum veal glacé: Combine the veal stock and sorghum syrup in a small saucepan and cook until hot. Keep warm.

7. Season the scallops with salt to taste. Heat the peanut oil in a
medium cast iron skillet over high heat until hot. Sear the scallops on
both sides until golden brown and just cooked through.

8. To serve, spoon some of the farro mixture into each of 4 individual Lodge Oblong Mini Servers. Top with a bacon cube, some of the
mushroom mixture, and 2 of the scallops. Drizzle the glacé over each
serving and serve immediately.

When Billie Cline Hill was a small child in the 1930s, her parents, Kate Belk and John Douglas Cline, opened a grocery store on Cedar Avenue in South Pittsburg, Tennessee. Mrs. Cline would cook the family meals in the rear of the store. Workmen at the Sequachee Valley Electric Cooperative building next door had a break at 9 a.m., and Billie's mother always put out a plate of leftovers from the previous night's dinner for the men to enjoy. Her fried chicken was such a favorite that she always cooked extra just for them.

MOTHER'S FAVORITE FRIED CHICKEN

serves 5 to 6

1 cup all-purpose flour	2 large eggs
1 tablespoon salt	¼ cup milk
1 teaspoon freshly ground black pepper	1 whole chicken, cut into 8 pieces
2 cups vegetable shortening	

1. Combine the flour, salt, and pepper in a bowl large enough to hold the largest piece of chicken.

2. Heat the shortening in a large cast iron Dutch oven or the fryer of a Lodge Combo Cooker over medium heat to 325°.

3. While the shortening heats, beat the eggs and milk in a bowl large enough to hold the largest piece of chicken. Dip the chicken pieces, one at a time, into the egg mixture, dredge them in the flour mixture, and then back into the egg mixture and the flour mixture.

4. Slowly fry the chicken until it is golden brown on all sides and cooked through. You may need to turn the heat down to prevent the chicken from getting too brown before it's done.

This simple dish comes from Patrick Reilly of the Majestic Grille in Memphis. The hardest part is deboning the chicken, but it is so worth the effort. You can do it yourself, or ask your butcher to do it for you. Make sure you save the bones and wings—they make the best chicken stock ever. Patrick likes to serve this with a tomato salad and Lyonnaise Potatoes (page 218).

SPATCHCOCK CHICKEN

serves 2

1 (3-pound) fryer chicken (look for a farm-raised organic bird—Patrick loves West Wind Farms from Deer Lodge, Tennessee)

1 tablespoon olive oil
Kosher salt and freshly ground black pepper

1. To debone the chicken, place the chicken on a cutting board, breast side up, with the legs pointing away from you. With a sharp knife, cut down the left center of the breast, keeping the tip of the knife along the edge of the breastbone, until you have cut the bird in half. Cut through the wing joint where it connects to the breast. Turn the chicken on its side and gently pull the leg back toward the breast until the leg joint pops out. Cut around the leg, removing the leg and the breast in one piece. Repeat with the other half of the chicken. Cut a slit down the length of the two bones in the legs; remove the bones, scraping the meat off as you go. Rub the chicken with the oil and season with salt and pepper to taste.

2. Heat a large cast iron grill pan over medium heat. Place the two chicken halves, skin side up, in the pan, and cook 8 minutes. Flip the chicken over, place a cast iron grill press on top, and cook until the juices run clear and the skin has turned golden brown and crispy, about 10 minutes. Let the chicken rest a few minutes. You can either serve each diner half a chicken or carve it into thick slices.

This recipe comes from cookbook author Diane Phillips's grandmother, Aleandra Ciuffoli Pasquini. Although her Nona used red wine vinegar, Diane prefers the sweeter flavor of good aged balsamic vinegar. Serve the chicken over sautéed potatoes like Nona did.

NONA'S CHICKEN

serves 6

6	thick bacon slices, cut into ½-inch pieces	1	teaspoon freshly ground black pepper
¼	cup olive oil, if needed (see Note below)	4	garlic cloves, sliced
1	(3-pound) whole chicken, cut into 8 pieces	2	tablespoons fresh rosemary leaves, finely chopped
2	teaspoons salt	¼	cup balsamic vinegar

1. Cook the bacon in a 12-inch cast iron skillet over medium-high heat, stirring often, until crisp. Add as much of the oil to the bacon and drippings in the pan as needed before adding the chicken (see Note).

2. While the bacon cooks, sprinkle the chicken pieces evenly with the salt and pepper. Add the chicken to the skillet and brown over medium-high heat on all sides, turning when each side is browned. While the chicken is browning, add the garlic and rosemary. When the chicken is browned, add the vinegar and turn the pieces of chicken to coat them with it.

3. Cover the skillet and cook over medium-high heat until a meat thermometer inserted into the thickest portion registers 165° and the chicken is cooked through, about 10 minutes.

note

If the bacon is quite lean, there will not be enough fat in the pan to brown the chicken; add as much of the olive oil to the pan as you think necessary before adding the chicken.

a cast iron memory

Sizzling bacon pieces hopped in the coal black skillet as Nona would gently cook it until crispy. When the bacon was crisp, she would add the chicken pieces, cut up and sprinkled liberally with salt and pepper, spitting and tossing up steam when they hit the pan. As the aromas rose from the skillet, Nona would slice several cloves of garlic and drop them in. Hearing the sizzle, she would grunt, turn to the fresh rosemary on the counter, and begin to chop. The pan was taking care of her ingredients; she knew that the chicken would release from the pan once it was browned, almost like a modern-day nonstick pan. The rosemary was tossed in, the chicken turned again, and then red wine vinegar was added. The hiss and bubble of the pan juices would erupt into a fog of garlic-rosemary aroma. Once the chicken was cooked, it was transferred to a platter and covered with aluminum foil.

If you were quite clever, you could sneak just a bit of chicken to taste or a scrap of bacon. Once the pan was free, more bacon fat went in, as well as diced potatoes. Sprinkled with salt and pepper and tossed in the fat, the potatoes turned translucent, then slowly golden, and then crusty brown, turned constantly to give them an even, crunchy crust. The chicken was arranged over the potatoes, its sauce spooned over everything. The coal black pan cooled to room temperature and was carefully cleaned, and then put back on the stove-top to dry and season.

Nona's skillet reminded her of Italy, the land she'd left as an 18-year-old with two children to come to a foreign country and make a home, without her extended family or the ingredients she knew. That skillet was her tie to Umbria; it was similar to those her mother had used and enabled her to make the dishes she remembered with love and longing.

Me, sitting between Nona and Grandfather

AUG • 59

The skillet made its way to my mother's house after Nona died; she would cook her chicken just as Nona had and make sure to carefully dry and reseason the pan before putting it away. And when she passed on, it came to me. —Diane Phillips

A resident of South Pittsburg, Tennessee, Wayne Gray, with his horse, Lady, participates in Civil War reenactments as an East Tennessee Federalist.

GRILLED CHICKEN WITH CITRUS SALSA

serves 4

1 jalapeño chile, sliced	1 small grapefruit, sectioned and cut into ¼-inch pieces
¼ cup plus 1 tablespoon fresh lime juice	4 green onions, thinly sliced
¼ cup plus 1 tablespoon olive oil	10 cherry tomatoes, seeded and diced
4 skinned and boned chicken breasts	Grated zest of ½ orange
Salt and freshly ground black pepper	Grated zest of ½ lime
	1 jalapeño chile, minced
1 navel orange, sectioned and cut into ¼-inch pieces	4 handfuls mixed greens

1. Combine the jalapeño slices with ¼ cup each of the lime juice and oil in a shallow bowl.

2. Rub the chicken with salt and pepper to taste and place in the jalapeño marinade, turning to coat both sides. Cover and refrigerate 30 minutes.

3. Combine the orange and grapefruit pieces, green onions, tomatoes, orange and lime zest, minced jalapeño, the remaining 1 tablespoon each lime juice and oil, and salt and pepper to taste. Set salsa aside.

4. Remove the chicken from the marinade; discard the marinade. Grease a 10-inch cast iron grill pan and heat over medium-high heat until hot. Add the chicken and cook 5 minutes on each side, until done. Remove the cooked chicken from the pan and let stand 5 minutes.

5. Divide the greens among 4 serving plates. Slice each chicken breast and place over the greens on each plate. Spoon the salsa over the top and serve immediately.

a cast iron memory

I love the South. I love the way we sit on porches and wave to whoever passes, whether we know them or not. And the way men wave to one another in their pickup trucks, raising their index finger without removing their hand from the steering wheel. And I love the way our mothers hand down recipes and their black-as-pitch cast iron skillets like they were passing down a country estate. The best recipes ("Simply the best, I tell you, darlin'") are passed along in a bit of a whisper while sitting on the front porch, like they contained "11 herbs and spices" otherwise kept in a vault. That's how this recipe came to me and my wife, Ann, whispered between waves to strangers while sitting on a porch. It's the best, darlin'. Trust me.

—Wayne Gray

Chef John D. Folse's grandfather grew beans of every variety in his garden on Cabanocey Plantation. "I vividly remember the eight Folse children circling a large washtub to shell the fresh beans," recalls Chef Folse, who is the founder and namesake of the John Folse Culinary Institute at Nicholls State University in Thibodaux, Louisiana. "They went into everything from shrimp dishes to casseroles, including this preparation, one of my grandfather's favorites." Serve it over steamed white rice. This recipe comes from Chef Folse's cookbook *The Encyclopedia of Cajun & Creole Cuisine.*

SMOTHERED CHICKEN WITH BUTTER BEANS

serves 6

¼ cup vegetable oil

¼ cup all-purpose flour

1 cup diced onion

1 cup diced red bell pepper

¼ cup minced garlic

1 (3-pound) fryer chicken, cut into 8 pieces

3 cups chicken stock, or as needed

4 cups shelled fresh butter beans

Salt and freshly ground black pepper

½ cup sliced green onions

1. Heat the oil in a large cast iron Dutch oven over medium-high heat. Slowly whisk in the flour and stir constantly until you have a light brown roux (it should be the color of peanut butter).

2. Add the onion, bell pepper, and garlic, and cook, stirring frequently, until the vegetables are wilted. Add the chicken and cook until well browned on all sides, 5 to 10 minutes. Add the stock and stir well; you may need to add more stock or water to achieve a stew-like consistency. Add the butter beans and season with salt and pepper to taste. Bring to a rolling boil; reduce the heat and simmer until the chicken is cooked through and tender, 30 to 45 minutes.

3. Stir in the green onions; taste and adjust the seasoning, if desired.

You get a double hit of garlic in this dish—in the chicken's creamy filling and in the sauce that tops it. This recipe was contributed by International Dutch Oven Society member E.T. Moore.

STUFFED GARLIC CHICKEN BREASTS

serves 4

4 ounces cream cheese, softened

4 garlic cloves, chopped

1 large onion, chopped

¼ teaspoon red pepper flakes

4 skinned and boned chicken breast halves

Salt and freshly ground black pepper

2 tablespoons canola oil

¼ cup (½ stick) salted butter

2 tablespoons white or cider vinegar

2 tablespoons barbecue sauce of your choice

⅓ cup (1½ ounces) shredded Parmesan cheese

1. Preheat the oven to 350°.

2. Combine the cream cheese, ¾ of the garlic and onion, and the red pepper in a medium bowl. Mix well.

3. Cutting into a long side of each chicken breast half, slice it almost in half. Open each breast up like a book and spread ¼ of the cream cheese mixture over one side. Fold the other side of the breast over it and secure the opening with wooden picks. Season both sides of each stuffed breast with salt and black pepper to taste.

4. Heat the oil in a 12-inch cast iron skillet or large Dutch oven over medium heat. Add the chicken and sear each side 3 to 4 minutes. Transfer to oven; cover and bake for 25 minutes.

5. Meanwhile, in an 8-inch cast iron skillet, melt the butter over medium heat. Add the remaining garlic and onion and cook, stirring often, until almost soft and translucent. Add the vinegar and barbecue sauce, stir well, and heat through.

6. Remove the skillet from the oven and pour the sauce over the chicken. Sprinkle the Parmesan over the chicken. Return the chicken to the oven and bake, covered, until done, another 10 to 15 minutes.

Cookbook author and *Bon Appétit* contributing editor Dede Wilson has made this with both boneless, skinless thighs as well as breasts. You can also substitute white wine for the red for a slightly less dark and rich dish. Serve it with rice or steamed potatoes—or, better yet, the next day with crusty bread.

CHICKEN WITH ARTICHOKE HEARTS, OLIVES, AND CAPERS

serves 4

8 skinned and boned chicken thighs or 2 skinned and boned chicken breasts (cut breasts into halves, and then cut in half crosswise)

Salt and freshly ground black pepper

2 tablespoons olive oil

1 large yellow or white onion, chopped

6 garlic cloves, minced

1 teaspoon fresh thyme leaves, crushed

¾ cup dry red wine

1 (28-ounce) can diced tomatoes, undrained

2 tablespoons balsamic vinegar

1 (9-ounce) package frozen artichoke hearts, thawed

¼ cup pitted green olives, such as Greek or French in brine, cut in half

¼ cup pitted black olives, such as kalamata, cut in half

2 tablespoons drained capers

¼ cup chopped fresh flat-leaf parsley

1. Season the chicken with salt and pepper to taste. Heat the oil in a 5-quart cast iron Dutch oven over medium-high heat. Brown chicken, a few pieces at a time, 4 minutes total for each batch (2 minutes for breasts). Remove browned chicken pieces to a platter.

2. Add the onion and cook, stirring occasionally, over medium-low heat until translucent and beginning to lightly brown, about 4 minutes. Add the garlic and thyme and cook 1 minute. Add the wine and bring to a boil, scraping the bottom of the pan to loosen browned bits and incorporate them into the liquid. Stir in the tomatoes and vinegar.

3. Return the chicken to the pan and add the artichokes, both kinds of olives, and the capers. Cover and simmer over medium-low heat until the chicken is done, about 30 minutes. Sprinkle with the parsley and serve.

TOM'S WIDELY KNOWN WAYFARER CHICKEN CURRY

serves 6 to 8

Peter Gerety offers up this recipe in remembrance of his brother-in-law, Tom Hill. When they were both actors (along with Peter's sister, Anne Gerety), they ended up in Portland, Oregon, running the Storefront Theater. In order to support themselves, Tom bought a macrobiotic restaurant, called the Wayfarer. He turned it into a curry house where they all worked, when not on stage, preparing the dishes Tom grew up with in India. Serve this curry over Tom's Pulao (page 115).

2 tablespoons canola oil
2 heaping tablespoons Tom's Curry Powder (see recipe)
1 tablespoon chopped peeled fresh ginger
2 medium onions, chopped
3 medium tomatoes, chopped (reserve the juices)

Salt
½ cup canned unsweetened coconut milk
8 skin-on, bone-in chicken thighs

1. Heat the oil in a large cast iron Dutch oven over medium heat until hot. Add Tom's Curry Powder and ginger; sauté just until they release their fragrances, about 1 minute or less.

2. Add the onions, stir, and let cook until softened. Add the tomatoes and their juices and salt to taste (you can also add a little water if the tomatoes aren't juicy enough). Reduce the heat to low and simmer, uncovered, 1 hour.

3. Stir in the coconut milk. Add the chicken, turning to coat the pieces with the sauce. Bring the curry to a boil; cover, reduce the heat to medium-low, and simmer until the chicken is done, about 1 hour.

Salmon Curry: Substitute 6 to 8 (6-ounce) pieces of salmon fillet for the chicken and simmer the salmon to desired degree of doneness, about 25 minutes.

TOM'S CURRY POWDER

makes a generous ¼ cup

4 teaspoons turmeric
4 teaspoons ground cumin
4 teaspoons ground coriander
1 teaspoon crushed fenugreek seeds

1 teaspoon cayenne pepper or more to taste

1. Stir together the spices in a small bowl. Store in an airtight container.

TOM'S PULAO

serves 4

¼ cup (½ stick) butter
1 cinnamon stick
1 bay leaf
1 teaspoon whole cloves
4 or 5 cardamom pods
½ cup raisins
2 cups rice

4 cups water
Toppings: slivered almonds, browned onion slivers, golden raisins, unsweetened grated coconut, and/or dry-roasted peanuts

A benefit to cooking rice in cast iron is that it keeps the cooked rice hot for a long time.

1. Melt the butter in a medium cast iron Dutch oven over medium heat. Add the cinnamon stick and next 4 ingredients; sauté 1 minute, until the spices release their fragrances. Stir to coat the raisins with the spiced butter.

2. Add the rice and stir 1 minute to coat with the spiced butter. Add the water and bring to a boil. Cover tightly, reduce the heat to the lowest setting, and cook 15 minutes.

3. Turn off the heat and let the rice steam 45 minutes (do not lift the lid during this time). Remove and discard cinnamon stick and bay leaf. Serve with the toppings.

This is an adaptation of a recipe that originally ran in *Coastal Living* magazine. Senior Food Editor Julia Rutland has changed it up to make it a little easier and healthier. "My kids really like breast meat, so instead of a whole chicken cut into pieces, I opted for four bone-in breasts. To save time and to lighten it, I used skinless chicken. If you prefer to use skin-on chicken, brown it first in about two tablespoons olive oil," says Julia. If you see Moroccan spice blend in the store, buy that rather than having to purchase four individual spices to rub on the chicken. And if you can't find preserved lemons, substitute the juice and grated zest of a fresh lemon, and season the dish with a little more salt.

CHICKEN TAGINE

serves 4

2 teaspoons ground ginger	Salt and freshly ground black pepper
1 teaspoon ground coriander	
1 teaspoon turmeric	2 fresh parsley sprigs
1 teaspoon ground cinnamon	2 fresh cilantro sprigs
4 skinned, bone-in chicken breasts	¾ cup water
	Pinch of saffron threads
2 tablespoons olive oil	½ cup pitted Moroccan purple or kalamata olives
1 onion, thinly sliced into half moons and pulled apart into strips	2 wedges preserved lemon, cut into thin strips
4 garlic cloves, chopped	Hot cooked couscous

1. Combine the ginger, coriander, turmeric, and cinnamon in a small bowl. Sprinkle evenly on the chicken; cover and refrigerate until ready to cook.

2. Heat the oil in a large cast iron Dutch oven over medium-high heat. Add the onion and garlic and cook, stirring occasionally, until tender and just starting to brown, about 3 minutes. Add the chicken and sprinkle with salt and pepper to taste; top with the parsley and cilantro sprigs.

3. Combine the water and saffron; pour over the chicken. Bring to a boil. Cover, reduce heat, and simmer 15 minutes; stir and cook until the chicken is done, about another 15 minutes.

4. Stir in the olives and preserved lemon; cook 5 minutes, until heated. Serve with hot couscous.

John Richard "Dick" Lodge, Jr., likes to serve this jambalaya with hot sauce, country-style bread, and a green salad. Dick based his recipe on several jambalaya recipes, none of them particularly authentic from a Louisianan's perspective. "It is called 'Tennessee Valley' because we live in the Valley, and because country ham is included for flavor, rather than andouille or another spicy Cajun sausage," explains Dick. This was a nod to the young Lodge children, who did not like the heat of more authentic Louisiana jambalaya.

TENNESSEE VALLEY JAMBALAYA

serves 6

1 small whole chicken	1 cup long-grain rice
8 links sweet or hot Italian sausage	½ teaspoon dried thyme
1 cup chopped onion	½ to 1 teaspoon chili powder
1 cup chopped green bell pepper	1½ teaspoons salt
2 to 4 garlic cloves, minced	½ teaspoon freshly ground black pepper
3 tablespoons olive oil	1½ tablespoons chopped fresh parsley
1 cup diced country ham	
1 (16-ounce) can whole tomatoes, undrained	

1. Place the chicken in a large saucepan and cover with water. Bring to a boil, reduce the heat to a simmer, and cook until the chicken is done, about 30 minutes. Drain, reserving 1½ cups of the broth.

2. Let the chicken stand until cool enough to handle; remove the meat from the bones and tear or cut it into bite-size pieces. Set aside.

3. While the chicken cools, place the sausage on a baking sheet and bake in a preheated 350° oven until browned and cooked through, about 30 minutes. Let stand until cool enough to handle, and then cut into ⅛-inch-thick slices. Leave the oven on.

5. In a 5-quart cast iron Dutch oven, cook the onion, bell pepper, and garlic in the oil over medium-high heat, stirring, just until tender. Add the chicken, sausage, ham, tomatoes, rice, reserved broth, thyme, chili powder, salt, and pepper. Bring to a boil, stirring once or twice. Cover tightly and bake for 1 hour. If the rice is still slightly crunchy, stir and bake 10 to 15 minutes longer.

6. Stir in the parsley and serve.

Wild duck can be a little tricky to prepare, but Paul McIlhenny, a game cook, knows that simplicity is often the best solution. "The reason I like this recipe so well is that it doesn't totally hide the flavor of the wild duck," Paul says. "The sauce is full, without being overpowering, and complements the richness of the bird." And it's quick and easy, which makes it even better.

SEARED TEAL BREASTS

serves 4

¼ cup Lea & Perrins Worcestershire sauce

1 teaspoon Tabasco sauce

Cracked black peppercorns

8 skin-on boneless teal breasts, plucked clean

2 tablespoons unsalted butter

Salt

1. Combine the Worcestershire, Tabasco, and cracked peppercorns to taste in a large shallow baking dish. Add the teal breasts, turning to coat both sides in the marinade. Refrigerate 2 hours.

2. Drain the teal breasts and pat dry. Heat a large cast iron skillet over medium-high heat until hot. Add the butter, followed quickly by the teal breasts, 4 at a time, skin side down; sear 4 minutes. Turn the breasts and sear the meat side for 2 minutes; the breasts should be cooked to no more than medium rare. Transfer breasts to a cutting board and let stand 5 minutes. Repeat cooking process with the remaining teal breasts.

3. Slice each breast, across the grain, into 4 pieces, and place 2 breasts on each plate. Lightly season with salt and additional cracked pepper to taste; serve immediately.

This recipe comes from environmental scientist Dr. Geraldine McGuire. Based in Queensland, Australia, she has worked with clients throughout Asia and the Pacific to blend sustainable economic, environmental, and social solutions. Also recognized as an excellent cook, she recommends serving this dish with a steamed green vegetable and potatoes fried in some of the fat you render when you sear the duck.

SAGE AND CITRUS-BRAISED DUCK

serves 4 to 6

2   free-range ducks
1   tablespoon olive oil
3   pink grapefruit
2   oranges
1   teaspoon dried or chopped
    fresh sage

¼   teaspoon freshly ground
    white pepper
Sea salt

1. Remove the breasts and legs from the ducks (discard the wings and carcasses or use them to make stock). Score the skin.

2. Heat the oil in a large cast iron skillet over medium heat. Add the duck pieces, skin side down, and sear until well browned. Turn over and brown the other side. Transfer the duck pieces to a large cast iron Dutch oven. When the drippings cool, strain the duck fat from the skillet; store the fat in the refrigerator or freezer—it adds wonderful flavor when frying potatoes.

3. Juice 2 of the grapefruit and 1 of the oranges; pour the juices over the duck pieces. Peel and cut the remaining grapefruit and orange into pieces, removing any seeds; place the pieces over the duck. Sprinkle with the sage, pepper, and salt to taste.

4. Cover the pan and cook over low heat until the duck starts to fall apart and is tender, 2 to 3 hours.

Duck breast is a treat to enjoy at fine restaurants, but many people are hesitant to try it themselves at home. This recipe from Al Hernandez, food and wine editor of *The Vine Times*, helps you bring that tasty and elegant meal home.

DUCK BREAST WITH SUGAR SNAP PEAS AND MUSHROOMS

serves 4

4   (6- to 8-ounce) duck breasts
Salt and freshly ground black
   pepper
4   garlic cloves, finely chopped
¾   pound sugar snap peas,
   ends trimmed

8   ounces mushrooms (cremini
   and button mushrooms
   preferred), thinly sliced
2   teaspoons sherry vinegar or
   red wine vinegar

1. Remove any silverskin from the duck breasts and pat dry with a paper towel. Score the duck skin approximately ½ inch apart in a crisscross pattern (be sure not to cut into the duck meat). Season both sides with salt and pepper to taste.

2. Heat a large cast iron skillet over medium heat. Place the duck breasts in the hot skillet, fat side down, and sear until golden brown, 7 to 9 minutes. Turn the breasts over and cook another 5 to 7 minutes. (The recommended serving temperature for duck is 145° for medium rare.)

3. Transfer the breasts to a plate. Pour the rendered duck fat into a heatproof container; measure 1½ tablespoons of the rendered duck fat back into the skillet (refrigerate any remaining fat and use it to cook potatoes). Add the garlic, sugar snap peas, and mushrooms to the skillet. Season with salt and pepper to taste. Add the vinegar and cook, stirring, over medium heat until heated through, 5 to 7 minutes.

4. Cut the duck breasts into ½-inch-thick slices. Serve the duck with the vegetables on the side.

This remembrance and its recipes on the following three pages were contributed by J. Wayne Fears. In his wide and varied career, he has been a wildlife specialist, developed and operated hunting lodges in Alabama, and served as the editor-in-chief of *Rural Sportsman* and *Hunting Camp Journal*.

Wayne is the author of more than 25 books on outdoor-related topics and a columnist and contributor to numerous outdoor- and hunting-related periodicals. More information can be found at his Web site, jwaynefears.com.

CAST IRON AND COUNTRY COOKING

Growing up on the side of one of the Cumberland Mountains in North Alabama, life was simple. My dad was a trapper, and we somewhat lived off the land. The one inspiring thing about that simple lifestyle was that my mom was a master at turning anything we brought in from the woods into delicious table fare.

When I was a youngster, it was a contest up and down the valley to see who could get the circuit preacher to have Sunday dinner at their house. He preached in the valley only twice a month, and it was bragging rights to the housewife whose cooking could keep the reverend coming back to that home for encore meals. My mom found out the reverend loved fried young groundhog, and she became a repeat winner. It was great for me since I was sent out to harvest "just the right groundhog," a chore I loved.

CAST IRON INDOORS AND OUT

My mom's cookware was, by our standards, "the best money could buy"—a cast iron skillet and a couple of flat-bottomed cast iron Dutch ovens. They were handed down to her from her mom, who got them from her mother, and now, many years later, they are doing service in my kitchen and still working their cast iron magic. They are treasured heirlooms that my children look forward to getting.

As I was growing up, I accompanied my dad on many outdoor expeditions, and his camp cook kit was comprised of a cast iron skillet and a 10-inch camp Dutch oven. His dishes, prepared over an open fire next to some remote creek, instilled in me the desire to be a lifetime student of cast iron cooking. I learned early that my dad's cast iron cookware was made by a company named Lodge, and over the years I came to trust the Lodge brand in remote camps over much of the globe. Whether cooking for hunting clients over a little willow and alder fire on the headwaters of the Canning River in the Brooks Range of Alaska, or in a bean hole (see *Bean Hole Cooking*, pages 186-191) in a remote fishing camp in the Colorado high country, or in a modern kitchen at Stagshead Lodge in Alabama, Lodge and its magic skillets and pots have produced dishes that have graced my magazine articles and books for more than four decades. The same dishes cooked in anything other than cast iron just aren't the same. As I said, there is magic in those black pots and skillets.

You try it for yourself, and you will see the difference. Here are some starter recipes featuring meats from the wild harvest.

SKILLET FRIED RABBIT WITH GRAVY

serves 4

Rabbit:
½ cup all-purpose flour
1 teaspoon salt
¼ teaspoon freshly ground black pepper
1 (2¼- to 2¾- pound) rabbit, cut into pieces
½ cup (1 stick) salted butter

Gravy:
3 tablespoons all-purpose flour
1 cup chicken broth
1 cup milk
½ teaspoon salt
⅛ teaspoon freshly ground black pepper
⅛ teaspoon dried thyme
⅛ teaspoon dried marjoram

This is a recipe I learned from George Prechter, one of New Orleans' master game chefs and a camp cook without equal. He has served this rabbit dish to many who professed how much they disliked wild game while dipping into the pan for second and third helpings.

1. Make the rabbit: Combine the flour, salt, and pepper in a large plastic or paper bag. Dredge the rabbit pieces by shaking them in the bag. Tap off any extra flour.

2. Melt the butter in a large cast iron skillet with a lid over medium heat; add the rabbit and cook until evenly browned on all sides, 5 to 6 minutes.

3. Cover, reduce the heat to low, and cook until the rabbit is fork-tender, about 1 hour, turning 2 or 3 times. Transfer the rabbit to a serving dish and keep warm.

4. Make the gravy: Blend the flour into the pan drippings, but do not brown. Add the broth, milk, and remaining ingredients. Cook over medium heat, stirring often, until thickened. Pour the gravy over the rabbit and serve.

TENDER VENISON ROAST

serves 8 to 10

1 (4-pound) venison or beef roast	1 (1-ounce) envelope dry onion soup mix (such as Lipton)
1 cup plus 2 teaspoons hot water	1 tablespoon Worcestershire sauce

1. Preheat the oven to 300°.

2. Place the roast in a 12-inch cast iron Dutch oven on a small wire rack. Add 1 cup water.

3. Make a paste with the soup mix and remaining 2 teaspoons water. Brush paste over roast; sprinkle with the Worcestershire.

4. Cover the pan and bake until the roast is fork-tender, about 3 hours.

I discovered this recipe back when I owned hunting lodges and served meals to dozens of guests each day. Often hunters complained of venison roast being tough and dry. Using a cast iron Dutch oven, this recipe can reliably take a less-than-tender roast, whether venison or beef, and make it fork-tender.

BRAISED BREAST OF GROUSE

serves 2

½ cup (1 stick) butter	1 celery rib, cut into ¼-inch-thick slices
2 grouse breasts	2 fresh parsley sprigs
Salt and freshly ground black pepper	½ bay leaf
1½ cups cold water	¼ cup all-purpose flour
1 small carrot, cut into ¼-inch-thick slices	¼ cup canned diced tomatoes
	1 teaspoon fresh lemon juice
1 small Vidalia onion, cut into ¼-inch-thick slices	1 teaspoon minced fresh parsley
	½ cup sautéed mushrooms

1. Melt ¼ cup butter in a 10-inch cast iron skillet over medium heat. Add breasts; brown both sides. Season with salt and pepper to taste. Pour the water over the top. Add the carrot and next 4 ingredients. Cover and simmer over low heat until tender, 20 minutes.

2. Remove the breasts from the pan, strain the stock, and set aside. Rinse and dry the skillet.

3. Melt the remaining ¼ cup butter in pan over low heat; stir in flour, whisking until golden brown. Add reserved stock and tomatoes gradually to the roux, stirring constantly. Add the lemon juice, parsley, and mushrooms; season with salt and pepper to taste. Remove and discard bay leaf. Reheat the grouse in the sauce and serve.

If ruffed grouse weighed 30 pounds, I would never hunt big game again. In my opinion, grouse is the most flavorful game bird and top table fare of all the wild harvest. Here is a recipe that, when coupled with the cast iron skillet, ensures your grouse breast of being all it can be. The recipe also works well for pheasant.

Contributed by Chris Schlesinger, chef/owner of the East Coast Grill in Cambridge, Massachusetts, this recipe was perfected by his father, who cooked it for special occasions. A cast iron skillet is the key to providing a flavor-packed crust, but beware: This technique also creates a lot of smoke. "My dad always claimed the smoke contributed to the atmosphere," recalls Chris. "Both the aroma and the flavor will always be embedded in my culinary memory."

SEARED PEPPER STEAK WITH BOURBON-SHALLOT SAUCE

serves 4

2 tablespoons kosher salt, plus more to taste

¼ cup cracked black peppercorns

4 (10-ounce) beef top loin steaks, about 1 inch thick

2 tablespoons olive oil

3 tablespoons chopped shallots

½ cup bourbon

½ cup beef stock

¼ cup heavy cream

1 tablespoon butter

2 tablespoons chopped fresh parsley

1. Rub the salt and cracked peppercorns on both sides of the steaks.

2. Heat the oil in a large cast iron skillet over medium-high heat until hot. Cook the steaks 3 to 4 minutes per side for medium rare or to desired degree of doneness. Transfer the steaks to a plate and loosely cover with foil.

3. Add the shallots to the skillet and sauté 30 seconds.

4. Remove the skillet from the heat and turn off the burner. Add the bourbon (there will be a lot of steam all at once). Carefully light the liquid in the skillet with a long match. Allow the flames to burn off on their own.

5. Return the skillet to the heat. Add the stock, bring it to a simmer, and cook until the liquid is reduced by half, about 3 minutes. Stir in the cream and simmer 3 minutes.

6. Remove the pan from the heat and stir in the butter until totally incorporated into the sauce. Stir in the parsley. Taste and add additional salt to taste, if desired.

7. Place a steak on each of 4 plates, top with the sauce, and serve.

For cooking instructor and food writer Jane Gaither, known in Tennessee as "Gourmet Gadget Gal," the secret to grilling restaurant-quality steaks at home means pulling out her Lodge grill pan, quickly searing the steaks on the stove, and finishing them in the oven. This recipe goes from stove-top to table in 10 minutes.

CAST IRON GRILLED STEAKS WITH BLUE CHEESE BUTTER

serves 2

Blue Cheese Butter:
½ cup (1 stick) unsalted butter, softened
1 (4-ounce) package crumbled blue cheese
1 teaspoon Worcestershire sauce
Pinch of salt
A few grinds of black pepper

Steaks:
2 (1-inch-thick) beef strip steaks
1 teaspoon vegetable oil
Salt and freshly ground black pepper

1. Cream the butter in a small bowl, then add the blue cheese, Worcestershire, salt, and pepper and beat until smooth. Using a 12-inch piece of plastic wrap, spoon out the butter mixture and roll it up like a log, twisting the ends. Freeze the butter until firm or for up to 1 month.

2. Preheat the oven to 350°.

3. Bring the steaks to room temperature. Heat a Lodge Grill Pan over high heat until smoking hot. Carefully brush the pan with the oil.

4. Season the steaks on both sides with salt and pepper to taste. Carefully place the steaks on the hot grill pan and grill 2 minutes per side.

5. Transfer the grill pan to the oven and bake for 2 minutes.

6. Remove the pan from the oven and let the steaks stand 5 minutes. Serve with a pat of Blue Cheese Butter on each steak.

PAN-FRIED FAJITA STEAKS

serves 4

Fajitas are a restaurant favorite, but John Meyer of Main Dish Media has started making them at home—and they've become a regular request when friends come over. He cooks the steaks and vegetables in cast iron skillets, and serves the fajitas straight out of the pans. "Unlike most fajita recipes, I use whole steaks, as well as big cuts of vegetables. If I wanted small slices and bites, I'd be doing stir-fry!" John explains. When left whole, the steaks develop a flavorful sear, while the whole vegetables retain their individual taste and texture.

2	tablespoons chili powder	3	tablespoons vegetable oil
1	tablespoon dried oregano	8	fajita-style flour tortillas
1	tablespoon ground cumin	2	yellow bell peppers, cut in
2	teaspoons kosher salt, plus		half and seeded
	more to taste	8	plum tomatoes, cut in half
2	teaspoons freshly ground	12	green onions, trimmed
	black pepper, plus more	2	limes, cut in half
	to taste		
4	(10- to 12-ounce) beef strip		
	steaks		

1. Preheat the oven to 350°. Preheat 2 large cast iron skillets over medium-high heat.

2. Combine the chili powder, oregano, cumin, salt, and pepper in a small bowl; rub the mixture evenly over the steaks.

3. Pour 1 tablespoon oil into each of the hot skillets. Add 2 steaks to each pan and sear, turning every minute, until the steaks reach desired degree of doneness (10 to 12 minutes or an internal temperature of 120° for medium rare). Transfer the steaks to a platter, cover loosely with foil, and let stand.

4. Wrap the tortillas in foil and warm in the oven as the vegetables cook.

5. Increase the heat under the skillets to high. Add some of the remaining 1 tablespoon oil to each pan, if necessary. Divide the bell peppers, tomatoes, green onions, and lime halves into 2 equal piles; add to the hot pans. Cook, tossing the vegetables and limes a few times, until slightly charred, 3 to 4 minutes. Transfer the mixture to the platter with the steaks.

6. To serve, heat both skillets over high heat; return the steaks and fajita vegetables to the pans and squeeze the charred lime halves over the top. Serve with the warm tortillas. Each diner gets their own steak and can help themselves to the vegetables in the pans.

SUKIYAKI

serves 4 to 6

Growing up in Sacramento, Michael McLaughlin especially looked forward to sukiyaki dinners out with his family. Whether served ready to eat, with the pot's contents ladled into the diners' waiting bowls, or the raw ingredients assembled on platters for diners to cook at the table using the sizzling broth from a Japanese hot-pot, sukiyaki is a festive meal. Michael invites you to try his favorite recipe adapted for the home cook.

❧ Asian flavor ❧

From an Asian market you will need shirataki noodles, also known as yam noodles. They come in a package, ready to use, and look similar to moistened glass noodles. The recipe also calls for the bonito-flavored soup stock known as dashi, and mirin, a sweetened cooking rice wine.

1½ cups dashi (¼ teaspoon instant bonito-flavored soup stock powder added to 1 cup lukewarm water), or vegetable or beef stock, or water
½ cup soy sauce
½ cup mirin (sweet rice wine)
2 to 4 tablespoons brown sugar
¼ cup sake (optional)
1 (7-ounce) block enoki mushrooms
5 baby bok choy or ½ head napa (Chinese) cabbage
2 teaspoons canola oil
1 (14-ounce) package firm tofu, drained and cut into ½-inch cubes
1 pound high-quality, well-marbled boneless sirloin or rib-eye steak, cut into ¼-inch-thick slices
1 bunch leafy greens (watercress, spinach, edible chrysanthemum leaves, Swiss chard, etc.), trimmed of heavy stems and cut into bite-size pieces
8 small to medium shiitake mushrooms, stemmed
2 green onions, trimmed and cut into 1-inch pieces
1 (8-ounce) package shirataki noodles

1. In a medium bowl, stir together the dashi, soy sauce, mirin, brown sugar to taste, and, if desired, sake, until the brown sugar dissolves.

2. Cut off and discard the connective bottom from the block of enoki mushrooms, pulling them apart under cool running water. Soak for about 2 minutes; drain and set aside. Trim the bottoms from the bok choy and slice across into ½-inch-wide strips.

3. Heat a cast iron Dutch oven over medium heat until hot. Heat the oil, and then sear the tofu until browned on all sides, about 8 minutes. Remove the tofu from the Dutch oven.

4. Add the steak to the Dutch oven and stir-fry until about 80% of the desired degree of doneness, about 3 minutes. Remove from the pot.

5. Add the bok choy and greens and stir-fry just until wilted, 1 to 2 minutes. Remove from the pot.

6. Add the enoki and shiitake mushrooms and green onions and stir-fry to soften, 1 to 2 minutes.

7. Return the greens, bok choy, and tofu to the Dutch oven. Add the shirataki noodles. Stir the dashi mixture; pour over mixture in Dutch oven and bring to a simmer. Add the steak and stir. Bring the pot to the table and let diners serve themselves.

BOURBON BARREL PEPPER POT ROAST

serves 4

1   (3½-pound) chuck roast
Coarse salt
Bourbon smoked pepper
2   tablespoons canola oil
2   cups beef stock
2   tablespoons tomato paste

4   cups (½-inch-thick)
    diagonally sliced carrots
2   tablespoons sorghum syrup
Hot seasoned rice

1. Preheat the oven to 325°.

2. Pat the roast dry with paper towels and season it liberally with salt and smoked pepper to taste.

3. Heat the oil in a large cast iron Dutch oven over high heat until hot but not smoking. (The oil will appear to be moving in waves across the surface of the pot and shimmer slightly.) Sear the roast in the hot oil, rotating it with tongs to brown all sides. Remove the roast from the pan.

4. Combine the stock and tomato paste in a bowl and stir until well blended; slowly add the stock mixture to the pan, scraping the pan bottom to loosen browned bits.

5. Reduce the heat to low, return the roast to the pan, and bring the liquid to a low boil. Cover the pan, transfer it to the oven, and bake until the roast is fork-tender, about 2¾ hours.

6. Transfer the roast to a cutting board. Place the Dutch oven on the stove-top; add the carrots and cook at a low simmer until tender, about 10 minutes. Whisk in the sorghum and bring to a simmer to thicken, no longer than 3 minutes; immediately remove from the heat.

7. Slice the meat thickly and serve in shallow bowls with seasoned rice. Spoon the sauce and carrots over the top and sprinkle on a bit more smoked pepper.

This recipe is from Francine Maroukian, an award-winning food writer and contributing editor to *Garden & Gun, Travel + Leisure,* and *Esquire* magazines.

sorghum syrup

Sorghum is a sweet syrup with a hint of exotic spice; it can be purchased (as can the bourbon smoked pepper) at *bourbonbarrelfoods.com.*

International Dutch Oven Society members Nicole and Taylor Baugh contributed this beautiful and tasty dish, perfect to present to guests.

ROLLED FLANK STEAK

serves 4 to 6

1 (2-pound) flank steak	4 thick bacon slices
½ cup olive oil	½ cup baby spinach
¼ cup soy sauce	½ cup sliced cremini
2 teaspoons steak seasoning	mushrooms
and more to taste	½ red bell pepper, seeded
2 tablespoons chopped garlic	and cut into strips
½ pound thinly sliced	½ cup chopped onion
provolone cheese	

1. Place the flank steak on a cutting board with a short end facing you. Starting from one of the long sides, cut through the meat horizontally to within ½ inch of the opposite edge.

2. Combine the oil, soy sauce, and steak seasoning in a 1-gallon zip-top plastic freezer bag. Add the steak, zip the bag shut, and squeeze to coat the steak. Marinate in the refrigerator 4 hours or overnight.

3. Preheat the oven to 350°. Grease a large cast iron Dutch oven.

4. Lay out the flank steak flat in front of you with the grain of the meat running from left to right. Spread the garlic evenly over the meat and sprinkle with steak seasoning to taste. Layer the provolone over the steak, leaving a 1-inch border on all sides. Arrange the bacon, spinach, mushrooms, bell pepper, and onion over the cheese in stripes running in the same direction as the grain of the meat. Roll the flank steak up and away from you so that when the roll is cut into the pinwheel shape, each of the filling ingredients can be seen; roll firmly, but be careful not to squeeze the fillings out the ends. Once rolled, tie with kitchen string, securing at 2-inch intervals.

5. Place the stuffed steak into the prepared Dutch oven and bake until a meat thermometer inserted in the center of the stuffed steak registers 145°, about 1 hour. Remove the stuffed steak from the Dutch oven and let stand 5 to 10 minutes before cutting into 1-inch-thick slices. Remove the string before serving.

Some cooks mistakenly shy away from cast iron when a recipe contains an acid like tomatoes or vinegar. The simple fact is that if your cast iron is well seasoned, the iron is impervious to whatever you decide to put into your pan. And for Nach Waxman, owner of Kitchen Arts & Letters bookstore in New York City, cast iron is his pan of choice when cooking up (or rather cooking down) this tomato reduction.

A SUMMER TOMATO REDUCTION

When I'm lucky and am faced with a good tomato season and a magnificent end-of-summer surplus of big, squishy tomatoes going soft faster than one could ever use them; the solution, of course, is to make sauce. But sauce, whether you can it or freeze it, requires a fair amount of prep work and, after you've made it, you've got quarts and quarts to be stored—no casual consideration in most modern homes.

So, with the help of cast iron, I've adopted a method of getting the bulk down, freezing it, and giving our household a terrific pantry resource for those difficult, tomato-deprived winter months. When you thaw this highly flavored base, you can add garlic, sausage, or whatever you like, simmer it together with good canned tomatoes, and bring a range of surprisingly fresh and interesting sauces to your winter table.

TOMATO REDUCTION RECIPE

makes 8 (4-ounce) containers

This recipe is for reducing 2 quarts (8 cups) of tomatoes at a time, which is a good, efficient cooking unit.

6   to 9 ripe tomatoes, depending on their size

2   to 3 tablespoons olive oil, plus 1 teaspoon, as needed

½   cup finely chopped white bottom portion of celery ribs

½   cup torn celery leaves

Up to 2 rounded tablespoons Part Pesto (see recipe) or about 20 large fresh basil leaves, torn into small pieces, to your taste

1   to 2 tablespoons water, as needed

Salt and freshly ground black pepper

1. Cut the stems and any bad spots out of the tomatoes. Cut the tomatoes into ⅛-inch-thick slices, and then cut each slice into ⅛-inch cubes. Do this over a plate to catch any juices.

2. Heat 2 to 3 tablespoons oil in a 10- or 12-inch cast iron skillet over medium heat. Reduce the heat slightly; add the chopped celery and leaves and cook until softened and the leaves start to darken (don't let them brown), stirring occasionally. Add the cubed tomatoes along with any spilled juices and pulp and start them bubbling slowly but steadily; reduce them for 30 minutes.

3. Add the Part Pesto and cook 5 minutes. Reduce the heat to the lowest setting and cook very slowly for at least 2 hours, stirring every half hour or so, making certain that there is no sticking. If there is, add the water and remaining 1 teaspoon oil, as needed, and scrape up any stuck portions. You will notice that the water will gradually evaporate until what remains is extremely thick but still damp with a small amount of oil. It will be about the density of a relish, and the tomatoes will appear to be a softer, much less intense version of the sun-dried product.

4. Season the reduction with salt and pepper to taste. Let cool completely; divide among airtight containers and freeze.

PART PESTO

Part Pesto is a pesto prepared in season, when fresh basil is abundant, and then frozen. It is made by blending basil leaves, olive oil, salt, pine nuts, and a little water, omitting the garlic and cheese, which do not survive the freezing very well. Because of its oil and salt content, it freezes nicely into an intense, pungent slurry, which has the texture of ice cream and can be conveniently spooned out as needed. For *2 cups fresh basil leaves,* I add *½ cup olive oil, ¼ cup pine nuts,* and *¼ cup water.* This preparation, intended for freezing, is a modified version of a suggestion by Paula Wolfert in her book *Mediterranean Cooking.*

STEAK, KIDNEY, AND MUSHROOM PIE

serves 4

Chef/owner Patrick Reilly, of the Majestic Grille in Memphis, is a huge fan of beef kidney, but he understands that not everyone shares his enthusiasm. If that's the case, he advises you to simply use more beef.

perfect crust

Traditionally in the making of steak and kidney pie, a pie pan is lined with pastry, the cooked meat is poured in, and then it is covered with the top pastry. Baked that way, Patrick Reilly always found the pastry to be soggy. His solution is to cook the filling in a cast iron skillet and chill it overnight. The next day, cover it with puff pastry right in the pan. The result—piping hot beef and a crispy, crumbly crust.

½ pound beef kidney (buy it from your local butcher)

¼ cup all-purpose flour

Kosher salt and freshly ground black pepper

2 tablespoons vegetable oil

1 pound beef stew meat, cut into 1-inch pieces (Patrick loves the beef from Neola Farms in Tipton County, Tennessee, but, failing that, advises that you buy your meat from a good local butcher and cube it yourself; avoid pre-packaged stew meat)

4 thick bacon slices, cut into 1-inch pieces

1 medium onion, cut into ¼-inch cubes

1 celery rib, diced

2 garlic cloves, chopped

4 ounces button mushrooms, quartered

½ of a (12-ounce) bottle beer (use a good brown ale such as Bass or Guinness Stout)

½ cup red wine

1 cup beef stock

2 bay leaves

1 fresh thyme sprig

1 (17.3-ounce) package frozen puff pastry sheets, thawed

1 egg yolk, beaten with 2 teaspoons water and a pinch of salt

1. Cut the kidney in half and remove any tubes and skin. Cut into 1-inch pieces and soak in ice water for about 1 hour. Drain and pat dry.

2. Place the flour in a shallow bowl and season generously with salt and pepper to taste.

3. Heat the oil in a 12-inch cast iron skillet over medium-high heat until hazy but not smoking.

4. Dredge the beef and kidney pieces in the flour, shaking off any excess. Brown the beef and kidney in the hot oil on all sides in 2 batches. Remove from the pan and keep warm.

5. Reduce the heat to medium, add the bacon, and cook for a few minutes. Add the onion and celery and cook until lightly browned, stirring a few times. Add the garlic and mushrooms and cook, stirring often, for a few minutes. Add the beer and wine and reduce by three-fourths. Add the stock, bay leaves, thyme, and browned meat. Cover, reduce the heat to low, and simmer until the beef and kidney pieces are tender, about 1 hour.

6. Remove the bay leaves and thyme. Allow the filling to cool in the pan to room temperature; cover with plastic wrap and refrigerate overnight.

7. Preheat the oven to 350°.

8. Roll the pastry into a 13-inch circle on a lightly floured surface with a floured rolling pin. Cover the chilled pan with the pastry; it should overhang the edge of the pan slightly, about ¼ inch. Brush the pastry with the egg wash. Bake until the pastry is golden brown and the filling is heated through, 20 to 30 minutes. Serve immediately or the crust will start to get soggy.

GRILLADES

serves 6

2	medium veal or beef round steaks (1 to 1½ pounds total)	
Salt		
Cracked black peppercorns		
1	cup all-purpose flour	
¼	cup vegetable shortening or bacon drippings	
1	cup minced onion	

1 cup minced celery
½ cup minced bell pepper
1 cup diced tomatoes
1 cup thinly sliced green onions
¼ cup minced garlic
3 cups beef stock
1 cup sliced mushrooms
¼ cup chopped fresh parsley

1. Cut the round steaks into 3-inch squares. Season with salt and cracked peppercorns to taste. Dust the pieces generously with the flour.

2. Melt the shortening in a large cast iron Dutch oven over medium-high heat. Brown the meat (in batches, if necessary) on all sides. Add the onion, celery, bell pepper, tomatoes, green onions, and garlic; cook, stirring, until the vegetables are wilted, 3 to 5 minutes. Pour in the stock and bring to a low boil; reduce the heat to a simmer. Cover the pan and cook the grillades slowly, stirring occasionally to prevent scorching, until the meat is tender, about 45 minutes.

3. Stir in the mushrooms and parsley. Adjust the seasonings, if necessary. Cook 10 minutes, and serve over grits or rice.

According to Chef John D. Folse, founder and namesake of the John Folse Culinary Institute at Nicholls State University in Thibodaux, Louisiana, it is believed this dish originated when South Louisiana butchers preparing the annual *boucherie* took thin pieces of fresh pork and pan-fried them with sliced onions. The cooking probably took place in black iron pots hung over the *boucherie* fires. The grillades were eaten over grits or rice throughout the day. Today, grillades and grits are a tradition on many Sunday brunch menus. To present grillades as an entrée, serve it over rice. Most recipes for grillades call for veal round pounded lightly and smothered in natural juices. This recipe is from Chef Folse's book *The Encyclopedia of Cajun & Creole Cuisine.*

SHEPHERD'S PIE

serves 8

This recipe is from Paul Kelly, a network instructor for Pitney Bowes. An excellent cook and lifelong devotee of Lodge cast iron, Paul regularly prepares dishes for family and friends in his Senoia, Georgia, home. Shepherd's pie is usually made using ground beef, but preparing it with tender pot roast makes it irresistible.

Filling:

4　tablespoons extra-virgin olive oil

2　pounds chuck roast or other beef stew meat with the fat trimmed, cut into 1-inch cubes

1　large Vidalia onion, chopped

4　garlic cloves, minced

2　teaspoons salt, plus more to taste

1　teaspoon freshly ground black pepper

1　teaspoon red pepper flakes (optional)

1　cup beef broth

1　teaspoon dried oregano

1　teaspoon dried thyme

1　tablespoon chopped fresh flat-leaf parsley

4　large carrots, cut into 1-inch pieces, or 1½ cups baby carrots

1½ cups frozen green peas

1　cup chopped celery

2　tablespoons all-purpose flour

1　cup water

Mashed Potato Crust:

2　pounds baking potatoes, peeled and cut into 1-inch cubes

4　quarts water

1　tablespoon salt

3　tablespoons salted butter

½　cup milk

½　cup half-and-half

1　teaspoon freshly ground black pepper

1. Make the filling: Preheat the oven to 325°. Heat 2 tablespoons oil in a 5-quart cast iron Dutch oven over medium-high heat. Add the beef, half the onion, half the garlic, the salt, black pepper, and, if desired, red pepper to the pan and cook until the beef is browned on all sides, about 5 minutes. Add the broth, oregano, thyme, and parsley. Cover the pan and transfer to the oven; bake until the meat is fork-tender, about 2 hours.

2. Remove the meat and broth and wipe the pan clean. Place the remaining 2 tablespoons oil in the pan and heat over medium-high heat. Add the remaining onion and garlic and cook, stirring often, 2 minutes. Add the carrots, peas, and celery and cook, stirring often, 2 minutes.

3. Return the meat to the pan, stir, and add enough of the broth to cover. Season with salt to taste. Cook over medium heat, stirring frequently, 5 minutes.

4. Place the flour in a cup and slowly add the water, whisking until smooth; if any lumps form, strain the flour mixture through a sieve. Add the flour mixture to the pan and stir well to blend.

5. Increase the oven temperature to 350°.

6. Make the mashed potato crust: Place the potatoes in a stockpot; add the water and salt and bring to a boil. Cook until potatoes are tender, about 10 minutes. Drain thoroughly. While the potatoes are still hot, stir in the butter until it melts. Add the milk, half-and-half, and pepper; mash until smooth.

7. Spoon the mashed potatoes over the filling in the Dutch oven. Bake on the center rack, uncovered, 30 minutes.

8. Turn on the broiler and broil until the potatoes are browned, about 5 minutes. Check often to prevent burning.

Tough and bony short ribs are delicious when braised until fall-off-the-bone tender. In this Southern-style version, from Joanna Pruess' *Cast-Iron Cookbook: Delicious and Simple Comfort Food*, the cooking liquid includes bourbon and molasses. (Joanna likes the robust, slightly less sweet taste of dark molasses, but you can also use the light variety.)

ALL-AMERICAN SHORT RIBS

serves 4

4 pounds bone-in beef short ribs, trimmed and blotted dry	1½ cups beef stock
Salt and freshly ground black pepper	1 (14½-ounce) can diced tomatoes, undrained
Grapeseed or canola oil	½ cup molasses
2 medium carrots, diced	3 large fresh thyme sprigs or 1 tablespoon dried thyme
1 medium yellow onion, diced	2 bay leaves
1 large celery rib, diced	2 tablespoons chopped fresh flat-leaf parsley
1 tablespoon minced garlic	
½ cup bourbon	

1. Preheat the oven to 350°.

2. Season the short ribs on both sides with salt and pepper to taste. Heat a large cast iron Dutch oven over high heat until hot, about 3 minutes. Pour in about 1 tablespoon oil and add as many ribs as can fit comfortably in the bottom of the pan without crowding (cook in batches, if necessary); sear them on all sides. Remove the browned ribs to a large bowl. Add oil as needed to the pan and repeat until all the ribs are cooked.

3. Drain all but 1 tablespoon of the drippings from the pan. Stir in the carrots, onion, and celery; cook over medium-high heat, stirring often, until lightly browned, about 5 minutes. Stir in the garlic and cook 30 seconds; pour in the bourbon and boil over high heat until almost evaporated, about 1½ minutes. Add the stock, tomatoes and their juice, molasses, thyme, and bay leaves; return the ribs to the pan and bring to a boil. Cover the pan and transfer it to the oven to bake until the meat is fork-tender, 1½ to 2 hours.

4. Remove from the oven. Using tongs, transfer the short ribs to a bowl. Pour the liquid through a strainer to catch vegetables, and then

⸙ short ribs ⸙

Short ribs are generally sold in 1- and 2-inch lengths. The shorter ones are easier to work with, but with either size, you should figure about a pound of uncooked ribs per person. You can make these several days ahead, refrigerate them, and then slowly reheat them before serving. Serve over grits or mashed potatoes.

pour the broth into a fat separator; discard the fat and return the liquid to the pan. (If you don't have a fat separator, cover the pan and refrigerate it overnight or until the fat congeals; scrape off the fat, return the sauce to the pan, and heat.) Return the meat and strained vegetables to the liquid in the pan; cover, heat, and set aside. If the sauce is too thin, gently boil to reduce and slightly thicken it, spooning it over the ribs and turning them occasionally. Add additional salt and pepper to taste, if desired. Discard the bay leaves and thyme stems; sprinkle with the parsley and serve.

In this recipe, Bri Malaspino, creative manager of Lodge Manufacturing, enhances New England-style pork chops with the crispy sear and sweet caramelized flavors only cast iron can provide. This recipe is traditionally made by layering the items in a roasting dish and baking it, which yields a more stewed flavor. By sautéing and searing the ingredients, you get a greater contrast in flavors and texture.

SEARED PORK CHOPS WITH CARAMELIZED APPLES AND ONIONS

serves 2

3   tablespoons butter
1   Granny Smith apple, cored and cut into ½- to 1-inch-thick slices
1   sweet onion, cut into ½-inch-thick rings
3   to 5 fresh sage leaves, chopped
2   large (1-inch-thick) bone-in pork chops
Salt and freshly ground black pepper

1. Melt 2 tablespoons butter in a 12-inch cast iron skillet over medium heat. Add the apple slices, onion rings, and sage; cook, turning the mixture occasionally, until the apple and onion are caramelized. Remove the mixture from the pan and keep warm.

2. Increase the heat to medium-high. Add the remaining 1 tablespoon butter to the pan.

3. Season the pork chops with salt and pepper to taste. Add the pork chops to the pan and sear 6 to 8 minutes per side for medium doneness or 10 to 14 minutes per side for well done. For the best results, cover the pan for the last 10 minutes of cooking time to trap as much moisture as possible.

4. Serve the chops with the sautéed apple and onion.

This recipe is from Francine Maroukian, an award-winning food writer and contributing editor to *Garden & Gun*, *Travel + Leisure*, and *Esquire* magazines. "Be sure to make this with small, firm squash," she advises. "Larger squash hold so much water that you'll get steamed rather than browned vegetables."

PAN PORK WITH RAPID RATATOUILLE

serves 4

1 (2½-pound) boneless pork loin	2 garlic cloves, minced
Salt and freshly ground black pepper	4 cups diced mixed pattypan squash and zucchini
2 tablespoons canola oil	1 cup diced tomatoes
2 tablespoons unsalted butter	Big pinch of torn fresh herbs (like basil, parsley, or thyme)
1 shallot, minced	

1. Preheat the oven to 375°.

2. Season the pork loin with salt and pepper to taste.

3. Heat a cast iron skillet over medium heat until hot. Add the oil and sear the pork loin on all sides. Transfer the skillet to the oven and roast until a meat thermometer inserted into the thickest portion registers 155° and the pork is cooked through but still juicy, about 25 minutes. Transfer the pork to a cutting board to stand.

4. Return the skillet to medium heat. Add the butter and let it melt, stirring frequently to scrape up any browned bits. When the butter is foaming slightly, add the shallot and garlic, stirring quickly to soften. As soon as they release their fragrances (about 1½ minutes), add the squash mix and stir to coat with the flavored butter. Cook, stirring occasionally, until golden brown, about 6 minutes. Add the tomatoes and herbs; stir only once or twice to soften the tomatoes and release the aroma of the herbs.

5. Slice the pork loin and place on 4 plates. Spoon the ratatouille onto the pork slices, adding salt and pepper to taste, if desired.

LOMO DE PUERCO ASADO
(Roasted Pork Loin)

serves 6 to 8

This recipe from *Sunset* food editor Margo True is a reimagining of a dish her father made frequently when their family lived for several years in Mexico—first in Guadalajara and later in Tijuana. It's an easy main course, and leftovers make good pork sandwiches—especially layered on a crusty Mexican *bolillo* or other white roll, with avocado, cilantro, tomato, and sweet onion.

1   cup olive oil
1½ tablespoons fresh lime juice
1½ teaspoons dried Mexican oregano or 1 tablespoon chopped fresh oregano
1   teaspoon dried crushed chile de arbol or red pepper flakes
1   teaspoon ground cumin
1   teaspoon salt
½   teaspoon freshly ground black pepper
3   garlic cloves, crushed
1   (3-pound) boneless pork loin roast
2   tablespoons vegetable oil

1. Whisk together the first 8 ingredients in a small bowl. Place the pork in a baking dish just big enough to hold it, pour the marinade over the top, and turn to coat. Marinate, covered, in the refrigerator at least 12 hours (preferably 24 hours), turning once or twice.

2. Let the pork stand 1 hour or until it reaches room temperature.

3. Preheat the oven to 350°.

4. Heat the vegetable oil in a large cast iron skillet over medium-high heat. Remove the pork from the marinade and discard the marinade. Pat the pork dry with paper towels; add the pork to the pan and brown well on all sides, about 10 minutes.

5. Transfer the skillet to the oven and roast until a meat thermometer inserted in the thickest portion registers 140° (the temperature will rise after the meat comes out of the oven), 45 to 60 minutes. Let the roast stand, covered loosely with foil, 15 minutes before slicing.

note

There was a time when folks worried about trichinosis in fresh pork and therefore overcooked it to eliminate these fears. Trichinosis has been all but eliminated from commercial pork. But even when an infestation is present, spores are killed when the meat reaches an internal temperature of 137°, well below the doneness recommended to produce juicy pork. Cook to 150° to 155°. Perfect pork will have a faint pink blush. Let it stand for 10 to 15 minutes after cooking to reabsorb juices and allow the meat to finish cooking (raising the internal termperature by 5° to 10°; the USDA recommends cooking pork to 160°).

Cooler weather is the perfect time for braised dishes, which fill the house with savory and comforting smells. This recipe from Al Hernandez, food and wine editor of *The Vine Times*, provides an easy and inexpensive option for a festive group.

CARNITAS *(Mexican Pulled Pork Tacos)*

serves 8 to 14, depending on the appetites!

2 tablespoons granulated garlic	2 tablespoons vegetable oil
2 tablespoons paprika	1 medium yellow onion, chopped
1 tablespoon kosher salt, plus more to taste	3 cups chicken stock
1 teaspoon freshly ground black pepper, plus more to taste	12 to 24 flour or corn tortillas, warmed
½ teaspoon cayenne pepper	**Toppings**: chopped onion,
1 (4- to 6-pound) bone-in pork shoulder (also known as Boston butt or picnic roast)	chopped cilantro, shredded cheese, chopped tomato, guacamole, and/or salsa

1. Preheat the oven to 225°.

2. Combine the granulated garlic, paprika, salt, black pepper, and cayenne in a small bowl. Rub the spice mixture over the pork shoulder.

3. Heat a large cast iron Dutch oven over medium heat. Add the oil and onion and cook, stirring often, until softened. Place the pork shoulder in the pan and pour in the stock. Cover and slow roast for 8 hours, turning the pork after 4 hours.

4. Transfer the pork to a cutting board or platter and shred with two forks. Season the pork and the cooking liquid (save this liquid and use it as a base for soup) with additional salt and pepper, if desired.

5. Serve the pork with the tortillas topped with your favorite taco toppings.

crazy for cast iron

I don't think I knew there was any type of skillet other than cast iron until I was 9 or 10 years old. Things were either cooked in cast iron or on the grill during the summer. I assumed everyone used cast iron. This, of course, was reinforced by my favorite Saturday morning cartoons—someone was bound to get hit with a frying pan at some point!

It wasn't until years later that I realized why it seemed to be the only type of skillet to me as a child. The versatility of cast iron crosses all boundaries, from searing to sautéing, baking to braising—one pan can do it all. As an added bonus, if properly taken care of, it will last for generations. Just ask Grandma or your favorite Saturday morning cartoon character!

—Al Hernandez

crazy for cast iron

One of the most efficient and satisfying ways of making a dressing for pasta that can be prepared in as little time as it takes to cook up and drain the pasta involves using a good heavy cast iron pan—a 10- or 12-inch, depending on the amount of pasta you are making.

Typically it involves heating olive oil over a relatively high flame and adding any of a number of ingredients to the oil and sizzling them a bit—cut-up anchovies or sardines, garlic, coarse black pepper, red pepper flakes, capers, chopped parsley, broccoli rabe, a handful of quartered cherry tomatoes, etc. Don't add too many different things, perhaps two or three, because this is meant to be a simple preparation. And, of course, the order and the timing depend on the ingredients used. For example, garlic normally goes in toward the very end so that it doesn't brown and begin to turn bitter.

I often prepare one of these for myself and my wife, Maron, to serve with a thin spaghetti. When the pasta is finished, but definitely al dente, I drain it and promptly dump it, still damp, into the hot flavored oil and the infused ingredients, tossing it for a minute or two over a good medium hot flame. I use tongs to keep it moving and well mixed. Then, I continue cooking it in the pan for about 5 minutes more, turning it only two or three times. In this way, some of the pasta surfaces begin to crisp and even brown a bit.

I serve it straight out of the pan at the table. It looks good, tastes zesty, and every mouthful contains a little bit of crunch. If you like, finish it off with a grating of cheese.

—Nach Waxman

This recipe is a favorite of mother and daughter cookbook authors Sharon Kramis and Julie Kramis Hearne, who serve it over polenta, mashed potatoes, risotto, or noodles. They like to use any leftover pork to make sandwiches with coleslaw and mango salsa the next day.

BRAISED PORK SHOULDER WITH STAR ANISE

serves 8 to 10

1 (3- to 4-pound) bone-in pork shoulder

1 teaspoon salt, plus more to taste

½ teaspoon freshly ground black pepper, plus more to taste

2 tablespoons olive oil

1 medium yellow onion, cut in half and medium diced

3 garlic cloves, slivered

1 cup beef broth

1 (14½-ounce) can fire-roasted diced tomatoes, undrained (such as Muir Glen)

½ cup full-bodied red wine

2 tablespoons brown sugar

1 cinnamon stick

3 star anise

1 bay leaf

1. Preheat the oven to 325°.

2. Score the fat side of the pork shoulder in a crisscross pattern. Pat dry and season all over with the salt and pepper.

3. Heat the oil in a 5-quart cast iron Dutch oven over medium to medium-high heat. Cook the pork, turning it using tongs or a long fork, until browned on all sides, 8 to 10 minutes. Transfer the pork to a large plate and set aside.

4. Add the onion to the pan drippings and cook over medium heat, stirring occasionally, 5 minutes. Add the garlic and cook, stirring often, 3 minutes. Add the broth, tomatoes (with their juice), and wine. Bring to a low boil and stir in the brown sugar; add the cinnamon stick, star anise, and bay leaf. Return the pork to the pan and cover with a tight-fitting lid. Transfer to the center rack of the oven and braise until the pork is fork-tender, 2½ to 3 hours.

5. Transfer the pork to a serving platter with tongs or a long fork. Bring the juices in the pan to a boil and cook until reduced and slightly thickened, about 3 minutes. Season with more salt and pepper, to taste, if desired. Discard the cinnamon stick, star anise, and bay leaf. Slice the pork and drizzle the sauce over the top.

INDOOR PULLED PORK WITH NORTH CAROLINA VINEGAR SAUCE

serves 8

Grilling expert and cookbook author Elizabeth Karmel dedicates this recipe to Lodge public relations and advertising manager, Mark Kelly. He loves Elizabeth's slow-smoked North Carolina pulled pork so much that he convinced her to try adapting it to a Dutch oven. "At first, I thought it would be blasphemy, but once I tried it, I had to agree that it was a quick and easy version that is great for winter, tailgates, and anyone who doesn't have outdoor space," says Elizabeth. If you cook it on top of the stove the entire time, you will need two to three times the liquid as you do for the oven method. This recipe is adapted from one in Elizabeth's cookbook *Taming the Flame: Secrets for Hot-and-Quick and Low-and-Slow BBQ.*

1 (4- to 7-pound) bone-in pork shoulder or Boston butt, trimmed
Olive oil
Kosher salt and freshly ground black pepper
North Carolina Vinegar Sauce (see recipe)
2 cups water
1 package hamburger buns (no sesame seeds)
North Carolina Coleslaw (see recipe)

1. Pat the pork dry with paper towels and then brush with a thin coating of oil. Season with salt and pepper to taste.

2. Heat about 2 tablespoons oil in a 9-quart cast iron Dutch oven over medium-high heat until hot. Gently lower the pork into the pan and sear 3 to 4 minutes on all sides; you want the pork to be golden brown. While the pork is searing, make the North Carolina Vinegar Sauce.

3. Once the pork is seared, arrange it in the pan so that the fat side is facing up. Pour the water over the pork and then pour 2 cups vinegar sauce over the top. Place the lid on the Dutch oven and cook 30 minutes over medium-high heat.

4. Preheat the oven to 350°.

5. Transfer the covered Dutch oven to the center rack of the oven. Cook slowly for 2 to 3 hours, depending on the size of the pork butt, until a meat thermometer inserted into the thickest portion registers 190° to 200°. The meat should be very tender and ready to be pulled apart. If there is a bone in the meat, it should come out smooth and clean, with no meat clinging to it (this is the real test for doneness on the barbecue circuit). Remember, there is no need to turn the meat during the entire cooking time.

6. At this point, the pork can be cooled in the Dutch oven and refrigerated overnight, if desired. (The advantage of doing this is that the extra fat will congeal and it will be very easy to lift off the top, leaving only the concentrated juices. Reheat the pork in the Dutch oven in a preheated 250° oven until hot all the way through; spoon the juices over the pork as it reheats, and then follow the rest of the instructions.)

7. Let the meat stand 20 minutes until cool enough to handle; wearing rubber food-service gloves, pull the meat from the skin, bones, and fat. Set aside any crispy bits. Working quickly, shred meat using two forks. (You can chop the meat with a cleaver if you prefer, but then you have "chopped" pork barbecue, not "pulled" pork.) Chop the reserved crispy bits and stir them into the pulled pork. While the meat is still warm, stir in about ¾ cup of the remaining vinegar sauce (depending on the meat) to moisten and season the meat. The recipe can be made in advance up to this point and reheated with about ¼ cup additional sauce in a double boiler or in a covered pan in a 250° oven.

8. Serve the pulled pork on buns topped with North Carolina Coleslaw. Serve additional sauce on the side, if desired.

NORTH CAROLINA VINEGAR SAUCE

makes about 6 cups

4	cups cider vinegar	
1	cup ketchup	
2	tablespoons kosher salt	
2	tablespoons ground white pepper	
½	to 1 tablespoon red pepper flakes	

¼ cup granulated sugar

½ cup firmly packed brown sugar

1 teaspoon freshly ground black pepper

1. Combine all the ingredients in a large bowl and stir well. Let stand at least 10 minutes or almost indefinitely in the refrigerator. The longer the sauce stands, the hotter it gets because the heat from the red pepper is brought out by the vinegar. Start with ½ tablespoon red pepper and add more to taste.

NORTH CAROLINA COLESLAW

serves 8

3 cups North Carolina Vinegar Sauce or as needed

1 medium head green cabbage, cored and chopped

1. Combine the sauce and cabbage in a medium bowl and stir until the cabbage is well coated with sauce but not quite wet. Let stand 2 hours or overnight in the refrigerator.

Grapes and sausage may seem like an odd combination, but you'll love this satisfying dish from award-winning cookbook author Clifford A. Wright. The sweetness of the grapes acts as a wonderful foil for the spiciness of the hot sausage and red pepper. Be sure to cook this dish over low heat the entire time. Add a green salad and you've got dinner.

PAN-ROASTED SAUSAGE, POTATOES, AND GRAPES

serves 4

6 tablespoons extra-virgin olive oil

2 large garlic cloves, crushed

3½ pounds potatoes, cut into small cubes and dried well with paper towels

Salt

1 (½-pound) link sweet Italian sausage, casing removed and meat crumbled into small pieces

2 (½-pound) links hot Italian sausage, casings removed and meat crumbled into small pieces

1 teaspoon red pepper flakes (preferably Chimayo chile flakes)

2½ cups seedless green grapes (about 1¼ pounds)

Freshly ground black pepper

1. Heat the oil and garlic in a 12- or 14-inch cast iron skillet over low heat. Once the garlic turns light golden, remove and discard it.
2. Add the potatoes and shake the skillet so they cover the bottom. Salt lightly to taste. Place both kinds of sausage on top of the potatoes, sprinkle with the red pepper and cook until the potatoes are sticking and golden on the bottom, about 15 minutes.
3. Turn the mixture by scraping with a metal spatula and cook, stirring occasionally, until golden brown, about 1 hour.
4. Add the grapes, season with salt and black pepper to taste, and cook until the grapes are soft, about 20 minutes. Serve hot.

Nothing is simpler to make for a quick dinner than a delicious sandwich served with a salad or a bowl of soup. In this recipe, Gourmet Gadget Gal cooking instructor, food writer, and blogger Jane Gaither twists together two classic Southern sandwiches, the pimiento cheese and the BLT, and presses them into an oozy melt sure to please your family. If you don't own a panini press, you can always use a smaller preheated cast iron skillet to press the sandwich down. This recipe makes enough pimiento cheese for eight sandwiches and it will keep in your refrigerator for up to two weeks.

PIMIENTO CHEESE PANINI SANDWICH

makes 1 sandwich

Pimiento Cheese Spread:

3　cups (12 ounces) shredded Cheddar cheese

1　(4-ounce) jar diced pimiento, drained

½　teaspoon minced garlic

1　teaspoon prepared horseradish

1　teaspoon hot sauce

1　teaspoon Worcestershire sauce

A few grinds of black pepper

6　tablespoons mayonnaise (Jane likes to use Duke's)

Panini:

Softened butter

2　(⅓-inch-thick) bread slices cut from a dense loaf

2　thick bacon slices (Jane uses Benton's from Madisonville, Tennessee), cooked until crisp

1　tomato, sliced

1. Combine the Pimiento Cheese Spread ingredients in a medium bowl and stir well.

2. Spread butter on one side of each bread slice.

3. Heat a 12-inch Lodge Grill Pan and Panini Press over medium-high heat.

4. Place 1 bread slice, buttered side down, on the hot grill pan. Spoon 3 tablespoons of the Pimiento Cheese Spread onto the bread and spread it to the edges. Add the bacon and sliced tomato and top with the second bread slice with the buttered side up.

5. Place the hot panini press on top of the sandwich for 2 minutes, pressing gently to flatten it.

6. Remove the press and transfer the sandwich to a plate. Enjoy!

COOKING OUTDOORS

This chapter harkens back to the origins of cast iron cookery,
when it was used to prepare meals over open flames. We've got
a tasty selection of recipes for you to try—on your grill, over a
campfire, or on top of live coals.

GRILLED MARGHERITA PIZZA

serves 2 to 4

Grilling expert and cookbook author Elizabeth Karmel loves grilled pizza with a capital "L!" While she was writing her book *Pizza on the Grill* she realized that it took only a second for pizza to go from under-done to overdone on a charcoal fire. The Lodge Pizza Pan changes all that and ensures a gorgeous, crispy, slightly smoky crust every time. The cast iron pan creates hot, consistent indirect heat that browns food beautifully and helps prevent burning. This recipe also provides directions for using it on a gas grill, but it's not as important as it is when cooking over charcoal. Try it—it will be the best "open-fire" pizza you have ever eaten!

Once you master the Margherita, add your favorite toppings. Remember, a grilled pizza crust is a blank canvas for all your favorite foods!

1 (14½-ounce) can crushed tomatoes with or without basil, drained
2 garlic cloves, minced
Sea salt and freshly ground black pepper
¼ cup uncooked grits or polenta (for rolling the dough)
1 ball prepared pizza dough, at room temperature
2 tablespoons olive oil
8 ounces fresh mozzarella cheese, cut into ¼-inch-thick slices, or 1 cup (4 ounces) shredded mozzarella (if fresh is unavailable)
10 fresh basil leaves

1. Preheat a gas grill by setting all burners on high. Close the lid and leave the grill on high for 10 minutes, then reduce the heat of all burners to medium—you don't want the heat too high, or the crust will burn. Place a Lodge Pizza Pan in the center of the cooking grates. (If you have a charcoal grill, let the coals burn to a gray ash and spread in an even layer. Place your pan on the cooking grate and let it preheat for 5 minutes.)

2. For the sauce, pour the tomatoes into a small nonreactive bowl. Add half the garlic and season with salt and pepper to taste.

3. Sprinkle work surface with the grits. Roll out and shape dough ideally into a thin, organically shaped piece of dough (about ¼-inch thick). Drizzle or brush both sides generously with the oil.

4. Pick up the dough by the two corners closest to you. In one motion, lay it down flat on the pizza pan from front to back. Grill, with grill lid down, until the bottom is nicely browned, about 3 minutes.

5. Using tongs, flip the crust. Spread the entire surface with 1 cup tomato sauce; sprinkle with the remaining garlic and top with the cheese.

6. If using a gas grill, switch to indirect heat by turning off the center burner(s) or one of the burners if you have a 2-burner grill. The pan will now be over the unlit section. (If using a charcoal grill, you won't change anything.) Grill, with the lid down, until the bottom of the crust is well browned and the cheese has melted, 7 to 10 minutes.

7. Using a pizza peel or a flat-sided cookie sheet, remove the pizza from the grill; garnish with the basil and season with salt and pepper to taste. Slice and serve immediately.

This dish creates an awful lot of smoke, so chef Patrick Reilly of the Majestic Grille in Memphis likes to cook it outside on the burner of his gas grill. "You can also use the burner of an outdoor fryer," says Patrick.

SEARED ROSEMARY AND GARLIC PORTERHOUSE WITH BROWNED BUTTER

serves 2

1 fresh rosemary sprig
1 garlic clove, sliced
¼ cup extra-virgin olive oil
1 (2-pound) Porterhouse steak (dry-aged Prime is always best but good Choice will also work)

Kosher salt and freshly ground black pepper
¼ cup (½ stick) unsalted butter
1 tablespoon chopped fresh curly parsley

1. Let the rosemary and garlic infuse in the oil for a few hours.

2. Take the steak out of the refrigerator 1 hour before you plan to cook it and allow it to come to room temperature.

3. Place a large cast iron skillet on the gas eye of one of the burners of a gas grill set on high and leave it for at least 20 minutes. (Patrick finds it best to go make a gin and tonic or a martini to pass the time.)

4. Using the rosemary sprig as a brush, brush the steak with the infused oil. Sprinkle with salt and pepper to taste. Place the steak in the hot skillet over high heat. Let cook (without moving) for about 3 minutes.

5. Using tongs, lift the steak out of the skillet and pour the drippings from the skillet into a heatproof container. (Use a grill mitt to grab the skillet handle—it's going to be incredibly hot.) Return the pan to the burner; place the steak, uncooked side down, back in the skillet and cook for 2 to 3 minutes.

6. Remove the steak to a cutting board. Let stand for 5 to 6 minutes to allow juices to settle. Using a sharp knife, carve the meat off the bone, then slice lengthwise and place on a platter.

7. Wipe skillet clean and add the butter. Reduce the heat to medium and cook until the butter is foamy and brown. Stir in the parsley and pour the butter mixture over the sliced steak. Serve immediately.

This recipe made for some unforgettable memories when *Good Eats* culinary director, Tamie Cook, prepared it over a campfire for her friends (see A Cast Iron Memory at right). Tamie recommends serving this with a baked potato and green salad.

PEPPER STEAK AL FRESCO

serves 4 happy campers

4 boneless strip steaks (1¼ inches thick), trimmed	Kosher salt
1 tablespoon olive oil	⅓ cup plus 1 teaspoon cognac
3 tablespoons coarsely cracked black peppercorns	1 cup heavy cream

1. Place a 10-inch cast iron skillet on a grate over a campfire until the pan is hot. (The pan is hot enough when you sprinkle a little water in it and it "dances.")

2. Rub the steaks on all sides with the oil and press on the black pepper. Sprinkle with salt to taste. Add the steaks to the hot pan and cook for 4 to 5 minutes per side for medium-rare (the only way to eat a steak, says Tamie). Place the steaks on a plate and let them stand while you prepare the sauce.

3. Place the pan at the end of the grate, away from the hottest part of the fire. The pan will be very hot, so proceed with caution! Carefully add ⅓ cup cognac. Tilt the edge of the pan closest to the fire to light the alcohol. Shake the pan until the flames die down. Add the cream to the pan and bring to a boil, stirring or whisking until the mixture thickens enough to coat the back of a spoon. Stir in the remaining 1 teaspoon cognac and season with additional salt to taste, if desired.

4. Serve the sauce over the steaks with a baked potato and salad.

a cast iron memory

I'll admit it—I'm not a camper and people closest to me know that my idea of roughing it is a hotel without room service. So when my "friends who camp" invited me to join them for a weekend in the great outdoors, I was quite surprised. I agreed on the condition that I would handle the food. I would do all of the shopping and bring all the necessary equipment as long as they carried everything to the campsite, set up my tent, and provided me with an air mattress. This was music to their ears. None of them like to cook, and, more often than not, their idea of camp food is a can of beans and a hot dog on a stick.

Imagine their surprise when I showed up with my well-seasoned 10-inch Lodge cast iron skillet and all the makings for a three-course meal for our first evening. Though I think they initially questioned the logic of this move, once they tasted that perfectly seared steak with its delectable sauce, they too were believers in the magic of the iron skillet. —Tamie Cook

GRILLED VEAL CHOPS

serves 6

Thick, luscious veal chops are seared in a salted, hot, dry skillet after marinating in herbs. The fat on the chops helps them grill to perfection. Says cookbook author Ellen Wright, "The only pan I would ever use to make these chops is my favorite cast iron skillet, which I've had for 50 years. It's got a half-inch-tall side, so it's basically flat. To clean it, I run it under hot water when it's still warm, then wipe it off with a paper towel."

1 tablespoon dried or fresh rosemary leaves

1 tablespoon dried or fresh thyme leaves

6 (1½-inch-thick) veal chops, trimmed of excess fat (don't remove all of it!)

1 to 2 tablespoons kosher salt

2 lemons, quartered

Watercress sprigs for garnish (optional)

1. Sprinkle the rosemary and thyme evenly on both sides of the chops and keep at room temperature for about 2 hours.

2. Heat a 14- to 16-inch cast iron skillet over medium-high heat on the grill. Sprinkle the salt in the pan. Sear the chops until golden brown on each side and slightly pink inside, 4 to 5 minutes per side.

3. Remove the pan from the grill. Serve the chops as soon as possible with a wedge of lemon and garnish with watercress, if desired.

Come summer, it's too hot to cook inside. Instead of grilling up the usual suspects, try this beer can chicken from Max Brody, chef/owner of the Night Kitchen in Montague, Massachusetts. The beer helps to keep the meat moist and flavorful, while the heat from the coals creates a crispy and delicious exterior. The cast iron pan gives your beer can-ensconced chicken added stability on the grill, plus the chicken benefits from the extra moisture provided by the beer evaporating from the pan.

CAST IRON BEER CAN CHICKEN

serves 4, or 2 with leftovers

½ cup (1 stick) butter, melted
2 tablespoons soy sauce
1 tablespoon Dijon mustard
1 tablespoon light brown sugar
Salt and freshly ground black
    pepper

1 (3- to 4-pound) whole
    chicken, giblets removed
2 (12-ounce) cans beer of your
    choice

1. Start the coals in a chimney. Whisk together the melted butter, soy sauce, mustard, brown sugar, and salt and pepper to taste. Rub the marinade over the outside and inside of the chicken.

2. When the coals are hot, pour them on the bottom rack of your grill and arrange them around the perimeter of the grate, creating an area of indirect heat in the center.

3. Open 1 can of beer and place it on a large cast iron skillet. Place the chicken on top of the can so that the can is inside the cavity of the bird, with the bird sitting upright on the can. Place the skillet on the grill, over the area of indirect heat. Open the remaining can of beer and pour half of it into the skillet.

4. Partially close the grill lid. Check the chicken occasionally to make sure there is always liquid in the skillet, adding more of the remaining beer as needed. Baste the chicken with the juices that accumulate in the pan. Cook until a meat thermometer inserted into the thickest portion of the thigh registers 165°, about 1 hour and 20 minutes. Remove the skillet with the chicken from the grill and let cool for a few minutes before carefully removing the chicken from the beer can. (Be careful: The can will still be hot.)

5. Open a few more beers and enjoy!

crazy for cast iron

Let's be honest. What you cook with is just as important as the ingredients you choose to cook. But that doesn't mean you need a department store full of pots and pans to get the job done effectively.

Case in point: the old, tried-and-true black cast iron pan. And there are so many noncooking uses for it, too. My grandmother used it as a weight when she wanted to squeeze the moisture out of eggplant, and her chicken cutlets were paper-thin after she pounded them with her pan.

I have had my pan for as long as I have been married. It was passed down to me from my mother, who got it from her mother. It is well seasoned and works like a charm.   —Mary Ann Esposito

Mary Ann Esposito, cookbook author and host of PBS's *Ciao Italia*, America's longest running cooking show, inherited her cast iron skillet from her mother. One of her favorite ways to use it is on the grill—no more scraping incinerated food off the grill grate. It works particularly well with fish.

PAN-GRILLED HALIBUT WITH TARRAGON BUTTER SAUCE

serves 4

6   tablespoons (¾ stick) butter
3   tablespoons minced fresh tarragon
Grated zest of 1 large lemon
1¼ tablespoons lemon pepper seasoning
1⅓ teaspoons fine sea salt
4   (6-ounce) small halibut steaks

1. Melt the butter in a small saucepan over low heat. Add the tarragon and lemon zest and keep warm.

2. Place a well-seasoned cast iron skillet on the cooking grate and heat the grill to 600°. Then lower the heat to medium-high.

3. Meanwhile, mix the lemon pepper and salt in a small bowl and sprinkle it onto a sheet of wax paper. Place the halibut pieces on top of the seasoning mixture, pressing it onto the fish to adhere. Repeat on the other side.

4. Place the fish in the hot skillet; cook for about 6 minutes per side, depending on the thickness of the fish. The fish is done when a meat thermometer inserted in the center of each steak registers 145° or the fish flakes with a fork.

5. Place 1 halibut steak on each of 4 dinner plates and pour the warm butter sauce over the top. Serve immediately.

"Even people who say they don't like seafood gobble these up!" says campfire cook Rita Phillips of Gilbert, Arizona, who received this recipe from her dear friend Ronda.

SANDY BEACH SHRIMP TACOS WITH MANGO SALSA

serves 6 to 10

2 pounds jumbo shrimp

Marinade:

¼ cup fresh lemon juice

¼ cup olive oil

4 teaspoons minced garlic

Salt and freshly ground black
   pepper to taste

Mango Salsa:

2 large soft ripe mangoes,
   peeled and diced

4 ripe avocados, peeled,
   pitted, and diced

¼ cup fresh lime juice

2 tablespoons chopped fresh
   cilantro

2 small chiles (optional),
   seeded and finely chopped

Salt and freshly ground black
   pepper to taste

Canola oil

Small corn tortillas

1. Peel shrimp; devein, if desired. Place in a large zip-top plastic freezer bag or airtight container and chill until ready to use.

2. Combine the marinade ingredients in a small bowl. Add to the shrimp and toss until coated. Seal and chill for at least 30 minutes but no more than an hour.

3. Meanwhile, combine the salsa ingredients in a medium bowl. The salsa can be left at room temperature up to an hour; otherwise, keep chilled up to 1 day.

4. Build a fire with medium-high heat; the coals should all be white, with no live flame. Rub a large cast iron griddle with canola oil to keep the shrimp from sticking. Preheat the griddle over the fire until it sizzles when a drop of water makes contact with it. Pour the shrimp on the griddle in a single layer and grill 1 to 2 minutes on the first side; turn shrimp and grill 1 minute on the second side (just until shrimp turn pink). You may need to cook the shrimp in batches. Carefully remove the shrimp from the griddle.

5. Place another cast iron griddle (or the lid of a camp Dutch oven, set upside down) on the grill and warm the tortillas on both sides.

6. To serve, place a few shrimp in the middle of each warm tortilla, top with the salsa, and enjoy!

ROSEMARY-AND-GARLIC GRILLED SHRIMP

serves 4

"I grew up in Savannah, Georgia, and, like most children of the Low Country, shellfish are a constant in my life," says Mark Kelly, public relations and advertising manager of Lodge Manufacturing. Here is one of his favorite ways to grill shrimp.

¼ cup olive oil, plus extra for brushing

2 tablespoons chopped garlic, mashed into a paste with 1 teaspoon sea salt

2 tablespoons crab boil spice

1 tablespoon chopped fresh rosemary

2 pounds medium shrimp, peeled and deveined

1. Combine the ¼ cup olive oil, the garlic paste, crab boil, and rosemary in a large bowl. Add the shrimp; toss to coat. Cover with plastic wrap and marinate overnight in the refrigerator.

2. Build a fire in a Lodge Sportsman's Grill and allow the coals to burn down to a medium heat. Place the shrimp on the grill and brush every few minutes with olive oil. Cook 3 minutes per side, just until shrimp turn pink—be careful not to overcook.

Says Jerry Clepper, "A big catch in the Tennessee River calls for a Clepper family gathering. The fried fish never makes it to the table because it's gobbled up by the cook and the samplers as soon as it gets done." You can also fry French fries and hush puppies in the oil after all the fish has been cooked (see Doc Havron's Hush Puppies, page 232). Serve it all up with coleslaw, tartar sauce, and ketchup. If you like, you can substitute 6 cups of Zatarain's Fish-Fri for the flour and cornmeal.

DEEP-FRIED CATFISH

serves 10 to 12

1 gallon canola oil	Salt and freshly ground black
3 cups all-purpose flour	pepper
3 cups cornmeal	1 small jar yellow mustard
5 pounds catfish fillets, all cut	Lemon wedges for garnish
to about the same size	

1. Mount a 17-inch cast iron skillet on a propane burner. Fill the skillet two-thirds full with the oil. Heat the oil to 360°. (Have a guest keep a watchful eye on it; it's best to use a deep-fry thermometer to track the temperature.)

2. Combine the flour and cornmeal in a clean paper grocery bag. Arrange the fish fillets in a single layer on wax paper-lined baking sheets. Season both sides of the fish with salt and pepper to taste. Brush each piece on both sides with about ½ teaspoon of the mustard. Drop each fillet into the flour mixture and shake the bag to coat well.

3. Before you start frying, have another clean paper bag lined with several paper towels and a slotted spoon ready at the cooker.

4. Place the fillets, one at a time, into the hot oil. Be careful not to overcrowd the pan or the temperature of the oil will drop and you won't get crispy fish. Using the slotted spoon, remove the fish soon after they float but not until they have turned light brown. Place the cooked fillets inside the clean grocery bag to drain and keep warm. Garnish with lemon wedges.

eggplant

Eggplant has been used in almost every culture around the globe for thousands of years. Most people don't even realize it's a fruit! It's also a wonderful natural source of fiber and minerals. Ahh, the mysterious eggplant…made easy!

For Mark Kelly, public relations and advertising manager of Lodge Manufacturing, one of the greatest pleasures of living in southeast Tennessee is enjoying the abundance it has to offer. He frequents the Chattanooga Market, which is open each Sunday, spring, summer, and fall, and provides a wide selection of fresh-off-the-farm produce. One of Mark's favorite veggies to grill on his Lodge Sportsman's Grill is okra.

This recipe, from culinary teacher Megan McCarthy of Healthy Eating 101, is a great side dish to accompany any meal.

HERBED GRILLED EGGPLANT

serves 2

1 large eggplant
3 tablespoons extra-virgin olive oil
2 tablespoons balsamic vinegar
½ teaspoon sea salt
Cracked black peppercorns
1 teaspoon dried herbes de Provence
Grated Sardo, Asiago, or Pecorino-Romano cheese (optional)

1. Cut the eggplant into ½-inch-thick slices. In a small bowl, whisk together the oil, vinegar, salt, pepper, and herbes de Provence. Brush both sides of the eggplant slices with the mixture.

2. Heat a large cast iron grill pan over medium-high heat on a gas grill or stove-top. Arrange the eggplant slices on the pan in a single layer and grill on each side for 5 to 6 minutes.

3. Serve hot, topped with grated cheese, if desired.

GRILLED OKRA

serves 3

1 pound large fresh okra pods
1½ tablespoons kosher salt
½ teaspoon freshly ground black pepper
½ teaspoon garlic salt
2 tablespoons olive oil

1. Build a fire in a Lodge Sportsman's Grill and allow the coals to burn low.

2. Meanwhile, rinse the okra under cold running water and pat dry. (KEEP THE TIPS AND BOTTOMS.)

3. In a large bowl, stir together the salt, pepper, garlic salt, and oil. Add the okra and toss until the pods are completely coated.

4. Place the okra on the grill using tongs and turn after about 3 minutes, allowing the okra to become nicely browned. Remove from the grill and serve.

crazy for cast iron

OK, I confess. I wasn't much of a cook until the spring of 2005. That's when this former sports writer began meeting chefs, food stylists, cookbook authors, and other foodies while promoting Lodge Cast Iron Cookware. The more I became entrenched in the food world, the more I realized, "I can do this."

Strangely enough, my stove-top efforts with skillets, grill pans, and Dutch ovens weren't complete disasters (at least no one said they were calories of mass destruction).

Where I really found my niche was with the Lodge Sportsman's Grill, a highly revered all cast iron hibachi. Designed with a pull-down drawer to assist in the adding of more coals and a sliding door for airflow, it's easier to use than a smart phone.

But the truly utilitarian feature I most admire are the thin grill grates, which allow for the preparation of veggies, shrimp, fish, etc., without skewers and without worrying about food falling into the fire. The grill is equally proficient in preparing barbecued chicken or grilling steaks.

In my travels with Lodge, I've realized that food culture is in a constant state of change. A skillet may have its roots in cooking fried chicken, but the grandchildren of the original owner may be preparing stir-fries or fajitas in the same pan. Our Sportsman's Grill has a similar story. My recipes have a noticeable nod to the Deep South. Traveling around the country, though, I've seen folks tailgating at Southeastern Conference football games using their grill to prepare wings, burgers, and hot dogs—many times their recipes featuring Cajun or other regional spices. In the Midwest, you'll find bratwurst, venison, and perch fillets. In Texas and the Southwest, people will fire up their Sportsman's Grill with mesquite briquettes to cook beef briskets and a small skillet of peppers and onions. On the West Coast, the grill cooks everything from bluefin tuna to salmon, as well as tomatoes, onions, and other seasonal vegetables at home, at campsites, or when tailgating.   —Mark Kelly

MARK'S SUMMER BEAN AND VEGETABLE SURPRISE

serves 4

Mark Kelly, public relations and advertising manager of Lodge Manufacturing, offers up his favorite combination, but recommends that you use whatever fresh vegetables are in season and look good.

2 ears fresh corn
½ cup fresh okra
½ cup fresh seasonal pole beans
1 (7-ounce) can black beans
½ cup diced bell pepper (any color)
1 lime, cut in half

2 tablespoons freshly grated Parmesan cheese
1 tablespoon olive oil
Kosher salt and freshly ground black pepper
1 cup hickory chips, soaked in water for 1 hour

1. Build a fire in a Lodge Sportsman's Grill and allow the coals to burn low.

2. Meanwhile, shuck the corn and cut the kernels into a medium bowl, scraping the cobs; drain off any liquid and discard cobs.

3. Trim the tops and bottoms off the okra and slice into ½-inch-thick rounds. Add to the corn.

4. String the pole beans, opening the pods just enough so the beans will fall out while cooking. Add to the bowl.

5. Pour the canned beans and their liquid into the bowl; add the bell pepper and squeeze the lime halves over the vegetables. Sprinkle with the cheese and oil. Season with salt and pepper to taste. Stir well to combine and pour into a 12-inch cast iron skillet.

6. Drain the hickory chips and toss them onto the coals; wait for them to begin to burn and for the hickory aroma to emerge.

7. Place the skillet on the grill and stir vegetable mixture occasionally until the vegetables are good and hot and the cheese is melted and thoroughly mixed. If the coals begin to fade too much, add more charcoal.

GRILLED SWEET POTATOES WITH LIME-CILANTRO DRESSING

serves 4

4 organic sweet potatoes
Olive oil
Lime-Cilantro Dressing:
¼ cup fresh lime juice
½ teaspoon kosher salt
¼ teaspoon freshly ground black pepper
¼ cup extra-virgin olive oil
¼ cup chopped fresh cilantro

This recipe, from culinary teacher Megan McCarthy of Healthy Eating 101, is made with one of her favorite "superfoods," the sweet potato. Kids love this recipe as much as grown-ups. The cilantro and lime really give the potatoes an addictive flavor.

1. Cut the sweet potatoes lengthwise into wedges, leaving the skins on. Place them in a large pot, cover with cold salted water, and bring to a boil. Reduce heat and simmer until the potatoes are just tender, about 10 minutes. Drain, rinse the potatoes with cold water, and pat dry.

2. Lightly coat a cast iron grill pan with olive oil and preheat over medium-high heat on a gas grill or stove-top. Arrange the sweet potato wedges on the hot grill pan and cook until grill lines appear before turning onto the other side of the wedge.

3. In a small bowl, whisk together the lime juice, salt, and pepper. Slowly add the oil, whisking constantly. Stir in the cilantro and taste for seasoning.

4. Arrange the grilled sweet potatoes on a platter and drizzle with the dressing to serve.

HEAT-WAVE BREAD

makes 1 loaf

Rose Levy Beranbaum, author of *The Bread Bible,* worked out this technique for the now ubiquitous no-knead bread one August day when the temperature soared to the upper 90s and she just didn't feel justified heating up the whole house in order to have homemade bread for her height-of-the-season tomato sandwiches and BLTs.

"I had been meaning to try this technique for years, but this unusually intense heat wave finally spurred me into action. I was stunned and delighted by how easy it was to transition from indoor oven to outdoor gas grill," recounts Rose. "I have a Weber Summit with four burners, which makes it possible to turn off the two center burners to avoid blackening the bottom of the bread. I'm reasonably sure that this method can be adapted to any four-burner gas grill but have my doubts about the charcoal grill, as it's difficult to get and maintain the high temperature necessary to bake this bread effectively. But as far as I'm concerned, the results on the gas grill surpass those using the oven method."

3 cups (16.5 ounces) Gold Medal Better for Bread flour, or half unbleached all-purpose and half bread flour

¼ teaspoon instant yeast
1½ teaspoons salt
1⅔ cups room-temperature water

1. In a large bowl, whisk together the flour and yeast, then stir in the salt. Add the water and stir with your fingers or a silicone spatula just until the dry ingredients are moistened. The mixture will be very sticky.

2. Cover the bowl tightly with plastic wrap and allow to stand at around 70° for 18 to 19 hours. (It will rise significantly and be filled with bubbles hours earlier, but it does not deflate up to 19 hours. This longer rising results in more flavor.)

3. Turn dough out onto a well-floured surface. (Silpat is ideal because you need very little flour to keep it from sticking.) There is no need to flour the top of the dough. Pat the dough down gently, then do two business letter folds, pinching together the dough at the bottom to form a nice taut shape. (Because the dough is so moist and sticky, a bench scraper will be helpful shaping the dough. Latex gloves will also keep the dough from sticking.) Place the dough on a piece of parchment paper or aluminum foil cut to 14 inches in diameter and sprinkled with flour. Let it rise at 80° for 2 hours or at 70° (which will take a little longer) until it is about 9 inches in diameter and 2 inches high and, when pressed lightly with a wet finger, fills in slowly.

4. Use heavy-duty potholders, preferably the mitten type that protect your lower arms. Place a covered 10-inch cast iron Dutch oven on the cooking grate of a gas grill while the grill preheats to high heat with the lid closed for 20 minutes. The grill will be about 550° after 10 minutes, but the Dutch oven requires an additional 10 minutes. Place a trivet or heavy-duty rack alongside the grill.

5. Remove the Dutch oven lid. (Rose places hers back on the grill.) Transfer the Dutch oven to the trivet and close the grill. Allow the Dutch oven to sit for about 1 minute to cool slightly. (Rose checked the temperature inside the oven with an infrared thermometer and it was 475°.) Transfer the dough to the Dutch oven, cover with the lid, and place it back on the cooking grate in the center of the grill. Work quickly so the heat does not escape or dissipate. Turn off the two center burners. Close the grill lid.

6. Bake for 20 minutes. (With the center burners off, Rose's grill maintained a temperature of 450° during this period.) Remove the Dutch oven lid, close the grill lid, and continue baking for 10 minutes. (The grill was 440° for this period.)

7. Remove the bread from the Dutch oven (turn over to unmold it) and place it directly onto the cooking grate in the center of the grill. Close the grill lid and bake for an additional 10 minutes. Turn off the burners and allow the bread to stand in the covered grill for another 10 minutes.

tip

No-knead bread is characteristically moist, bordering on pasty. If you prefer a slightly drier bread, as Rose does, slice the bread and let the slices sit for about an hour on wire racks. Freeze any leftovers. When ready to serve, remove slices and toast them very lightly to restore them to the consistency of perfectly fresh-baked bread.

CAMP DUTCH OVEN COOKING

A camp Dutch oven is specifically designed for outdoor cooking. It has three stubby legs that lift it off the ground just enough so that hot coals can be set underneath it, as well as a flat, flanged lid so coals can be set on top of it with no worry that they will roll off. You can choose between shallow and deep Dutch ovens; they range in size from 8 to 16 inches in diameter. The shallow Dutch ovens are also known as "bread ovens," as they are the preferred pot when cooking bread or biscuits. The deeper Dutch ovens are perfect for chili, stews, and meat dishes of all sorts.

Camp Cooking 101

1. Prepare your cooking area. You want to choose a site with as much wind shelter as possible. If need be, build up a windbreak around where you will set your pot using patio stones, brick, or concrete block. If you are using a camp Dutch oven in your backyard, be sure to clear the cooking area of twigs and other flammable materials. You may also want to lay out an area of brick to use for your fire site.

2. Determine how many briquettes you'll need for the temperature you want and get them going in a chimney starter. (See the chart below or your recipe.)

3. Place the hot coals. Draw an outline of the bottom of your pot where it will be cooking. Using the chart (or your recipe) as your guide, place the appropriate number of bottom briquettes in a checkerboard pattern within that outline. Set the oven over those coals. Then place the top coals in a checkerboard pattern on the lid of the oven, if your recipe calls for them.

4. Rotate your oven. To maintain an even oven temperature and prevent hot spots, lift and rotate the oven a quarter turn every 15 minutes. Then rotate the lid a quarter turn in the opposite direction. You'll find that a pair of welding gloves and a lid lifter are necessities for camp cooking.

baking in your dutch oven

Oven Size	Briquettes	325°	350°	375°	400°	425°	450°
8"	Total briquettes	15	16	17	18	19	20
	Top/bottom	10/5	11/5	11/6	12/6	13/6	14/6
10"	Total briquettes	19	21	23	25	27	29
	Top/bottom	13/6	14/7	16/7	17/8	18/9	19/10
12"	Total briquettes	23	25	27	29	31	33
	Top/bottom	16/7	17/8	18/9	19/10	21/10	22/11
14"	Total briquettes	30	32	34	36	38	40
	Top/bottom	20/10	21/11	22/12	24/12	25/13	26/14
16"	Total briquettes	37	39	41	43	45	47
	Top/bottom	25/12	26/13	27/14	28/15	29/16	30/17

campfire cooking and cast iron

Cooking over the fire seems to be a lost art these days, but not for campfire cooking expert Johnny Nix. He has perfected his techniques over the past 30 years using a cooking system he fashioned from equipment used by chuckwagon cooks in the 1800s.

It consists of two side poles and a crossbar with a set of five varying length hooks from which to hang cast iron camp Dutch ovens. He compares the hooks to the settings on your oven or stove-top, ranging from the longest hook (high heat), which allows the Dutch oven to hang the closest to the fire, to the shortest hook (simmer), which holds the Dutch oven farthest from the fire, with medium-high, medium, and medium-low in between.

"It's the heat from the coals you need for cooking," Nix says. "A great 'cook fire' is one that has been burning for around one hour, with a low flame and the coals generating most of the heat." Placing a layer of wood coals on the top of the Dutch oven generates top heat, creating an oven effect. For more information on cooking over fire, go to *yalleatyet.com*, or try out Johnny's recipes on pages 173-175.

Nix's laid back Southern charm and culinary skills delighted viewers of the popular television series *Campfire Café*, which he hosted for more than four years, and on his new show, *Cookin' Outdoors*. Johnny Nix's goal is to encourage everyone to slow down, get outside, and enjoy nature and the company of family and friends. "Nothing is better than the aroma of good food and the crackle of the campfire to bring family and friends together."

Sweet potatoes are a Southern tradition, especially for the holidays, and campfire cooking expert Johnny Nix makes his unforgettable in this light and fluffy soufflé. "Our family would never let us live it down if we forgot to serve this dish with our holiday meal," says Johnny.

SWEET POTATO SOUFFLÉ

serves 8

3 or 4 sweet potatoes
¾ cup firmly packed dark brown sugar
½ cup (1 stick) unsalted butter, softened
2 large egg yolks
1 cup heavy cream
1 teaspoon vanilla extract
½ teaspoon ground cinnamon
⅛ teaspoon ground nutmeg

Grated zest of 1 orange
4 large egg whites

Topping:
½ cup firmly packed light brown sugar
6 tablespoons (¾ stick) unsalted butter
1 cup crushed cornflakes
½ cup chopped pecans

1. Place the sweet potatoes in a 12-inch cast iron camp Dutch oven (an oven with a flat lid). Cover and place the oven over a campfire at medium heat (see page 172; 350°). Bake the potatoes until they are soft, about 1 hour. Remove from the oven and let cool.

2. Spoon out the potato pulp (you'll need 4 cups) and place in a medium bowl. Add the dark brown sugar, ½ cup butter, and egg yolks and stir until thoroughly blended. Stir in the cream, vanilla, cinnamon, nutmeg, and orange zest.

3. In another medium bowl, beat the egg whites until stiff peaks form; fold into the sweet potato mixture. Pour sweet potato mixture into a lightly greased 12-inch cast iron camp Dutch oven. Put the lid on, top with an even layer of coals, and cook over the campfire at medium heat (350°) until set, about 45 minutes. Remove from the fire.

4. Meanwhile, in a medium cast iron skillet over a medium-low fire (300°), heat the light brown sugar and 6 tablespoons butter for the topping, stirring constantly, until melted. Remove from the fire and add the cornflakes and pecans, stirring until well coated.

5. Spread the warm topping evenly over the soufflé; cover and bake for another 15 minutes over medium heat.

Traditional Sunday chicken dinner is taken up a notch with this great dish. The orange glaze adds a perfect citrus touch to the hens and rice. Campfire cooking expert Johnny Nix says, "Serving these small hens keeps everyone from fighting over their favorite piece of the chicken."

ROAST CORNISH GAME HEN WITH WILD RICE STUFFING

serves 6

2 tablespoons butter

1 medium onion, finely diced

1 cup finely diced celery

1 cup chopped mushrooms

1½ cups wild rice, cooked according to package directions using chicken broth instead of water

½ teaspoon dried thyme, crushed

½ teaspoon dried marjoram, crushed

Salt and freshly ground black pepper

1 (12-ounce) jar orange marmalade

½ cup orange juice

6 Rock Cornish game hens

1. Melt the butter in a large cast iron skillet over a medium fire. Add the onion, celery, and mushrooms and cook, stirring occasionally, until tender. Remove from the fire and let cool. Stir in the cooked rice, thyme, and marjoram and season with salt and pepper to taste.

2. In a small saucepan, bring the marmalade and orange juice to a boil and cook until the mixture is reduced by half.

3. Stuff the cavity of each hen loosely with the rice mixture; tie the legs together and place, breast side up, on a trivet in a 14-inch cast iron camp Dutch oven (an oven with a flat lid). Put the lid on, top with an even layer of coals, and roast over a campfire at medium heat (see page 172; 350°) until the juices run clear when cut at the joint between the leg and thigh, 45 minutes to 1 hour. Begin basting the hens with the marmalade glaze once they begin to brown; baste two or three times.

"Everything is better with bacon," says Johnny Nix, campfire cooking expert. The wonderful flavor of bacon mixed with the herbs and cheese makes this dish a real crowd-pleaser.

BACON-WRAPPED STUFFED TURKEY BREAST

serves 10

1 (3-pound) boneless turkey breast
¼ cup (½ stick) unsalted butter, softened
1 tablespoon mashed roasted garlic
2 teaspoons dried basil, crushed
1 (10-ounce) package frozen chopped spinach, thawed and squeezed dry
½ cup (2 ounces) shredded Asiago cheese
1 pound thin bacon slices

1. Place the turkey breast, skin side down, on a cutting board, spreading the skin out as much as possible so it can wrap around the breast.

2. In a small bowl, stir together the butter, garlic, and basil. Spread the flavored butter over the inside of the breast. Arrange the spinach lengthwise down the center and top with the cheese. Pull the skin around the breast, taking care not to tear it, to make a roll.

3. Lay the bacon slices on the cutting board, slightly overlapping each slice. Place the turkey breast on top of the bacon and wrap the bacon around the breast. Make sure to overlap the ends of the strips; this will keep the bacon from curling as it cooks.

4. Place the turkey breast on a roasting rack inside a 14-inch cast iron camp Dutch oven (an oven with a flat lid). Put the lid on, top with an even layer of coals, and cook over a campfire at medium-high heat (see page 172; 450°) until a meat thermometer inserted in the center of the breast reads 170°.

5. Remove the turkey breast from the oven and let stand 10 minutes before carving.

STUFFED FRENCH TOAST

serves 10 to 12

Camp cook Rita Phillips of Gilbert, Arizona, likes to mix this up the night before, refrigerate it in an airtight container, and pour it into a Dutch oven in the morning. Served with Buttermilk Syrup (below), she declares that "your guests will be calling you the 'Kitchen Diva.' "

1 French bread loaf, cut into
   1-inch cubes
1 dozen large eggs
2 cups milk
1 tablespoon vanilla extract
⅓ cup maple syrup
1 (8-ounce) package cream
   cheese, cut into ½-inch
   cubes and softened

1. Line a 12-inch cast iron camp Dutch oven (an oven with a flat lid) with heavy-duty aluminum foil all the way to the top edge (the French toast will rise). You will need a total of 32 charcoal briquettes (20 on top of the lid and 12 under the legs).

2. Place the bread cubes in a large bowl. Whisk together the eggs, milk, vanilla, and maple syrup in a medium bowl and pour over the bread cubes. Stir in the cream cheese. Let stand 10 to 30 minutes to let the bread absorb the egg mixture.

3. Pour the mixture into the prepared Dutch oven. Cover and add the coals to the top and bottom of the oven (see page 170). Bake for 50 to 60 minutes. Insert a table knife into the center to check for doneness; if it comes out clean, it's ready. Rita advises, "Don't worry if it deflates when you do this; the casserole is going to drop some anyway. It's also okay if it rises to the top of the Dutch oven and gets a browned crust; some people think that's the best part!"

4. Serve with Buttermilk Syrup (recipe follows) or your favorite topping.

BUTTERMILK SYRUP

makes about 3 cups

Use less of this than you would maple syrup—it's REALLY sweet.

1 cup (2 sticks) butter (Rita
   prefers to use unsalted butter,
   but says salted works fine as
   well)
1 cup buttermilk
1½ cups sugar
2 teaspoons baking soda
2 teaspoons vanilla extract

1. Combine the butter, buttermilk, and sugar in a large saucepan with tall sides over medium-high heat and stir occasionally until the butter melts and the sugar is dissolved.

2. When the mixture starts to boil, remove from the heat and add the baking soda and vanilla. Stir; it will foam up a lot. Serve hot or let cool. Store in an airtight container in the refrigerator up to 2 weeks.

Cacciatore means "hunter" in Italian, and this contribution from cast iron enthusiast Paul Kelly takes "hunter-style chicken" to its logical conclusion. Paul uses his prized camp Dutch oven to prepare the dish over a campfire, but charcoal with hickory or mesquite wood chips may be substituted if there is not a campfire handy.

CAMPFIRE CHICKEN CACCIATORE

serves 8

¼ cup extra-virgin olive oil

1 large Vidalia onion, chopped

4 garlic cloves, minced

2 teaspoons salt

2 teaspoons freshly ground black pepper

2 fryer chickens, each cut into 8 serving pieces

Hickory or mesquite wood chips, soaked in water at least 1 hour

2 pounds mushrooms, cut into quarters

4 large carrots, cut into 1-inch pieces, or 1½ cups baby carrots

1 cup chopped celery

1 (28-ounce) can ground peeled tomatoes

¼ cup chopped fresh flat-leaf parsley

2 teaspoons fresh rosemary leaves

Hot cooked rice

1. Prepare a campfire using wood up to 2 inches thick. Allow the fire to die down to coals.

2. Place a well-seasoned 12-quart cast iron camp Dutch oven (an oven with a flat lid) directly on the coals. Add the oil, onion, garlic, salt, and pepper and cook, stirring, 2 minutes. Add the chicken and cook until browned, 3 to 5 minutes per side.

3. Remove the Dutch oven from the fire and add the drained wood chips to the fire to add more smoke flavor (especially if you're cooking with charcoal). Place the Dutch oven back on the fire. Add the mushrooms, carrots, celery, tomatoes, parsley, and rosemary. Cook, uncovered, 15 minutes. Cover and shovel coals onto the lid. Cook 30 minutes.

4. Remove the lid carefully, making sure no coals fall into the interior of the Dutch oven. Check to see that the chicken is cooked through. If it is, remove the pot from the fire. Serve the chicken and vegetables over rice.

These tenderloins are pungent with fresh herbs and garlic and made even more richly delicious with the addition of bacon. This recipe earned Lisa and Brian Blodgett first place for a main dish at the 2010 International Dutch Oven Society World Championship Cook-off.

BACON-HERB WRAPPED PORK TENDERLOIN

serves 6 to 8

2   (1-pound) pork tenderloins
Salt and freshly ground black
    pepper
2   tablespoons minced garlic
2   tablespoons chopped fresh
    thyme

3   tablespoons chopped fresh
    rosemary
20 fresh sage leaves, chopped
8   to 10 bacon slices
2   tablespoons olive oil

1. Place the tenderloins on a cutting board. One at a time, slice each tenderloin almost in half along a long edge and open each up like a book. Place between 2 sheets of heavy-duty plastic wrap and pound each tenderloin into a long, thin cutlet. Season each with salt and pepper to taste, then divide the garlic between the two, spreading it evenly over each. Combine the chopped herbs in a small bowl and rub over the top of each tenderloin, saving a little to rub on the outside of the meat.

2. Roll up each tenderloin, jelly-roll fashion; rub with the remaining herbs and wrap each tenderloin with 4 or 5 bacon slices. Use kitchen string to tie the bacon in place.

3. In a 12-inch cast iron camp Dutch oven (an oven with a flat lid), heat the oil, then sear the meat over a medium hot fire for 2 minutes on each side. Cover the Dutch oven. Place it on top of 8 coals (see page 170) and place 18 coals on top of the lid. Cook until a meat thermometer inserted into the thickest portion of each tenderloin registers 140°, 45 to 60 minutes.

4. Remove the Dutch oven from the heat and let stand for 10 minutes. Remove the string before slicing and serving the pork.

HAM, TURKEY, AND CHEESE BREAD

serves 4 to 6

Dough:

3½ to 4½ cups all-purpose flour

1 package active yeast

1 tablespoon vital wheat gluten

¼ cup sugar

1½ teaspoons salt

2 tablespoons Mrs. Dash seasoning blend

¼ cup (½ stick) butter

¾ cup water

¼ cup milk

2 large eggs

Filling:

1 (8-ounce) tub onion-and-chive cream cheese

1 pound shredded Colby-Jack cheese blend

½ cup cubed ham

½ cup cubed turkey

1 large egg white, lightly beaten (optional)

This hearty, cheesy bread is a filling choice for lunch, brunch, or an afternoon snack. The recipe was contributed by International Dutch Oven members Wil and Jen Ward, who took third place with it in the Bread category at the 2010 International Dutch Oven Society World Championship Cook-off.

1. Make the dough: Combine 2 cups flour, the yeast, wheat gluten, sugar, salt, and seasoning blend in a large bowl and set aside.

2. In a small cast iron Dutch oven, heat the butter, water, and milk over the fire just until the butter is melted, stirring well. Remove from the fire. Add the eggs to the milk mixture and stir. Add the egg mixture to the flour mixture and stir well with a wooden spoon. Add as much of the remaining flour as needed to yield a dough that is not sticky.

3. Place the dough in a lightly greased 12-inch cast iron camp Dutch oven (an oven with a flat lid) and let dough rise in a warm spot until doubled in bulk.

4. Turn the dough out onto a lightly floured surface and roll or press dough into an 18- x 12-inch rectangle.

5. Make the filling: Combine the filling ingredients in a medium bowl. Spread the filling down the center of the dough. Cut strips horizontally into the dough on both sides every 2 inches up to the filling. Braid the dough by folding one strip over the other toward the center of the filling.

6. Grease the Dutch oven you let the dough rise in, then place the braided dough inside. Brush the top of the dough with the egg white for color, if desired. Cover the Dutch oven and place on a ring of 8 coals (see page 170). Place 16 coals on the lid. Bake until golden brown, 35 to 45 minutes. Serve hot or cold.

These campfire rolls are delicious served with butter and honey—homemade jam is tasty as well. This recipe was contributed by Sandy and Jack Wallace and Maureen Knapp of the International Dutch Oven Society.

FEATHER LIGHT ROLLS

makes about 24 rolls

1 tablespoon instant yeast (SAF)	¼ cup light vegetable oil
1¼ cups warm milk (110° to 115°)	2 large eggs
	3½ cups bread flour
¼ cup sugar	1 teaspoon salt
	¼ cup (½ stick) butter

1. Combine the yeast, milk, sugar, oil, and eggs in a large bowl, stirring well. Add 2½ cups flour and stir well for 1 minute. While stirring, slowly add the salt. Add the remaining 1 cup flour, or as much of it as needed, to create a soft dough.

2. Turn the dough out onto a lightly floured surface and knead for 5 minutes or strongly whack the dough with a large spoon 30 times. Shape the dough into a round and place it into a copper, glass, or plastic bowl. (Avoid stainless steel or sheet metal bowls, as both can have a negative reaction with the yeast.) Cover the bowl with a clean cloth, place in a warm spot (but out of direct sun during hot weather), and let rise until doubled in bulk. (The warmer it is, the faster the dough will double—20 to 30 minutes at 75°.)

3. While the dough is rising, melt the butter in a warm 12-inch cast iron camp Dutch oven (an oven with a flat lid). Spread the butter over the bottom and up the side of the pot. Allow any excess butter to pool in the bottom.

4. After the dough has risen, place it on a clean, lightly greased, flat surface. Shape the dough into a round ball. Pinch off a 1½- to 2-inch ball of dough; roll the piece of dough between your palms to round it up, then seal the seams. Drop the dough ball into the prepared Dutch oven. Roll it around in the butter to coat it on all sides, then place the roll seam side down, leaving a nice rounded top. Repeat with the remaining dough, arranging the rolls so they touch each other.

5. Cover the Dutch oven with a clean cloth or its lid and place in a warm spot (but out of direct sun during hot weather). The Dutch oven should be warm, but not hot. Allow the rolls to rise until

almost doubled. Again, depending on the temperature, it will take from 20 to 40 minutes. Watch them!

6. Arrange 8 coals in a ring underneath the Dutch oven and place 16 coals on the lid (see page 170); your target temperature inside is 325° to 350°. Let your rolls bake; it may take 25 to 40 minutes, depending on the ambient temperature. Keep in mind, every time you lift the lid to check on your rolls, you need to add 5 more minutes of cooking time. Be patient and trust your nose. When you can smell yeasty bread, the rolls are close to being done—about 5 more minutes. When it smells more like baked bread, the rolls are done.

7. The butter used earlier will allow the rolls to lift, slide, or dump out onto a cooling rack. They can be served hot out of the Dutch oven as well. Remember, the Dutch oven will keep cooking them, so the bottoms and sides may get a little crunchy if you leave them in. You can also let the rolls cool on a rack, then return them to the Dutch oven to serve and to keep warm.

how to bake bread in a camp dutch oven

Baking bread (any favorite free-form or country bread recipe will work) in a cast iron camp Dutch oven is a real taste treat. Whether rafting the Colorado, camping in the Sierras or the Alleghenys, or picnicking at a campsite, the combination of hot cast iron radiating heat from all sides, glowing coals, and fresh air contributes to a loaf similar in consistency to one baked in an enclosed outdoor oven. The crust is exceptionally thin and crisp and the interior sweetly fragrant. Cookbook author Beth Hensperger became familiar with this technique while river rafting the Stanislaus and American rivers and perfected it in her backyard. This recipe requires a camp Dutch oven (one with a flat lid) so that coals can be placed on top of it.

1. Grease the inside of the lid and the inside of a 12-inch (6-quart) cast iron camp Dutch oven (with a flat lid) with butter. Line the bottom with parchment paper, if desired. Add a ball of dough at any point in its rising cycle. Cover the pot with the lid and let the dough rise at room (or outdoor) temperature until doubled in size, about 1½ hours.

2. Burn a wood, charcoal, or combination fire until you have a good supply of coals. Sweep the coals into a shallow depression in the ground dug next to the fire, saving some larger coals. Set the Dutch oven on a grill, or balance it on three stones ½ inch above a ring of 6 to 8 evenly spaced hot coals. Place 12 to 16 larger coals directly on the pot lid around the edge and in the middle for even heat distribution from the top as well as the bottom of the pot.

3. Bake, fanning the coals periodically, until the bread is golden brown, crisp, and hollow sounding when tapped. Check the bread after 35 minutes but it may take 45 to 50 minutes total. Please note that the handle of the Dutch oven will be very hot. Use a pair of pliers to lift the lid and wear leather gloves to avoid burns.

4. Remove the loaf with care using oven mitts. Let it cool to just warm or room temperature; slice and serve.

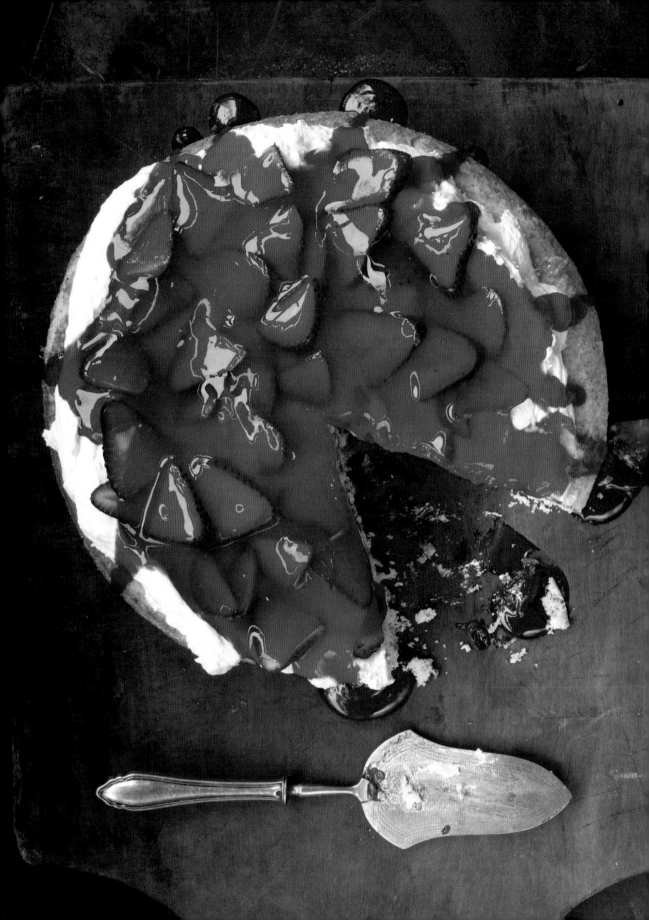

DUTCH OVEN DANISH CAKE

makes one (12-inch) layer cake; serves 10 to 12

Cake:

3 cups cake flour
4 teaspoons baking powder
½ teaspoon salt
¼ cup vegetable shortening
1¼ cups granulated sugar
1 cup milk
1 teaspoon vanilla extract
½ teaspoon almond extract
5 large egg whites

Topping:

1 (4¾-ounce) package
   strawberry-flavored Danish
   dessert mix (such as Junket
   Danish Dessert)
2 cups confectioners' sugar
1 (16-ounce) tub Cool Whip
1 (8-ounce) package cream
   cheese
1 pound fresh strawberries,
   hulled

After a long day of enjoying the outdoors, you can knock everyone's socks off by serving this showstopper of a cake. International Dutch Oven Society members Melissa and Rebecka Boyer contributed this recipe.

1. Grease 2 (12-inch) cast iron camp Dutch ovens (ovens with flat lids).
2. Make the cake: Sift and measure the flour into a medium bowl. Add the baking powder and salt and sift again. In a large bowl, beat the shortening. Gradually add the granulated sugar and beat until fluffy. Add the flour mixture to the shortening mixture alternately with the milk and extracts. Beat until blended after each addition.
3. In another large bowl, beat the egg whites with an electric mixer until stiff peaks form; gently fold into the batter until no white streaks remain. Divide the batter between the prepared Dutch ovens and bake with 8 coals evenly arranged underneath each oven and 17 coals on top of the lids of each oven (see page 170). Cook until a wooden pick inserted into the center of each comes out clean, 25 to 30 minutes.
4. Make the topping: While the cakes cool, make the Danish dessert following package directions for the pie glaze.
5. Flip the cakes out of the Dutch ovens onto their lids. Stir together 1 cup of the confectioners' sugar with the Cool Whip. In a separate bowl, beat together the remaining 1 cup confectioners' sugar and the cream cheese. Combine the cream cheese and Cool Whip mixtures. Spread about half the Cool Whip mixture on the top of one of the cakes. Arrange half the strawberries on top. Place the other cake layer on top and spread the remaining Cool Whip mixture over the cake layer. Arrange the remaining strawberries attractively over the topping and spread the Danish dessert over the strawberries.

HOT LAVA CHOCOLATE CAKE FOR TWO

serves 2

This is the perfect sweet ending to a romantic campfire meal. You can share it straight from the Dutch oven, topped with a little whipped cream. This recipe was contributed by International Dutch Oven Society member David Herzog.

1 (1-ounce) square semisweet chocolate
2 tablespoons butter
¼ cup confectioners' sugar
½ large egg, lightly beaten
½ large egg yolk, lightly beaten
4½ teaspoons all-purpose flour

1. Butter a 5-inch cast iron camp Dutch oven (an oven with a flat lid). Melt the chocolate and butter together in a small bowl placed over hot water; whisk until completely melted and smooth. Stir in the confectioners' sugar until well blended. Add the egg and egg yolk and whisk well. Stir in the flour.

2. Pour the batter into the prepared Dutch oven and cover. Set the Dutch oven on 3 or 4 coals and place 6 coals on the lid (see page 170). Cook for 15 to 18 minutes; it's done when a wooden pick inserted in the center comes out clean.

COW PATTY RASPBERRY FUDGE CAKE

makes one (12-inch) layer cake

Who says you can't have your campfire AND cake and eat it too? This fudgy creation was contributed by International Dutch Oven Society member Vicky Stegal.

Cake:
3 cups sugar
3 cups all-purpose flour
1 cup unsweetened cocoa
1¼ teaspoons baking soda
1 teaspoon baking powder
1 teaspoon salt
3 large eggs
1 cup vegetable oil
1½ cups hot water
2 teaspoons vanilla extract

Ganache:
1 (12-ounce) package milk chocolate chips
½ cup heavy cream
½ cup raspberry jam or jelly

Glaze:
6 ounces semisweet chocolate chips
½ cup heavy cream
Fresh raspberries and shaved chocolate for garnish

1. Grease and flour a deep 12-inch cast iron camp Dutch oven (an oven with a flat lid); set aside.

2. Make the cake: Combine the sugar, flour, cocoa, baking soda, baking powder, and salt in a large bowl. In a medium bowl, stir together the eggs, oil, hot water, and vanilla until thoroughly blended; pour into the dry mixture, stirring until well blended. (The batter will be runny.)

Cow Patty Raspberry Fudge Cake

Pour batter into the prepared Dutch oven and cover. Place the oven on 8 coals arranged in a ring and place 16 coals on the lid (see page 170). Let bake until the cake pulls away from the side of the oven, about 30 minutes. Let cool 10 minutes in the oven with the lid off; remove from the oven and cool completely.

3. Use dental floss to cut the cake in half horizontally. Carefully remove the top layer and set aside.

4. Make the ganache: Pour the milk chocolate chips into a 10-inch cast iron camp Dutch oven and place over 5 coals. Stir the chocolate until it is melted and smooth. Let cool briefly and stir in the cream and jam. Beat with a wooden spoon until smooth. Spread the ganache over the bottom cake layer and let it ooze over the sides.

5. Make the glaze: Wipe the Dutch oven, pour in the semisweet chocolate chips, and place over the coals again. Stir until the chocolate is melted and smooth. Let cool a little; stir in the cream and beat with a wooden spoon until smooth. Place the top layer of cake on the ganache-covered bottom layer and spread the glaze over the top and sides. Garnish with raspberries and shaved chocolate.

The description, directions, and recipes that follow (pages 186-191) for this technique of Dutch oven cookery were contributed by J. Wayne Fears. In his wide and varied career, he has been a wildlife specialist, developed and operated hunting lodges in Alabama, and served as the editor-in-chief of Rural Sportsman *and* Hunting Camp Journal. *He is the author of more the 25 books on outdoor-related topics and is a columnist and contributor to numerous outdoor- and hunting-related periodicals. Visit him at* jwaynefears.com.

BEAN HOLE COOKING

A favorite method of cooking in hunting and fishing camps in the northeastern U. S., High Rockies, and Canada is what is commonly called "bean hole cooking." Bean hole cooking, according to historians, dates back for centuries to the early days of the Penobscot Indians of Maine. They found they could slow cook food by placing it in a hole dug in the earth that had been heated by building a fire in it. The food to be cooked was set in the hot coals, then the hole was covered with rocks and earth to seal in the heat. At the end of the day, they returned to a prepared meal.

Early settlers learned this method of cooking and added the cast iron pot as the vessel to hold the food. French voyagers carried this cooking technique into Canada, mountain men took it to the Rockies, and explorers took it to other parts of North America. Think of it as the early American version of the slow cooker.

It was in New England that the technique got its name "bean hole cooking." Back before stoves were common in logging camps, cooks did much of their cooking in cast iron Dutch ovens, often in holes in the ground, just like the Penobscot Indians. This was especially true of the cooks who followed the log drives down the rivers. Beans were the common table fare for these hard-working men, often three times a day. Because beans were the most common dish baked this way, the term "bean hole" cooking became the name used to describe the method.

For many years I hunted and fished with Pam and Ken French at their log cabin camp in central Maine. Outside their cabin, down near the lakeshore, Ken built a permanent bean hole. Miss Pam would prep her tasty dishes, and Ken placed the loaded Lodge cast

make your own bean hole

Following Ken's instructions, I have built a permanent bean hole at my cabin. It's the center of attention anytime I'm cooking for a group of guests. Here is how you can build your own permanent bean hole.

1. Take a clean 55-gallon drum and cut it in half. Save the lid and discard the upper half.

2. In a safe area, away from any flammable material, near your cabin or campsite, dig a hole a little deeper and wider than the half drum. Line the bottom and sides of the hole with firebricks.

3. Next, drill several small holes in the bottom of the drum to allow water to drain in the event water should ever get inside. Place about three inches of sand in the bottom of the drum to prevent it from burning out. Put the drum in the firebrick-lined hole. Fill in the spaces between the bricks and the drum with sand. Place the lid on top of the drum, and you have a permanent bean hole.

iron Dutch oven (or ovens) into the hot coals in the bean hole. A top was placed on the hole and it was covered with dirt. After a day of hunting or fishing, we returned, and the evening meal was hot and ready to eat.

PAM'S BEAN HOLE BEANS

serves 8

2 pounds dried red kidney beans

½ pound bacon, cut into pieces

½ cup dark molasses

1¼ cups firmly packed light brown sugar

2 medium onions, chopped

2 teaspoons dry mustard

Salt and freshly ground black pepper

1. Soak the beans in water to generously cover for about 12 hours.

2. Pour the soaking water and beans into a 14-inch cast iron camp Dutch oven (an oven with a flat lid). Add enough additional water so that it just covers the beans. Bring the beans to a boil; stir in the bacon, molasses, brown sugar, onions, and mustard until well combined. Let cool.

3. Cover the entire coverless pot tightly with heavy-duty aluminum foil, allowing just enough give so the lid will fit snugly on top of the oven, over the foil. Put the lid on; cover the entire Dutch oven tightly with foil.

4. Bury the Dutch oven in the hot coals of the bean hole, cover, and cook overnight or all day (see *Cooking in a Bean Hole*, right). Season with salt and pepper to taste before serving.

BEAN HOLE PEACH COBBLER

serves 6

Cobbler crust:

2 cups all-purpose flour

½ teaspoon salt

1 teaspoon baking powder

1 teaspoon granulated sugar

6 tablespoons vegetable shortening

½ cup ice water

Filling:

1 cup (2 sticks) unsalted butter

6 cups peeled, pitted, and sliced ripe peaches

1 cup firmly packed light brown sugar

1 cup granulated sugar

1 teaspoon ground cinnamon

1½ cups whipping cream

½ cup whiskey (such as Jack Daniel's)

1. Make the crust: Stir together first 4 ingredients. Cut in shortening with a pastry blender or fork until it resembles small peas and is crumbly. Add water gradually to make a dough ball. Divide dough into 2 balls for a top and bottom crust. Refrigerate the dough.

2. Make the filling: Melt the butter in large saucepan. Add the peaches, both kinds of sugar, the cinnamon, and cream. Bring to a boil, reduce the heat, and let bubble for 10 minutes. Add the whiskey and stir gently. Simmer for 15 minutes.

3. Turn the dough out onto a lightly floured surface. Roll out 1 dough ball with a floured rolling pin into a 9-inch circle. Fit the dough in the bottom of a 9-inch aluminum baking pan with 3-inch-high sides.

4. Roll out the second ball of dough into a 9-inch circle. If desired, cut it into strips for a lattice top, or leave it as is.

5. Carefully pour the filling into the dough-lined pan. Fit the top crust over the filling, or arrange the dough strips in a lattice design over filling.

6. Place the pan into a 12-inch cast iron camp Dutch oven (an oven with a flat lid). Cover the entire coverless pot tightly with heavy-duty aluminum foil, allowing just enough give so the lid will fit snugly on top of the foil. Put the lid on and cover the entire Dutch oven tightly with foil again.

7. Bury the Dutch oven in the hot coals in the bean hole; cover and cook overnight or all day (see *Cooking in a Bean Hole*, below). Place the cobbler in the bean hole with the main-meal Dutch oven and they will both slow cook at the same time. Remove them from the bean hole and you have a complete meal.

cooking in a bean hole

Go hiking or fishing for the day and return to a hot meal. As with most cooking techniques, it will take a few trials to get the method perfected, but it's fun and, once it's worked out, it'll become a favorite way to bake in your camp.

1. When you want to bake a pot of beans or any other dish, simply build a fire in the drum. Leave the top off and let the hole get hot.

2. Place a camp cast iron Dutch oven, with a tight-fitting flat lid, filled with beans, stew, a roast with veggies, or a cobbler into the bed of coals in the bean hole.

3. Place a shovel of hot coals on top of the Dutch oven lid. Put the cover on top of the drum and cover with dirt or sand. This will keep the temperature even for a long period of time.

GEORGE'S BEAN HOLE ROAST AND VEGGIES

serves 8

1	(3- to 4-pound) beef chuck roast	2	tablespoons extra-virgin olive oil
2	pounds small red or Yukon Gold potatoes, cut in half	2	teaspoons dried rosemary, crushed
1	pound carrots, cut into 2-inch pieces	1	teaspoon dried sage, crushed
1	large onion, cut into wedges		Salt and freshly ground black
1	cup beef broth		pepper

1. Spray a 12-inch cast iron camp Dutch oven (an oven with a flat lid) with nonstick cooking spray. Place the roast in the Dutch oven and arrange the potatoes, carrots, and onion wedges around it; pour beef broth over ingredients. Drizzle the oil evenly over the roast and vegetables; sprinkle with the rosemary, sage, and salt and pepper to taste.

2. Cover the entire coverless pot tightly with heavy-duty aluminum foil, allowing just enough give so the lid will fit snugly on top of the oven over the foil. Put the lid on and cover the entire Dutch oven tightly with foil again.

3. Bury the Dutch oven in the hot coals of the bean hole, cover, and cook overnight or all day (see *Cooking in a Bean Hole*, page 189).

4. Remove the Dutch oven from the bean hole. Serve the roast and vegetables in individual serving bowls.

SIDES

Because cast iron has the superb ability to heat evenly with
no hot spots, it's the perfect cookware for making quick-
cooking vegetable sautés and stir-fries. It also works well for
accompaniments that require a little stove-top prep before going
into the oven to bake into golden goodness.

POKE SALAT

Louis Fuqua learned to cook this dish as a child growing up in Gainesboro, Tennessee.

§ poke §

Poke grows wild near the edges of fields and along fence lines and roadways; in Tennessee the young leaves are picked in March and April. When cooked, poke salat resembles spinach and tastes like asparagus.

serves 6 to 8

2 gallons fresh-picked young poke leaves
5 cups water
½ cup chopped green onions
3 tablespoons bacon drippings
Salt
1 large egg, lightly beaten

1. Wash the poke greens well; drain. Add the greens to a large pot with 4 cups water. Bring to a boil, stir them down, and boil for 5 minutes. Drain off all the water and rinse the greens.
2. Return the greens to the pot; add the green onions and the remaining 1 cup water. Cover, bring to a boil again, and let boil 20 minutes. Drain again.
3. Heat the bacon drippings in a 12-inch cast iron skillet over medium heat. Add the drained greens and season with salt to taste. Cook, stirring frequently, for 5 minutes. Add the beaten egg and cook until the egg is done.

WILTED LETTUCE SALAD

This is a springtime favorite of Marion and Bertha Gonce, who have farmed the Joseph Lodge farm in South Pittsburg, Tennessee, since 1934. Bertha says it's the best when the lettuce, radishes, and onions are grown in your own garden and picked just before preparing.

serves 6

Salad:
1 head leaf lettuce (or spinach), torn
6 radishes, thinly sliced
4 to 6 green onions, thinly sliced
4 hard-cooked eggs, sliced

Dressing:
5 bacon slices
2 tablespoons red wine vinegar
1 tablespoon fresh lemon juice
1 teaspoon sugar
½ teaspoon freshly ground black pepper

1. Toss together the lettuce, radishes, and green onions in a large bowl.
2. Cook the bacon in a 10-inch cast iron skillet over medium-high heat until crisp. Remove to paper towels to drain, reserving drippings in skillet; crumble bacon. Add the vinegar, lemon juice, sugar, and pepper to the drippings; stir well. Immediately pour the dressing over the salad and toss gently. Top with the sliced eggs and sprinkle with the crumbled bacon. Serve immediately.

Wilted Lettuce Salad

This recipe, from Scott Jones, former executive food editor of *Southern Living*, is an update to his grandmother's recipe (and a childhood favorite). "My Mema used a smoked hock in her greens, along with a generous shake of hot sauce and pinch of sugar. I get my subtle sweet-tart pop from balsamic vinegar and the heat from red pepper flakes." Scott made the recipe a tad healthier by using bacon and fat-free chicken broth, which also creates a cleaner-tasting pot likker. Scott has been known to ladle the greens and pot likker over a bowl of creamy stone-ground grits.

SCOTT'S COLLARDS

serves 8

4   bacon slices
1   large carrot, chopped
1   large onion, chopped
2   garlic cloves, minced
2   to 3 tablespoons balsamic
    vinegar
4   (1-pound) packages fresh
    collard greens, washed,
    trimmed, and chopped

1½ cups low-sodium fat-free
    chicken broth
½   teaspoon red pepper
    flakes
½   teaspoon salt
¼   teaspoon freshly ground
    black pepper

1. Cook the bacon in a cast iron Dutch oven over medium-high heat until crisp. Remove the bacon to paper towels to drain, reserving 2 tablespoons of the drippings in the pot. Crumble the bacon.

2. Cook the carrot in the hot bacon drippings over medium-high heat, stirring occasionally, for 5 minutes. Add the onion and cook, stirring occasionally, until the carrot and onion begin to caramelize, about 5 minutes. Add the garlic; cook 30 seconds, stirring constantly. Add the vinegar and cook 30 seconds. Add the collards, crumbled bacon, broth, red pepper, salt, and black pepper. Bring to a boil; cover, reduce the heat to a simmer, and cook until the collards are tender, about 1 hour.

SQUASH PUPPIES

makes 24 squash puppies; serves 8

Summertime in the South means yellow summer or crookneck squash, crowder peas, sliced vine-ripened tomatoes, and steamy hot cornbread for dinner. Here is a recipe from Cindy Schoeneck of San Diego, California, that combines squash and cornbread.

3 medium yellow squash or zucchini	⅛ teaspoon cayenne pepper (optional)
1½ cups self-rising cornmeal mix	¼ cup buttermilk
¼ teaspoon salt	½ cup minced onion
¼ teaspoon freshly ground black pepper	1 large egg, lightly beaten
¼ teaspoon paprika	⅛ to ¼ teaspoon Tabasco sauce
	Vegetable oil for frying

1. Cut the squash into ¼-inch-thick rounds; place in a large saucepan and add water to cover. Bring to a boil; reduce the heat to a simmer and cook the squash until soft enough to mash with a potato masher, about 20 minutes. Drain; mash the squash and set aside.

2. Combine the cornmeal mix, salt, black pepper, paprika, and, if desired, cayenne in a large bowl. In a medium bowl, combine the mashed squash, buttermilk, onion, egg, and Tabasco. Add the mashed squash mixture to the cornmeal mixture and blend well.

3. Heat 2 to 3 inches of vegetable oil in a large cast iron Dutch oven to 350°. (You can test to see if the oil is hot enough by dropping in a small amount of batter; if it starts bubbling, the oil is hot enough. If the oil doesn't immediately start to bubble and sizzle around the batter, wait a few more minutes for the oil to heat completely.)

4. Drop the batter by tablespoonfuls into the hot oil, being careful not to overcrowd the pan. Fry until golden brown, about 3 minutes. Remove from the oil using a slotted spoon. Drain on paper towels or a clean paper bag. Repeat with the remaining batter.

SUMMER SQUASH CASSEROLE

serves 8   *(pictured on page 192)*

8   yellow squash
¼   cup (½ stick) unsalted butter
1½ cups sliced Vidalia onion
2   garlic cloves, chopped
½   cup chopped fresh flat-leaf parsley
Salt and freshly ground black pepper
½   cup 1-inch pieces white bread slices with crusts removed
Ice water
2   large eggs, lightly beaten
1   sleeve saltine crackers, crushed into crumbs
2   tablespoons unsalted butter, cut into small pieces

This recipe comes from Linton Hopkins, chef/owner of Restaurant Eugene and Holeman & Finch Public House in Atlanta.

1. Preheat the oven to 350°. Butter 8 individual cast iron Lodge Round Mini-Servers.

2. Peel, then cut the squash crosswise into ⅛-inch-thick rounds. Cut the rounds into half moons. Bring a large pot of salted water to a boil, add the squash, and boil just until tender; drain.

3. Melt the ¼ cup butter in a medium cast iron skillet over medium-high heat. Add the onion and cook until softened, stirring occasionally; add the garlic and cook for 1 minute. Stir in the parsley, season with salt and pepper to taste, and remove the skillet from the heat.

4. Soak the bread in ice water to cover until softened, then squeeze out the moisture and chop. Add to the onion in the pan and cook over medium-high heat for 3 minutes, stirring occasionally. Add the squash, cook 3 minutes, stirring occasionally, and remove from the heat. Stir in the eggs and season with salt and pepper to taste.

5. Divide the mixture between the prepared mini-servers. Sprinkle each with the crushed crackers, then dot with the pieces of butter. Bake until hot and golden brown on top, 20 to 25 minutes.

Serve these pancakes, as a side dish or a nibble before a meal, with a dab of Red Pepper–Yogurt Sauce or, as the Turks do, with plain yogurt on top. This recipe is from Joanna Pruess' *Cast Iron Cookbook: Delicious and Simple Comfort Food.*

ZUCCHINI PANCAKES WITH RED PEPPER-YOGURT SAUCE

serves 6

1 pound zucchini, coarsely shredded	⅓ cup chopped fresh dill or 1½ tablespoons dillweed
Coarse or kosher salt	⅓ cup chopped fresh mint or flat-leaf parsley
Red Pepper–Yogurt Sauce (recipe follows; optional)	Freshly ground black pepper
2 large eggs, lightly beaten	½ cup all-purpose flour
1 cup chopped green onions (white part and most of the green)	½ cup crumbled feta cheese
	½ cup pine nuts
	Olive oil for frying

1. In a colander, toss the zucchini with about ½ tablespoon salt and drain for 20 to 25 minutes. Meanwhile, prepare the yogurt sauce, if desired, and set aside.

2. Working in batches, squeeze the zucchini with your hands to remove as much moisture as possible, then transfer to a dish towel or several layers of paper towels and squeeze again. In a large bowl, combine the zucchini, eggs, green onions, dill, mint, about ½ teaspoon salt, and a generous amount of pepper, and mix well. Stir in the flour. Add the feta, stirring to blend. Just before cooking, stir in the pine nuts.

3. Preheat the oven to 300°. Line a baking sheet with paper towels and put it in the oven.

4. Heat a 12-inch cast iron skillet or griddle over medium-high heat. Add enough oil to coat the bottom of the pan. Drop the zucchini mixture by generous soup-spoonfuls into the skillet (about 3 tablespoons) and flatten with the back of a metal spatula into 3-inch discs, cooking only as many pancakes as will fit comfortably without crowding. Fry until golden brown, 2½ to 3 minutes, then turn and fry the other side the same length of time. Transfer the pancakes to the prepared baking sheet to keep warm while frying the remaining pancakes.

5. Serve hot with the yogurt sauce offered on the side, if desired.

Many vegetables other than potatoes can be shredded and fried into tasty pancakes. Joanna particularly likes this combination of zucchini, green onions, dill, mint, feta, and pine nuts, as it reminds her of a pancake-like hors d'oeuvre called mücver *that she ate in Turkey.*

RED PEPPER-YOGURT SAUCE

makes about ⅔ cup

2 large roasted red bell peppers (jarred or fresh roasted), blotted dry

2 garlic cloves, peeled

½ teaspoon salt

¼ cup plain Greek-style yogurt

2 tablespoons extra-virgin olive oil

¼ cup chopped fresh mint

1. In a blender or food processor, purée the roasted pepper, garlic, salt, and yogurt until smooth. Scrape into a small bowl and stir in the oil. Stir in the mint just before serving.

Gladys Streeter Wooten's favorite food has always been corn. Her mother, Margaret Streeter, taught her how to make this dish.

FRIED CORN

serves 4

6 large ears fresh corn (yellow or white), husks removed

3 tablespoons bacon drippings

1 tablespoon all-purpose flour

1 tablespoon sugar

1 cup water

½ cup milk

3 tablespoons butter

Salt and freshly ground black pepper

1. Cut the kernels off the cobs. Discard cobs.

2. Heat the bacon drippings in a 10-inch cast iron skillet over medium heat.

3. In a medium bowl, combine the corn, flour, sugar, water, and milk. Add the mixture to the hot drippings and stir to mix. When the mixture is hot, add the butter and season with salt and pepper to taste. Stir until the butter is melted and mixed in, and cook until the corn is tender.

In the summer, corn is so abundant that, at times, it's a struggle to keep up with the bounty. Corn pudding combines a number of things Oxford, Mississippi-based restaurateur and chef John Currence loves: the flavor of corn on the cob, the sweetness of creamed corn, and the lightness of a soufflé. It's just perfect and it goes with everything!

ROASTED CORN PUDDING

serves 6

4 ears fresh corn with husks
¼ cup chopped bacon
¼ cup diced yellow onion
1½ teaspoons minced garlic
1 jalapeño chile, seeded and minced
¾ cup whole milk
¼ cup heavy cream
3 large eggs

¼ cup (½ stick) unsalted butter, melted
3 tablespoons masa harina
1½ teaspoons cornstarch
2 tablespoons fresh thyme leaves
1½ tablespoons sugar
Salt and freshly ground black pepper

1. Preheat the oven to 325°. Place the unshucked ears of corn on the center rack of the oven and roast for 35 minutes. Let cool until they can be handled, then cut the kernels off the cobs (about 2 cups kernels). Set aside. Discard cobs. Grease a 12-inch cast iron skillet.

2. Cook the bacon in a medium cast iron skillet over medium heat until crisp. Remove the bacon to a paper towel to drain, reserving drippings in skillet.

3. Add the onion and garlic to the bacon drippings and cook, stirring occasionally, until softened. Add the jalapeño and cook, stirring, until softened, about 1 minute. Stir in the roasted corn and heat thoroughly.

4. In a small saucepan over medium heat, combine the milk and cream and cook until bubbles form around the edge of the pan. Remove from the heat and let cool briefly.

5. In a large bowl, whisk together the eggs, melted butter, masa, and cornstarch. Drizzle in the warm milk mixture, whisking constantly. Stir in the corn mixture until well blended. Stir in the thyme, sugar, and reserved bacon. Season with salt and pepper to taste.

6. Pour the mixture into the prepared 12-inch skillet and bake until the center is still jiggly but set, about 25 minutes.

Cookbook author Beth Hensperger swears by cast iron when it comes to fried rice. This dish is a favorite of hers when catering sit-down dinner parties and has become a summer standard. You can make it with a 50-50 combination of wild rice and long-grain brown rice, or cook up a brown rice blend. You want a hearty-flavored rice, not white rice.

SAUTÉ OF CORN, BROWN RICE, AND FRESH BASIL

serves 4

6 to 7 medium ears fresh white corn, husks removed, or 1 (12-ounce) package frozen baby white corn, thawed (to make 3 to 3½ cups)

⅓ cup fresh basil leaves

2 tablespoons unsalted butter

2 tablespoons olive oil

2 tablespoons minced shallots

2 cups cooled cooked wild rice and long-grain brown rice blend

3 tablespoons minced sun-dried tomatoes in oil

Salt and freshly ground black pepper

1. Cut the kernels off the cobs. Discard cobs. Finely chop the basil. Set both aside.

2. In a 10- to 12-inch cast iron skillet, melt the butter with the oil over medium-high heat. Add the shallots and stir-fry for 1 to 2 minutes to soften. Add the corn and cook for 1 to 2 minutes. Add the rice, breaking up any clumps with your fingers, if necessary. Stir-fry the rice and corn until heated and fragrant, about 2 minutes. Add the tomatoes and basil. Stirring constantly, cook another few minutes to heat all the ingredients. Season with salt and pepper to taste and serve hot.

a cast iron memory

On my first visit to France in 1977, I was invited to dine in a 200-year-old country house set in the midst of a truffle oak orchard south of Albi. It was rustic and rundown, built of the local white limestone. Steep external stairs led to a small landing, then directly into a main room with a large open fireplace, and the rectangular dining table sat in front of it. The room was quite dark, as there were no electric lights, but it was the hub of the farmhouse.

I sat at the end of the rough-hewn plank table in amazement at the makings of a true country feast. A gigantic rump of Auvergne beef encrusted with coarse sea salt and Dijon mustard was roasting over an open hearth fire in an even more gigantic lidded cast iron kettle, certainly the largest Dutch oven I have ever seen, about 14 inches in diameter and almost just as deep. In the far corner stood a small four-burner gas range with two ancient oversized pitch-black cast iron frying pans pushed to the rear of the stove; both contained vegetables waiting to be sautéed in

sweet butter. One was heaped with French-cut green beans, and the other a mound of sliced local fresh cèpes mushrooms. My mind's eye can still see the handles of these huge pans set at offset parallel angles with a sloping pyramid of vegetables rising up out of each of them.

In the center of the table was coarse homemade duck *pâté de campagne* with crisp sticks of crust-shatteringly fresh baguette to start, and a salad glistening with a pungent Dijon mustard and *le midi* golden olive oil vinaigrette to follow the roast. Unlabeled dark wine bottles were filled with a wonderful Languedoc red wine; we drank the wine out of squat tumblers, not stemware. An immense cut-crystal bowl was filled to the rim with tiny *fraises des bois* to accompany the cheese course of a Roquefort and a young Brie. The hinged wooden shutters opened to let in the only light, which reflected the bountiful sunlight through the crystal and sent fragments of rainbows onto the clay walls while we ate. That, and the conversation, was the entertainment. —Beth Hensperger

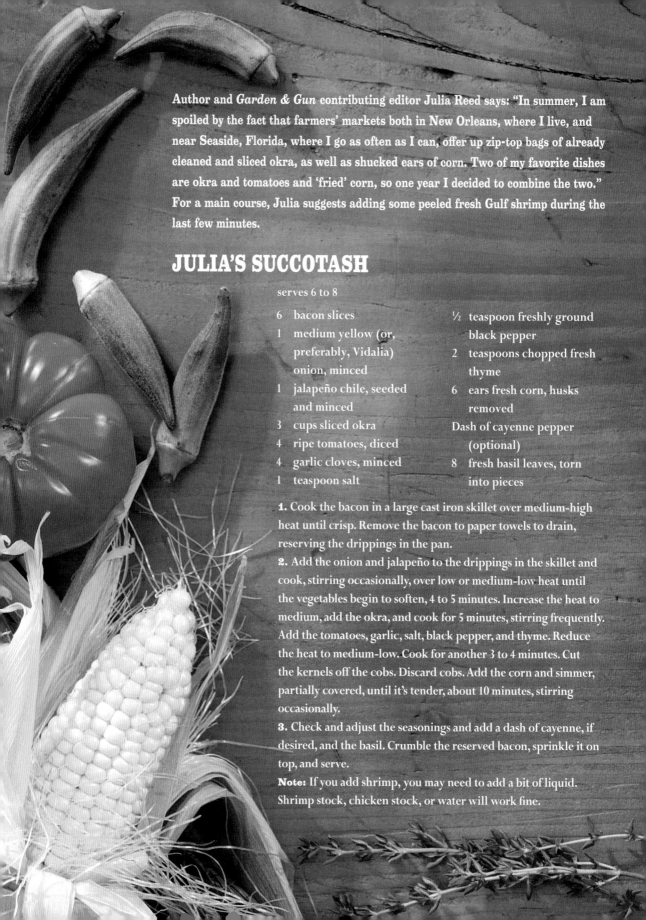

Author and *Garden & Gun* contributing editor Julia Reed says: "In summer, I am spoiled by the fact that farmers' markets both in New Orleans, where I live, and near Seaside, Florida, where I go as often as I can, offer up zip-top bags of already cleaned and sliced okra, as well as shucked ears of corn. Two of my favorite dishes are okra and tomatoes and 'fried' corn, so one year I decided to combine the two." For a main course, Julia suggests adding some peeled fresh Gulf shrimp during the last few minutes.

JULIA'S SUCCOTASH

serves 6 to 8

6 bacon slices	½ teaspoon freshly ground black pepper
1 medium yellow (or, preferably, Vidalia) onion, minced	2 teaspoons chopped fresh thyme
1 jalapeño chile, seeded and minced	6 ears fresh corn, husks removed
3 cups sliced okra	Dash of cayenne pepper (optional)
4 ripe tomatoes, diced	
4 garlic cloves, minced	8 fresh basil leaves, torn into pieces
1 teaspoon salt	

1. Cook the bacon in a large cast iron skillet over medium-high heat until crisp. Remove the bacon to paper towels to drain, reserving the drippings in the pan.

2. Add the onion and jalapeño to the drippings in the skillet and cook, stirring occasionally, over low or medium-low heat until the vegetables begin to soften, 4 to 5 minutes. Increase the heat to medium, add the okra, and cook for 5 minutes, stirring frequently. Add the tomatoes, garlic, salt, black pepper, and thyme. Reduce the heat to medium-low. Cook for another 3 to 4 minutes. Cut the kernels off the cobs. Discard cobs. Add the corn and simmer, partially covered, until it's tender, about 10 minutes, stirring occasionally.

3. Check and adjust the seasonings and add a dash of cayenne, if desired, and the basil. Crumble the reserved bacon, sprinkle it on top, and serve.

Note: If you add shrimp, you may need to add a bit of liquid. Shrimp stock, chicken stock, or water will work fine.

SOUTH COAST HOMINY

serves 6 to 8

3 tablespoons butter
1 small onion, minced
½ cup chopped green bell pepper
3 tablespoons all-purpose flour
½ teaspoon salt
½ teaspoon dry mustard
Dash of cayenne pepper
1½ cups milk

1 cup (4 ounces) shredded Cheddar cheese
½ cup chopped pitted ripe olives
2 (15½-ounce) cans yellow hominy, drained
¼ cup fine, dry breadcrumbs, tossed with 2 tablespoons melted butter

1. Preheat the oven to 375°.

2. Melt the butter in a 10-inch cast iron skillet over medium-high heat. Add the onion and bell pepper and cook, stirring, until the vegetables soften, 4 minutes. Stir in the flour, salt, mustard, and cayenne. Add the milk and cook, stirring constantly, until the mixture thickens and comes to a boil. Remove from the heat.

3. Add the cheese to the milk mixture and stir until melted. Stir in the olives and hominy. Sprinkle the breadcrumbs evenly over the top. Bake until the breadcrumbs are browned, about 25 minutes.

Carolyn Gonce LeRoy recalls, "Every fall in the late 1930s, Edith Lodge Kellermann would send her son Leslie down to the Joseph Lodge farm, where I was born, to get corn for making their hominy. Leslie later became president of Lodge."

SOUTHERN STYLE STRING BEANS

serves about 8

½ pound salt pork
2 pounds fresh green beans, ends trimmed and snapped into 1- to 2-inch pieces

½ pound October or butter beans, shelled and rinsed
Salt

1. Fill a 5-quart cast iron Dutch oven half full with water. Add the salt pork and bring to a boil. Add the beans. Cover and cook slowly over low heat for 1 hour. Uncover and continue to cook until the water has all boiled away and the beans are tender, about 2½ hours. Season with salt to taste.

Cooking Kentucky Wonder green beans using this recipe has been a tradition for more than 150 years in Jeanne Mynatt Scholze's family. If you can't find October beans, you can substitute another kind of fresh shelled bean, like butter beans or scarlet runner beans. Serve this with hot cornbread.

a cast iron memory

Both my mother's family and my dad's family are from Knoxville, Tennessee, with years of upper East Tennessee historical roots. Both families used the same recipe to cook Kentucky Wonder green beans, which are wide and flat. It was my privilege to know two of my great-grandmothers, whose mothers had taught them how to cook Kentucky Wonder green beans, always adding some October beans. My dad's father kept an enormous garden, and his Kentucky Wonders were especially delicious—but watching him in his garden is an even more delicious memory.   —Jeanne Mynatt Scholze

Enjoy this recipe the way *Sunset* magazine food editor Margo True does—with steamy basmati rice, another vegetable dish or two (like curried okra or spicy eggplant), and cool, fresh yogurt. This recipe makes a lot, but it'll keep in the fridge for up to three days and in the freezer for two months (but don't freeze if you've used frozen beans).

RAJMA *(North Indian Red Kidney Beans)*

makes 12 cups; serves 12 to 14

1 (16-ounce) package dried red kidney beans (about 2¼ cups), rinsed and picked over	1 cinnamon stick (2 inches)
	1 bay leaf
	2 teaspoons cumin seeds
4 garlic cloves, minced	1 tablespoon ground coriander
1 large onion, finely chopped	1 teaspoon turmeric
2 teaspoons minced peeled fresh ginger	4½ cups water
	1 (15-ounce) can tomato purée
1 serrano chile, minced	1 teaspoon salt, plus more to taste
3 tablespoons safflower, canola, or vegetable oil	
6 whole cloves	Chopped fresh cilantro (optional)
4 allspice berries	

1. Place the kidney beans in a large bowl and add water to cover by 1 inch. Soak overnight, or use the quick-soak method: Bring the beans and water to a boil, turn off the heat, and let stand 1 hour. Drain and rinse. (You can refrigerate the drained soaked beans for 2 days or freeze up to 2 months before cooking them.)

2. Purée the garlic, onion, ginger, and chile in a blender with a few tablespoons of water until supersmooth. Set aside.

3. Heat the oil in a large cast iron Dutch oven or wok over medium-high heat. Put the cloves, allspice, cinnamon stick, bay leaf, and cumin seeds in a small cup and toss all together into the oil. Let sizzle for 3 to 4 seconds.

4. Lower the heat to medium and stir in the onion purée. Cook, stirring often, until the purée tastes sweet and is starting to brown, 6 to 7 minutes.

5. Stir in the coriander and turmeric; cook 30 seconds, stirring constantly.

a cast iron memory

I met him in college when I was 19. We were together for 11 years, and his family—even though we were from entirely different cultures—became like my own. His mother, kind, funny, and generous, taught me how to cook some of his favorite foods. She'd sizzle whole spices in hot oil for just a second, then layer in the ginger, chile, onions, and, lastly, the powdered spices; then she'd add the main vegetable. Her cooking went straight to my head and my heart, just like he did, and India itself.

This recipe was one he (and I) especially loved. It's velvety smooth, brick red, and earthy. One of the worst things about not being with him anymore is that I've lost his family, too. I make this whenever I miss them, especially her.

—Margo True

6. Add the drained beans and water. Stir well, increase the heat to high, and bring almost to a boil; reduce the heat and simmer, covered, until the beans are tender, about 1 hour.

7. Stir in tomato purée, salt, and some hot water if the beans look too thick (they should be quite soupy). Simmer, covered, until the beans are very tender, about 30 minutes more.

8. Season with salt to taste and serve sprinkled with cilantro, if you like. Discard bay leaf.

More than 75 years ago, Oacie Lee Hart Haney was given an iron Dutch oven as a wedding present by one of her brothers. Until she passed away at the age of 93, she was still using the same Dutch oven. This recipe takes a long time, but it's worth the effort.

OACIE'S BAKED BEANS

serves 6 to 8

1 (16-ounce) package dried Great Northern beans, rinsed and picked over	1½ teaspoons dry mustard
	1½ teaspoons salt or to taste
1 medium onion, chopped	3 bacon slices, cut into 1-inch pieces

1. In a large bowl, cover the beans with water to 2 inches above the beans and soak at least 6 hours or overnight.

2. Preheat the oven to 350°.

3. Drain the beans and rinse until the water runs clear. Place the drained beans in a 5-quart cast iron Dutch oven and add water to cover the top of the beans by 1 inch. Add the remaining ingredients and stir well. Cover and bake for 3 hours.

4. Reduce the oven temperature to 200° and bake until the beans are very tender, about another 3 hours. If the beans start to get dry before they're done, add boiling water.

This recipe is from Beth Duggar, a member of the Executive Committee of the National Cornbread Festival, which is held each year in Lodge's hometown of South Pittsburg, Tennessee. Beth offers this tip for freezing okra from the garden: "Take it straight from the garden, and put it directly into freezer bags. When ready to use, thaw and wash. This way the okra holds its 'slime,' which is what makes it great!"

SOUTHERN FRIED OKRA

serves 4 to 6 people who love okra

2 quarts fresh okra
1 to 2 large eggs, lightly beaten
About 1 cup cornmeal
1 teaspoon salt or to taste
¼ teaspoon freshly ground black pepper or to taste
½ teaspoon onion powder or garlic powder (optional)
½ to ¼ cup bacon drippings or vegetable oil (enough to fill the skillet ¼ inch deep)

1. Wash the okra with lots of water and let dry. Remove the ends and slice into ¼- to ½-inch-thick rounds; place in a large bowl. (If the okra is tough, throw it out.) Pour the beaten egg(s) over the okra and stir gently until the rounds are coated. Add the cornmeal, salt, pepper, and, if desired, onion or garlic powder, stirring gently to coat.

2. Heat the bacon drippings in a 12-inch cast iron skillet over medium-high heat until hot. To test, add a slice of okra to the skillet to see if it really sizzles. Pour half the okra into the skillet and cook until golden brown all over, turning it with a metal spatula. (Some people like it almost burned.) You may need to add more bacon drippings.

3. Remove the okra from the skillet and repeat with the remaining okra, adding more drippings if needed.

When honey and vinegar plus a handful of dried cranberries are reduced to glaze young carrots, the combination becomes a memorable side dish to enjoy for the holidays or anytime you want a special vegetable. Joanna Pruess likes to use thyme honey because it adds a slightly bitter taste to the complex flavors, but any variety works. This recipe from Joanna's *Cast Iron Cookbook: Delicious and Simple Comfort Food* can be made ahead and reheated.

SWEET AND TANGY GLAZED CARROTS WITH CRANBERRIES

serves 4

1½ pounds young carrots, peeled, or large carrots, cut lengthwise into quarters and then in half crosswise

1 tablespoon canola or vegetable oil

1 teaspoon salt

½ cup good quality chicken stock

1 tablespoon unsalted butter

¼ cup dried cranberries

2 tablespoons thyme honey or other variety

2 tablespoons sherry vinegar or white wine vinegar

1 tablespoon finely chopped fresh flat-leaf parsley

1. Combine the carrots, oil, and salt in a bowl. Heat a cast iron skillet large enough to hold the carrots in a single layer over medium heat just until hot, about 3½ minutes. Scrape the carrots into the pan and cook for 2 minutes, stirring once or twice. Stir in the stock and butter, cover the skillet, reduce the heat to low, and cook until the carrots are almost tender when pierced with the tip of a knife, about 15 minutes.

2. Uncover and stir in the cranberries, honey, and vinegar; bring to a boil and cook until the liquid reduces to glaze the carrots, about 5 minutes, shaking the pan occasionally. Stir in the parsley and serve.

You don't like Brussels sprouts? Don't be so sure! "This is one of my favorite ways to make fresh Brussels sprouts," says Stacey Ballis. "It's converted many a person who thought they hated them. My five-year-old goddaughter is addicted to them!" Stacey is the author of *Good Enough to Eat* and blogs about food at *Polymath Chronicles*.

CARAMELIZED BRUSSELS SPROUTS

serves 6 to 8

2   tablespoons unsalted butter
1   tablespoon olive oil
2   pounds fresh Brussels sprouts, bottoms trimmed and halved lengthwise
1   tablespoon sugar
Salt and freshly ground black pepper
Toppings *(optional; pick one of the following):*
⅓   cup toasted nuts (walnuts, pistachios, and pine nuts are good options)
⅓   cup chopped crisp-cooked bacon, pancetta, or prosciutto
1   teaspoon grated lemon or orange zest
⅓   cup grated ricotta salata or crumbled feta cheese
⅓   cup dried currants
⅓   cup crispy fried onions or shallots
⅓   cup toasted buttered bread crumbs
⅓   cup packed fresh herbs (mint, basil, tarragon, and sage are all good), chopped

1. Melt the butter with the oil in a large cast iron skillet over medium-high heat until the bubbling subsides. Reduce the heat to medium. Place the Brussels sprouts, cut side down, in a single layer in the skillet. Cook, checking to ensure the sprouts aren't burning, until they have achieved a deep golden brown color, about 3 minutes depending on the heat of your burner. Using tongs, turn the sprouts over and brown the other side in the same way.

2. Reduce the heat to medium-low, sprinkle the sprouts with the sugar, and toss to evenly distribute the sugar. Continue to cook, tossing often, until the sprouts reach the desired level of doneness. (Stacey likes hers soft but not mushy, with a little give in the center.) Season with salt and pepper to taste.

3. If desired, sprinkle one of the optional toppings over the Brussels sprouts and serve.

This recipe is from cookbook author Ellen Wright's sister-in-law Nurit. The dish is slightly sweet and crispy, and they both like to serve it as a side for beef, pork, fish, or chicken. A bit of advice from Ellen: "Don't substitute butter for the margarine thinking butter will be better—it isn't. Margarine combines better with the egg mixture. I have done it both ways, and I know."

NURIT'S NOODLE PUDDING

serves 8 to 10

2 (16-ounce) packages wide
   egg noodles
½ cup (1 stick) plus
   2 tablespoons margarine,
   melted
5 large eggs
½ cup sugar
1 (8-ounce) package cream
   cheese, softened

3 cups whole milk
½ cup golden raisins
1 tablespoon vanilla extract

Topping:
½ cup cornflakes mixed with
   1 tablespoon sugar and
   1 teaspoon ground cinnamon
1 cup canned crushed
   pineapple, drained

1. Preheat the oven to 350°. Lightly butter a 12-inch cast iron skillet.

2. Cook the noodles in lightly salted boiling water with a little oil until they are soft but not mushy. Drain and toss with 2 tablespoons melted margarine. Set aside.

3. Combine the eggs and sugar in a large bowl and beat with a fork until blended. Add the cream cheese, milk, raisins, vanilla, and remaining ½ cup melted margarine and blend with a fork or an electric mixer just until combined. (Combine gently and do not overmix because of the raisins.)

4. Transfer the cooked noodles to the prepared skillet. Add the egg mixture, stirring to coat the noodles. Sprinkle the cornflake mixture and crushed pineapple on top.

5. Bake the pudding until crunchy and golden on top, 45 minutes to 1 hour.

Chef Patrick Reilly of the Majestic Grille in Memphis likes to serve these potatoes with his Spatchcock Chicken (page 105).

LYONNAISE POTATOES

serves 4

2 pounds fingerling or baby potatoes

½ cup (1 stick) unsalted butter

1 large onion, cut into ⅛-inch-thick half moons

2 cups vegetable oil for frying

Kosher salt and freshly ground black pepper

1. Cook the potatoes in a large pot of salted boiling water until almost tender, about 10 minutes. Drain well, let cool, and cut into ¼-inch-thick slices.

2. In a large cast iron skillet, melt 2 tablespoons butter over medium heat. Add the onion and cook, stirring often, until softened and caramelized. Remove the onion from the skillet and wipe the skillet clean with a paper towel.

3. Heat the oil in the skillet to 350°; use a deep-fry thermometer to check the temperature. Carefully add half the potatoes to the hot oil and cook over medium heat until browned and crispy. Using a metal slotted spoon, remove the potatoes from the oil. Repeat with the remaining potatoes. Pour off the oil.

4. Melt the remaining 6 tablespoons butter in the skillet over medium heat. Add the potatoes and onion, toss well in the melted butter, and season with salt and pepper to taste. Serve hot.

This recipe from Jane Gaither, who blogs at *Gourmet Gadget Gal*, brings back old kitchen memories: "The first task I was ever given in the kitchen was peeling potatoes with a rusty old vegetable peeler that my mother was loath to replace. I never enjoyed that chore and wanted to move quickly to using a knife, so I graduated to chopping the onions." This recipe is just the ticket, made with skin-on red potatoes and chopped onions.

CAST IRON-ROASTED RED POTATOES WITH ROSEMARY AND ONION

serves 4 to 6

1½ pounds red potatoes, quartered

1 large sweet onion, chopped

2 tablespoons olive oil

1 teaspoon fresh rosemary leaves

1 teaspoon salt

Freshly ground black pepper

1. Place a 12-inch cast iron skillet in the oven and preheat oven to 350°.

2. When the skillet is hot, add the potatoes and onion and drizzle with the oil. Add the rosemary, salt, and pepper to taste, and roast until the potatoes are browned and tender when tested with a knife, stirring occasionally, about 45 minutes.

Cast Iron-Roasted
Red Potatoes with
Rosemary and Onion

NOTHIN' BUT CORNBREAD

Cornbread and cast iron——a match made in heaven. This chapter offers up a satisfying selection of traditional recipes as well as tasty new twists. We're also proud to include the recipes of every Grand Winner of the National Cornbread Cook-off, held each year in Lodge's hometown of South Pittsburg, Tennessee.

This Ain't No Yankee
Cornbread

THIS AIN'T NO YANKEE CORNBREAD

serves 2 (4 if you're not a real cornbread fan)

2   tablespoons bacon drippings
1   cup white cornmeal
1   teaspoon baking powder
1   teaspoon salt
1   large egg, lightly beaten
1   cup buttermilk, or more if needed

1. Place 1 tablespoon bacon drippings in a 6½-inch Lodge cast iron skillet; place skillet in the oven while it preheats to 425°.
2. Whisk together the cornmeal, baking powder, and salt in a small bowl. Whisk together the egg, buttermilk, and remaining 1 tablespoon bacon drippings in a medium bowl. Add the dry ingredients to the buttermilk mixture and stir just until combined. (The mixture should pour like pancake batter; if not, add a little more buttermilk.)
3. Pour the batter into the hot skillet. Bake until the crust is dark golden brown, 15 to 20 minutes. Serve hot, no chaser.

This recipe is a favorite of Christine Rogers' family. They like this cornbread with a pot of pinto beans and turnip greens. A registered nurse, Christine grew up in South Pittsburg, and now lives in Chattanooga, Tennessee.

SOUR CREAM CORNBREAD

serves 8

½   cup vegetable oil
1   cup sour cream
1   (8-ounce) can cream-style corn
3   large eggs, lightly beaten
1   cup self-rising white cornmeal mix
¼   teaspoon salt or seasoned salt, or to taste

1. Pour ¼ cup oil into a 9-inch cast iron skillet; place the skillet in the oven while it preheats to 400°.
2. In a large bowl, combine the remaining ¼ cup oil, the sour cream, corn, eggs, cornmeal mix, and salt until well blended.
3. Remove the skillet from the oven and pour the hot oil into the batter, stirring to combine. Pour the batter into the hot skillet and bake until the top is lightly browned, about 45 minutes. Cut into wedges.

An homage to her Aunt T (see A Cast Iron Memory below), This Ain't No Yankee Cornbread was contributed by Tamie Cook, culinary director of Alton Brown's *Good Eats* program on the Food Network.

a cast iron memory

Everyone has a story about cornbread. Or at least, if you're from the South you do. Mine has to do with Aunt Henrietta Beatrice, or Aunt T as she was affectionately called. I didn't realize it until I was an adult, but she made the best cornbread I've ever eaten. Before she passed away, I told her how much I loved it and asked her for the recipe. She kind of chuckled and assured me that she never followed a recipe or even made it the exact way twice, but there were a few rules you needed to follow:

No. 1 Cornbread does not contain sugar. If it has sugar, it's called cake!

No. 2 You have to use bacon grease, the kind in the grease jar on the stove.

No. 3 You have to use a Lodge cast iron skillet—It just makes it taste good!

Every time I make cornbread, I can feel her smiling down on me.

—Tamie Cook

Elizabeth Adams has many pieces of cast iron that she uses every day, but her favorites are the two pieces that were the only things left after her house burned down 25 years ago. This is an old family recipe from Tunica, Mississippi.

ELIZABETH'S SCALDED CORNBREAD

serves 8

1 to 2 tablespoons bacon drippings or vegetable oil	1 cup buttermilk
½ cup boiling water	2 or 3 large eggs, lightly beaten
2 cups white cornmeal	1 teaspoon baking soda
	½ teaspoon salt

1. Place the bacon drippings in a 10-inch cast iron skillet and place in the oven while it preheats to 400°.

2. In a medium bowl, pour the boiling water over the cornmeal to scald it. Stir to cool the mixture and prevent lumps from forming. Gradually stir in the buttermilk. Add the eggs, baking soda, and salt and mix well with a wooden spoon.

3. Remove the skillet from the oven and pour the hot drippings into the batter. Stir to combine. Pour the batter into the hot skillet and bake until browned around the edges, about 25 minutes. Cut into wedges.

MAYONNAISE CORNBREAD FOR TWO

serves 2

Charles Cagle liked to make his cornbread in a Lodge Wonder Skillet, which is 5 inches square and ¾ inch deep. If you prefer your cornbread thicker, use a 4-inch round skillet. Charles enjoyed his cornbread best crumbled hot into a glass of milk.

1 tablespoon bacon drippings	2 tablespoons mayonnaise
½ cup self-rising white cornmeal mix	½ cup milk

1. Place the bacon drippings in a Lodge Wonder Skillet and place in the oven while it preheats to 450°.

2. In a small bowl, combine the cornmeal mix, mayonnaise, and milk.

3. Remove the skillet from the oven and pour the hot drippings into the batter. Stir to combine. Pour the batter into the hot skillet and bake until the top is lightly browned, about 15 minutes.

AUNT JIMMIE'S YEAST CORNBREAD

serves 8

½ cup corn oil
2 cups self-rising white cornmeal mix
1 package active dry yeast
½ teaspoon baking soda
1½ cups buttermilk
1 large egg

1. Pour the oil into a Lodge 10½-inch square cast iron skillet and place in the oven while it preheats to 400°.

2. In a large bowl, combine the cornmeal mix, yeast, and baking soda. In a large measuring cup, beat the egg into the buttermilk. Add to the dry ingredients and stir until well blended. Remove the skillet from the oven and pour the hot oil into the batter. Stir to combine.

3. Pour the batter into the hot skillet and bake until the top is browned, about 25 minutes. Flip the cornbread onto a platter and serve hot with butter.

Jimmie Russell was a "Yankee" who joined the Women's Army Corps during World War II. While stationed in Washington State, she met and fell in love with a Southerner from Tennessee. After moving home with him, she became one of the best Southern cooks in South Pittsburg.

This recipe is from Mary Virginia Loyd—it yields a moist, cheesy bread.

MRS. LOYD'S MEXICAN CORNBREAD

serves 8

1¼ cups self-rising cornmeal mix
½ teaspoon salt
¾ cup milk
⅓ cup canola oil
2 large eggs
1 (8¼-ounce) can cream-style corn
¾ cup (3 ounces) shredded Cheddar cheese
1 medium onion, finely chopped
½ green bell pepper, seeded and diced
2 small hot chiles, seeded and finely chopped

1. Preheat the oven to 400°. Grease a Lodge 10½-inch square cast iron skillet.

2. In a large bowl, combine all the ingredients until well blended. Pour the batter into the prepared skillet and bake on the bottom rack until browned, about 30 minutes.

Mary Virginia and David Loyd lived in the Bridgeport, Alabama, Loyd family home where David's parents had reared six sons. Virginia had a complete canning kitchen in the basement and a large modern kitchen with multiple ovens on the main floor. She was very generous with sharing both her recipes and her wonderful food. At the holidays David and Virginia entertained their families and many friends with gourmet meals that Virginia lovingly prepared.

Carolyn Gonce LeRoy, who grew up on the Joseph Lodge farm in South Pittsburg, Tennessee, has had this recipe for more than 40 years and makes it often.

VIDALIA CORNBREAD

serves 8

❧ vidalia onions ❧

Vidalia onions grow only in south Georgia and are available from late April until mid-September. Sweet and juicy, the onions can be found in most grocery stores during these months.

2 cups self-rising white cornmeal mix

1 tablespoon sugar

1 teaspoon baking powder

2 cups milk

2 tablespoons vegetable oil

1 large egg, lightly beaten

2 cups finely chopped Vidalia onions

1. Preheat the oven to 350°. Grease a 9-inch Lodge Wedge pan.

2. In a large bowl, combine the cornmeal mix, sugar, baking powder, milk, oil, and egg until well blended (the batter will be thin). Add the onions, stirring until well blended.

3. Pour the batter into the prepared pan and bake until golden brown, about 40 minutes. Let cool 10 minutes before serving.

Growing up, I both loved and hated fish night. Like most kids, I wasn't the biggest fan of fish—which of course I now love—but my grandmother's cornbread sticks were one of the best things that I ever put in my mouth. Even now, I can see and smell and taste the hot cornbread, crunchy on the outside and custardy on the inside, steaming as I broke it apart and slathered it with sweet butter. It was swoon-worthy cornbread. I still have her cast iron cornbread molds but most often use either a regular cast iron skillet or the Lodge Wedge Pan because I can bake and serve the cornbread in the same pan. —Elizabeth Karmel (See Elizabeth's recipes on pages 148 and 154)

CRANBERRY-ORANGE CORNBREAD WITH ORANGE "BUTTER"

serves 6 to 8

Here's a fun and sweet twist on traditional cornbread from cookbook author and baking expert Julie Hasson. Try it for breakfast, as part of your Thanksgiving lineup, or for dessert. This cornbread is not only delicious, but vegan too.

Cornbread:

1½ cups medium-grind yellow
    cornmeal
1½ cups unbleached all-purpose
    flour
½ cup granulated sugar
4   teaspoons baking powder
¼   teaspoon salt
1   cup orange juice
1   cup soymilk
¼   cup canola oil

1⅓ cups fresh or frozen
    cranberries
Grated zest of 1 orange

Orange "Butter":

⅓   cup nonhydrogenated
    margarine (such as Earth
    Balance), softened
¼   cup confectioners' sugar
1   tablespoon thawed orange
    juice concentrate

1. Make the cornbread: Preheat the oven to 400°. Grease a 10-inch cast iron skillet well with shortening.

2. Combine the cornmeal, flour, granulated sugar, baking powder, and salt in a large bowl. In a medium bowl, whisk together the orange juice, soymilk, and oil. Add the soymilk mixture to the flour mixture, stirring just until combined. Add the cranberries and orange zest and fold in, being careful not to overmix the batter.

3. Scoop the batter into the prepared skillet. Bake until lightly browned on top and a tester inserted in the center comes out clean, 40 to 50 minutes. Remove the cornbread from the oven and place on a rack to cool slightly.

4. Make the orange "butter": In a small bowl, whisk together the margarine, confectioners' sugar, and orange juice concentrate until smooth.

5. Serve the cornbread warm, spread with the "butter."

BACON AND GREEN ONION SKILLET CORNBREAD

serves 6 to 8

¼ pound best-quality sliced bacon, cut into ¼-inch strips

1 bunch green onions (white part and half the light green part), trimmed and cut into ¼-inch pieces

1 cup all-purpose flour (spoon flour into dry-measure cup and level off)

1 cup stone-ground yellow cornmeal

2 tablespoons sugar

1 tablespoon baking powder

1 teaspoon salt

¾ cup whole milk or buttermilk

3 large eggs

¼ cup (½ stick) unsalted butter, melted

1. Position oven rack in the center of the oven and preheat to 400°.

2. Cook the bacon in a 9-inch cast iron skillet over medium heat until it starts to sizzle. Regulate the heat so that it cooks slowly and evenly, stirring occasionally. Once the bacon has started to color, stir in the green onions and continue to cook until the bacon is crisp, about 5 minutes longer.

3. As soon as you start cooking the bacon, combine all the dry ingredients in a medium bowl and stir well to mix. In a 2-cup measuring cup, whisk together the milk and eggs and set near the bowl.

4. Once the bacon is ready, add the egg mixture and melted butter to the dry ingredients. Add the contents of the skillet and use a large rubber spatula to mix the batter smooth.

5. Heat the skillet over medium heat (it doesn't matter if a few pieces of bacon and onion have remained behind) for 1 minute. Pour in the batter. Bake the cornbread until it is risen and firm, about 20 minutes.

6. Cool on a rack for 5 minutes, then use a flexible spatula such as a pancake turner to help slide the cornbread onto a platter. Serve immediately, cut into wedges.

Baking cornbread in a well-seasoned cast iron skillet is an old Southern tradition. Just leave a little of the bacon fat clinging to the pan before pouring in the batter, and the bread releases perfectly after baking and has a bonus of a crunchy bottom crust. This version is from Nick Malgieri, adapted from *How to Bake,* one of his ten cookbooks. He is director of the baking program at the Institute of Culinary Education in New York City.

CORN FINGERS

makes 12 to 13   *(pictured on page 220)*

These corn fingers, baked in a corn finger mold to resemble little individual corn on the cob, are tender, fine-grained, and slightly sweet with little nubbins of corn in each bite and the glad surprise of occasional hot pepper flakes. They seem to dissolve in the mouth yet have a full corn flavor. Rose Levy Beranbaum makes these every summer when Jersey corn is in season, but sometimes in the winter, when she has the craving, she resorts to canned corn "niblets," which she finds to have the best flavor and texture of processed corn kernels. This recipe is adapted from her cookbook *The Bread Bible*.

✄ notes ✄

To cook the corn, boil it in unsalted water until just tender when pierced with a cake tester or skewer, 5 to 7 minutes. Fresh corn needs to be cooked in order to remove some of its moisture; otherwise it would make the batter too liquid. Blue cornmeal can be substituted for the yellow cornmeal but a few teaspoons of liquid should be added to compensate for the higher absorption of the blue cornmeal.

½ cup (2.25 ounces) yellow cornmeal, preferably stone-ground, such as Kenyon's (see Notes below)

½ cup plus ½ tablespoon (2.5 ounces) bleached all-purpose flour (preferably Gold Medal)

2 tablespoons plus 2 teaspoons sugar

1¼ teaspoons baking powder

½ teaspoon salt

½ to 1 teaspoon red pepper flakes, to taste

1 cup cooked corn, cut off the cob (2 small ears; see Notes below)

⅓ cup heavy cream

⅓ cup whole milk

¼ cup (2 ounces) unsalted butter, melted

1 large egg yolk

1 large egg white

1. At least 20 minutes before baking, preheat the oven to 425°. Position the rack in the center of the oven. Lightly grease 2 cast iron corn finger molds with nonstick cooking spray or oil. Five to ten minutes before the batter is ready, preheat the molds in the oven.

2. Stir the cornmeal, flour, sugar, baking powder, salt, and red pepper in a medium bowl. Add the corn; stir until coated with the mixture.

3. In a 2-cup glass measuring cup or bowl, lightly whisk together the cream, milk, melted butter, and egg yolk.

4. In a medium bowl, beat the egg white with an electric mixer until soft peaks form when the beater is lifted slowly.

5. Stir the cream mixture into the flour mixture just until moistened. There will still be lumps. Fold in the beaten egg white just until incorporated. You should still see little lumps.

6. Spoon or pipe the batter into the hot molds, almost to the top of each depression. Use a small metal spatula or the back of a teaspoon to smooth the batter, if necessary. If piping, use a pastry bag with a plain ½-inch-wide tube. Fill any empty depressions in the mold half full with water. Bake the corn fingers until the tops are golden brown, about 15 minutes.

7. Unmold the corn fingers; loosen the sides of each finger with a small metal spatula. Place a wire rack over one mold and invert so that they are all supported by the rack. Repeat with the second mold. These corn fingers are wonderfully tender, so they require care while still warm to avoid breaking them. Serve warm or room temperature. They also freeze well, up to several weeks. Let cool completely, then wrap each one airtight in plastic wrap, and place in heavy-duty zip-top freezer bags. To reheat from frozen, bake in a preheated 400° oven for 7 minutes.

crazy for cast iron

My passion for cast iron cookware goes back to when I was a freshman at the University of Vermont. My boyfriend at the time, David Gibbs, who was a native Vermonter, introduced me to the 11-inch cast iron skillet for frying and baking, and it became the first of my now large collection.

My cast iron collection includes a rare Bundt pan, a small square frying pan, an aebleskiver pan (for making the traditional Scandinavian round pancake puffs), a 7-depression blini pan, muffin pans of various shapes, corn finger pans, Dutch ovens, and even a trivet with George Washington's bust that I found years ago when living in Washington Crossing, Pennsylvania. One of my favorite memories about cast iron is of a friend who reported firing his cleaning lady for washing his treasured, well-seasoned frying pan.

Most of my collection resides in my country home, where the pans decoratively hang from the dining room walls. The one dearest to my heart is a 6-inch frying pan I purchased from my grandmother's yard sale when she decided to "go modern" at the age of 93! It's perfect for making a single fried egg for breakfast. I also have a square frying pan that I love to use to make a square-shaped fried egg to put on a square slice of bread. I can't imagine making corn fingers without the special pans that resemble ears of corn. And I would never dream of making bacon in anything other than my 11-inch frying pan. I also use this pan, heated as hot as I can get it, to fry slices of onion to a crisp golden brown. And perhaps my very favorite use for it is making steak in my New York apartment where I don't have access to a grill. I heat the pan as hot as possible and sear the steak on both sides, mopping up the fat with a folded paper towel held by tongs to prevent the smoke alarm from blasting in my ears. Then I transfer the steak in the pan to a hot, hot oven to finish cooking.

Oh yes, and for making French fries or any other deep-fat cooking, the Dutch oven or the smaller saucepan is the absolute best for maintaining the heat of the oil, resulting in the crispiest fries.

There is simply no equal to cast iron's ability for keeping a perfectly even heat, whether at high or low temperatures.

—Rose Levy Beranbaum

SMOKED SAUSAGE HOT WATER CORN CAKES

makes 20 to 25 cakes

In the early years of the National Cornbread Festival, held in South Pittsburg, Tennessee, the First Baptist Church had the Baptist Bread booth at the festival. Ibbie Bennett added sausage, onion, and pimiento (for color and flavor) to the hot water cornbread recipe passed down by Nettie Bennett, her mother-in-law, to make these delicious corn cakes.

Canola oil
3 cups self-rising white cornmeal mix
1 tablespoon sugar
1¼ cups boiling water
1 cup chopped onion
1 cup finely chopped smoked sausage
2 tablespoons pimientos, drained

1. Pour ½ inch of oil into a large cast iron Dutch oven or the fryer of a Lodge Combo Cooker and heat over high heat to 375°.
2. Meanwhile, combine the cornmeal mix and sugar in a large bowl. Pour the boiling water over the top and stir until sticky. Add the onion, sausage, and pimientos and stir well.
3. Working in batches, drop the batter into the hot oil by the ¼ cupfuls and fry until evenly browned on both sides, 1 to 2 minutes per side. (Don't crowd the oil with too many cakes at one time.)
4. Using a slotted spoon, remove the cakes from the oil to paper towels to drain. Repeat with the remaining batter.

DOC HAVRON'S HUSH PUPPIES

makes about 32 hush puppies

An avid outdoorsman, Dr. James B. "Jimmy" Havron liked to fry the fish he caught at his favorite fishing holes on Guntersville Lake near Hollywood, Alabama, or in the Everglades. He would cook his hush puppies in 2 inches of the corn oil left over from the fish fry.

2 cups self-rising white cornmeal mix
1 tablespoon sugar
1 tablespoon canola oil
1 large egg
1 small onion, diced
½ red bell pepper, seeded and diced
½ green bell pepper, seeded and diced
⅔ cup milk
Corn oil for frying

1. Combine the cornmeal mix, sugar, canola oil, and egg in a medium bowl. Stir in the onion and bell peppers. Stir in the milk.
2. Heat 2 inches of corn oil in a large Dutch oven or the fryer of a Lodge Combo Cooker to 365°. Carefully drop the batter by rounded tablespoonfuls into the hot oil, without crowding them, and fry until browned on all sides.
3. Using tongs or a slotted spoon, remove the hush puppies to paper towels to drain. Repeat with the remaining batter. Enjoy hot.

Sarah Reed had a small bakery for many years in South Pittsburg, Tennessee. When anyone would ask her if she ever got tired of baking, she would reply, "I get tired, but never of baking."

MRS. REED'S CORNBREAD DRESSING

serves 8

1 skillet of cornbread (use your favorite recipe)
½ cup chopped green onions
½ cup shredded carrots
1 tablespoon chopped fresh parsley
1 tablespoon rubbed sage
1 teaspoon freshly ground black pepper
¼ teaspoon salt
2 large eggs
6 cups chicken broth, or as needed
6 hard-cooked eggs, peeled and chopped

1. Cool the cornbread completely. Store it in a tightly covered bowl in the refrigerator overnight.

2. When you are ready to make the dressing, grease two Lodge 10½-inch square cast iron skillets and place in the oven while it preheats to 400°.

3. Crumble the cornbread in a large bowl (you should have 12 cups when crumbled). Add the green onions, carrots, parsley, sage, pepper, salt, and eggs. Stir in enough of the broth to make a slightly thin mixture. Gently stir in the chopped hard-cooked eggs.

4. Pour the mixture into the hot skillets. Reduce the oven temperature to 375° and bake until browned on top, about 35 minutes.

Sandi Klingler of Auburn, Alabama, took home the grand prize at the National Cornbread Cook-off in 2005 for this Thanksgiving-themed meal in a skillet.

AMISH CHICKEN CORNBREAD BAKE

serves 8

Filling:

½ cup (1 stick) butter

⅓ cup Martha White all-purpose flour

1 cup low-sodium chicken broth

1 cup half-and-half

½ teaspoon freshly ground black pepper

2 cups chopped cooked chicken breasts

1 (4-ounce) can sliced mushrooms, drained

½ cup dried cranberries

¼ cup (1 ounce) shredded Parmesan cheese

Topping:

1 cup mashed baked sweet potatoes or 1 (15-ounce) can sweet potatoes, drained and mashed

2 tablespoons sugar

1 large egg

3 tablespoons milk

1 (6-ounce) package Martha White Cotton Country Cornbread Mix

Fresh rosemary sprigs (optional)

1. Preheat the oven to 400°.

2. Make the filling: Melt the butter in a 10½-inch cast iron skillet over medium heat; gradually add the flour, whisking until smooth. Cook, whisking constantly, 1 minute. Gradually add the broth and half-and-half; cook, whisking constantly, until the mixture thickens. Stir in the pepper. Stir in the chicken, mushrooms, cranberries, and cheese. Cook, stirring occasionally, until hot, about 3 minutes. Reduce the heat to low while preparing the topping.

3. Make the topping: Combine the sweet potatoes, sugar, egg, and milk in a medium bowl; stir until blended. Add the cornbread mix; stir until blended. Carefully spread the topping over the chicken mixture to cover as a crust.

4. Bake until the cornbread is golden and the chicken mixture is bubbly, 25 to 30 minutes. Remove from the oven and let stand 5 minutes. Garnish with rosemary sprigs, if desired.

This recipe, the 2009 first-place winner of the National Cornbread Cook-off from Sonya Goergen of Moorhead, Minnesota, is a study in cool and spicy. The refreshing iceberg salad adds a welcome crunch.

BUFFALO CHICKEN CORNBREAD WITH BLUE CHEESE SALAD

serves 8

Buffalo Chicken Cornbread:

1 large egg

¾ cup milk

2 tablespoons olive oil

1 (6½-ounce) package Martha White Yellow Cornbread Mix

1 cup (4 ounces) shredded Cheddar cheese

½ cup crumbled blue cheese

2 cups frozen cooked boneless Buffalo-style hot wings, thawed and diced

½ teaspoon red pepper flakes

2 tablespoons chopped fresh cilantro

Blue Cheese Salad:

½ small head iceberg lettuce, cored and chopped

1 cup thinly sliced celery

½ red onion, thinly sliced into half moons

½ cup crumbled blue cheese

⅔ cup blue cheese salad dressing

Toppings (optional):

½ cup diced tomatoes

Chopped fresh cilantro

1. Preheat the oven to 400°. Spray a 10½-inch cast iron skillet with nonstick cooking spray.

2. Make the buffalo chicken cornbread: In a large bowl, stir together the egg, milk, and oil. Add the cornbread mix, Cheddar and blue cheeses, diced hot wings, red pepper, and cilantro. Stir until well blended. Pour the mixture into the prepared skillet, spreading it evenly. Bake until golden brown, 20 to 30 minutes. Remove from the oven. Cool on a wire rack while you prepare the salad.

3. Make the blue cheese salad: Combine the lettuce, celery, onion, and blue cheese in a medium bowl. Toss with the blue cheese dressing until the salad is well coated.

4. To serve, cut the cornbread into 8 wedges. Top each wedge with an even amount of salad. Top with tomatoes and/or cilantro, if desired.

Buffalo Chicken Cornbread with Ranch-Style Salad: Omit the blue cheese from the cornbread and salad. Substitute ranch dressing for the blue cheese dressing in the salad.

Sue Gulledge of Springville, Alabama, won the very first National Cornbread Cook-off in 1997 with this skillet full of tasty good flavor.

CHICKEN AND DRESSING SKILLET BAKE

serves 6

2 tablespoons butter	3 cups cubed cooked chicken,
1 cup chopped onion	seasoned with salt and
1 cup chopped celery	pepper
1 tablespoon vegetable oil	1 cup frozen corn kernels
2 (6-ounce) packages	1½ teaspoons poultry
Martha White Cotton	seasoning
Country or Buttermilk	1¼ cups milk
Cornbread Mix	2 large eggs, lightly beaten

1. Preheat the oven to 400°. Melt the butter in a 10-inch cast iron skillet over medium heat; cook the onion and celery, stirring occasionally, until tender, about 10 minutes. Remove the vegetable mixture to a large bowl.

2. Pour the oil in the same skillet; place in the oven to heat for about 5 minutes.

3. Add the cornbread mix, chicken, corn, poultry seasoning, milk, and eggs to the vegetable mixture; blend well. Carefully remove the skillet from the oven; pour the batter into the hot skillet. Bake until golden brown, 30 to 35 minutes. Cut into wedges and serve.

Gaynell Lawson of Maryville, Tennessee, came up with a first-place winner at the National Cornbread Cook-off in 2003. It's the perfect answer to "What's for dinner?" on a cold night.

WHITE CHICKEN CHILI WITH CHEDDAR HUSH-PUPPY CRUST

serves 6

White Chicken Chili:

1   tablespoon olive oil

1   cup finely chopped onion

2   garlic cloves, minced

1   medium green bell pepper, seeded and chopped

1   tablespoon chili powder

½   teaspoon ground cumin

2   tablespoons fresh lime juice

1   (19-ounce) can cannellini (white kidney) beans

2   cups chopped cooked chicken

1   (14½-ounce) can chicken broth

1   (4½-ounce) can mild green chiles, drained

Cheddar Hush-Puppy Crust:

1   large egg

½   cup milk

3   tablespoons butter, melted

1   (6-ounce) package Martha White Cotton Country Cornbread Mix

¼   cup finely chopped onion

1   cup (4 ounces) shredded Cheddar cheese

Toppings:

Sour cream, salsa, and chopped fresh cilantro (optional)

1. Preheat the oven to 400°.

2. Make the white chicken chili: Heat the oil in a 10½-inch cast iron skillet over medium heat. Add the onion, garlic, bell pepper, chili powder, and cumin; cook, stirring occasionally, until the vegetables are tender, 3 to 5 minutes. Stir in the lime juice, beans, chicken, broth, and chiles; simmer about 10 minutes.

3. Make the cheddar hush-puppy crust: Beat the egg in a medium bowl. Add the milk, melted butter, and cornbread mix, stirring until blended. Stir in the onion and cheese. Pour over the chicken chili in the skillet.

4. Bake until the crust is golden brown, 25 to 30 minutes. Top with sour cream, salsa, and/or cilantro, if desired.

CHICKEN TACO CORNBREAD WEDGES WITH RANCHERO CILANTRO DRIZZLE

serves 6

Ranchero Cilantro Drizzle:

½ cup ranch dressing

½ cup salsa verde

1 cup tightly packed fresh
   cilantro leaves

Chicken Filling:

2 tablespoons vegetable oil

½ cup finely chopped onion

¼ cup finely chopped red bell
   pepper

1 tablespoon finely chopped
   jalapeño chile

2 cups shredded rotisserie
   chicken

3 tablespoons finely chopped
   fresh cilantro

½ teaspoon salt

½ teaspoon ground cumin

¼ teaspoon freshly ground black
   pepper

1 (14½-ounce) can diced
   tomatoes with green chiles,
   undrained

Crust:

1 large egg, lightly beaten

1 (7-ounce) package Martha
   White Sweet Yellow
   Cornbread Mix

½ cup milk

¾ cup crushed corn tortilla
   chips

½ cup (2 ounces) shredded
   mozzarella cheese

½ cup (2 ounces) shredded
   Cheddar cheese

Toppings:

3 cups shredded romaine
   lettuce

1 cup chopped tomatoes

This first-place winner of the 2007 National Cornbread Cook-off from Jenny Flake of Gilbert, Arizona, is a bold contrast of flavors and textures. The southwestern-style chicken filling has a cornbread crust that's crunch-enhanced with the addition of crushed tortilla chips. Covered with melty good Cheddar and mozzarella cheese, the dish is served up in wedges with a zippy ranch dressing, shredded romaine, and tomatoes.

1. Preheat the oven to 400°.

2. Make the ranchero cilantro drizzle: Process all the ingredients in a blender or food processor until smooth. Cover and refrigerate.

3. Make the chicken filling: Heat the oil in a 10-inch cast iron skillet over medium heat. Add the onion, bell pepper, and jalapeño; cook, stirring frequently, until the vegetables are tender, 3 to 5 minutes. Stir in the chicken, cilantro, salt, cumin, pepper, and tomatoes with chiles; cook 5 minutes. Transfer the mixture from the skillet to a large bowl. Wipe out the skillet with paper towels; grease.

4. Make the crust: Combine the beaten egg, cornbread mix, and milk in a bowl; mix well. Place the tortilla chips in the prepared skillet, spreading them evenly over the bottom. Pour the batter over the chips. Spoon the chicken mixture over the batter; sprinkle with the cheeses.

5. Bake until golden brown, 16 to 20 minutes. Cut into wedges. Serve topped with the romaine and tomatoes and drizzled with the dressing.

Diane Sparrow of Osage, Iowa, used spicy hot Buffalo chicken wings as her inspiration for this 2002 grand winner at the National Cornbread Cook-off.

BUFFALO CHICKEN CORNBREAD WITH BLUE CHEESE MAYONNAISE

serves 6

1½ pounds chicken breast tenders, cut into 1½-inch pieces, if desired	3 tablespoons butter
⅓ cup Louisiana-style hot sauce	½ cup chopped red onion
½ cup mayonnaise	⅔ cup chopped celery
¼ cup plain yogurt	1 (6-ounce) package Martha White Cotton Country Cornbread Mix
2 ounces blue cheese, crumbled	½ cup milk
2 teaspoons fresh lemon juice	1 large egg
½ teaspoon salt	

1. Preheat the oven to 425°. Combine the chicken and hot sauce in a medium bowl, tossing to coat. Marinate at room temperature 20 minutes.

2. Stir together the mayonnaise, yogurt, blue cheese, lemon juice, and salt in a small bowl; mix well. Cover and refrigerate until ready to serve.

3. Melt 1 tablespoon butter in a 10½-inch cast iron skillet over medium heat. Cook the onion and celery in the butter, stirring often, until tender. Remove the vegetable mixture from the skillet.

4. Melt the remaining 2 tablespoons butter in the same skillet over medium heat. Add the chicken and its marinade. Cook, stirring frequently, 5 minutes. Reduce the heat to low while preparing the topping.

5. Combine the vegetable mixture, cornbread mix, milk, and egg in a medium bowl; mix well. Spoon evenly over the chicken mixture in the skillet.

6. Bake until the topping is golden brown and set, 15 to 20 minutes. Cut into wedges and top each serving with a dollop of the blue cheese mayonnaise.

You can enjoy this casserole, the National Cornbread Cook-off 2006 first-place winner from Janice Elder of Charlotte, North Carolina, as a part of a brunch or for dinner.

MONTE CRISTO CORNBREAD SKILLET SUPPER

serves 4

1 (6-ounce) package Martha White Cotton Country Cornbread Mix
¾ cup water
1½ cups chopped cooked turkey
½ cup chopped cooked ham
1½ cups (6 ounces) shredded Swiss cheese
4 large eggs
1 cup milk
2 tablespoons mayonnaise
2 tablespoons honey mustard
1½ teaspoons salt
½ teaspoon freshly ground black pepper
½ cup currant jelly
Confectioners' sugar

1. Preheat the oven to 450°. Following the package directions, combine the cornbread mix and water in a medium bowl and pour into a 10½-inch cast iron skillet. Bake for 15 to 20 minutes (the cornbread will be thin). Remove the cornbread from the skillet; cool and cut into cubes. Wipe out the skillet with paper towels; spray generously with nonstick cooking spray.

2. Reduce the oven temperature to 350°.

3. Place the cornbread cubes in the prepared skillet. Top with the turkey, ham, and cheese. In a medium bowl, whisk together the eggs, milk, mayonnaise, 1 tablespoon mustard, the salt, and pepper until well blended. Pour evenly over the ingredients in the skillet. Bake until set and lightly browned, 30 to 35 minutes.

4. Melt the jelly in a small saucepan over very low heat. Whisk in the remaining 1 tablespoon mustard to blend.

5. Remove the skillet from the oven. Cut cornbread mixture into wedges; sprinkle with the confectioners' sugar and serve with the honey mustard-currant sauce.

Two-time National Cornbread Cook-off winner Lori Stephens of Hendersonville, Tennessee, won in 2010 with her over-the-top version of sliders.

BACON AND GORGONZOLA CORNBREAD SLIDERS WITH CHIPOTLE MAYO

serves 6 (2 sliders each)

Slider Buns:

2 (6½-ounce) packages Martha White Yellow Cornbread Mix
½ cup Martha White all-purpose flour
1½ cups milk
¼ cup sour cream
1 large egg
3 tablespoons chopped fresh chives
8 bacon slices, cooked until crisp and crumbled
¾ cup crumbled Gorgonzola cheese

Chipotle Mayo:

½ cup mayonnaise

1 canned chipotle chile in adobo sauce, chopped, with 1 teaspoon sauce

Burgers:

2 tablespoons butter
1 medium yellow onion, cut into thin rings
1½ pounds ground chuck
1 large egg
½ cup Italian-style breadcrumbs
2 garlic cloves, minced
1 teaspoon salt
½ teaspoon freshly ground black pepper
12 thin slices Cheddar cheese, (½ ounce each)

1. Make the buns: Preheat the oven to 400°. Lightly grease 2 cast iron straight-sided muffin pans (6 cups each) with nonstick cooking spray. Stir together the cornbread mix, flour, milk, sour cream, and egg in a large bowl until well blended. Stir in the chives, crumbled bacon, and cheese. Fill each of the wells in the prepared muffin pans three-quarters full. Bake until golden brown, 10 to 12 minutes. (Any remaining batter can be made into additional muffins.)

2. Make the chipotle mayo: Combine the mayonnaise, chipotle, and adobo sauce in a small bowl until well blended. Set aside.

3. Make the burgers: Melt the butter in a 12-inch cast iron skillet over medium-low heat. Add the onion rings and cook, stirring occasionally, until softened, 8 to 10 minutes. Remove from the skillet; wipe the skillet clean.

4. Combine the ground chuck, egg, breadcrumbs, garlic, salt, and pepper in a large bowl. Blend well. Divide into 12 equal portions. Pat out into thin burgers. Heat the skillet over medium to medium-high

heat until hot. Cook the burgers, in batches, to desired degree of
doneness. Top each burger with a slice of cheese.

5. To serve, slice the cornbread muffins to make buns. Spread a
thin layer of the Chipotle Mayo on the tops and bottoms. Place
a burger on each bottom half. Top with onion rings. Place the
tops on the burgers and serve.

Fran Pickens of Hendersonville, Tennessee, took home first-place honors at the National Cornbread Cook-off in 2001 with this spicy entry.

UPSIDE-DOWN SALSA CORNBREAD

serves 6

Filling:

1   tablespoon vegetable oil
1   pound lean ground beef
½   cup chopped onion
1   teaspoon chili powder
1   teaspoon salt
½   teaspoon garlic salt
1   medium green or red bell
    pepper, seeded and cut
    into rings

Topping:

2   cups Martha White
    Buttermilk Self-Rising Corn
    Meal Mix
1   cup (4 ounces) shredded
    Cheddar cheese
1   tablespoon sugar
1   (16-ounce) jar chunky-style
    salsa
1¼ cups milk
3   tablespoons vegetable oil
1   large egg, lightly beaten

1. Preheat the oven to 425°.

2. Make the filling: Heat the oil in a 10½-inch cast iron skillet over medium heat until hot. Add the ground beef, onion, chili powder, salt, and garlic salt; cook until the beef is no longer pink, stirring frequently and breaking up any clumps of meat. Remove the beef mixture from the skillet to a bowl. Place the bell pepper rings in a single layer in the bottom of the skillet. Spoon the beef mixture over the rings.

3. Make the topping: Stir together the corn meal mix, cheese, sugar, salsa, milk, oil, and egg in a medium bowl; stir until well blended. Spread the batter evenly over the beef mixture in the skillet. Bake until golden brown, 32 to 38 minutes.

4. Place a serving plate over the skillet; carefully invert and remove the skillet. Cut into wedges. If desired, this can be served from the skillet: Cut into wedges and carefully turn each wedge upside down onto a serving plate.

Enjoy this dish, the 1999 first-place winner of the National Cornbread Cook-off from Janice Carver of Bartlett, Tennessee, for dinner or as a hot lunch.

REUBEN CASSEROLE WITH CORNBREAD

serves 6 to 8

Filling:

2   (10-ounce) cans sauerkraut, drained and rinsed

2   ripe medium tomatoes, cored and thinly sliced

⅓   cup Thousand Island dressing

1   (2¼-ounce) can sliced ripe olives, drained

6   ounces sliced corned beef, shredded

1½ cups (6 ounces) shredded Swiss cheese

Crust:

1   large egg

1   cup buttermilk

⅓   cup milk

3   tablespoons vegetable oil

1   cup Martha White Self-Rising White Corn Meal Mix

⅓   cup Martha White self-rising flour

1   tablespoon sugar

Mustard Sauce:

½   cup mayonnaise

½   cup prepared mustard of your choice

1   teaspoon finely chopped onion

1. Preheat the oven to 425°. Layer the sauerkraut, tomatoes, dressing, olives, and corned beef in a 10½-inch cast iron skillet. Top with the cheese. Set aside.

2. Make the crust: Beat the egg in a medium bowl. Whisk in the buttermilk, milk, and oil; mix well. Add the corn meal mix, flour, and sugar; stir until smooth. Pour the batter evenly over the filling in the skillet. Bake until golden brown, 30 to 35 minutes.

3. Make the mustard sauce: Combine the mayonnaise, mustard, and onion in a small bowl; stir to blend.

4. Cut the casserole into wedges and serve with the mustard sauce.

Start your new year right with black-eyed peas for good luck, as well as collards for a dose of good health, with this 1998 National Cornbread Cook-off first-place winner from Karen Shankles of Knoxville, Tennessee.

FESTIVE GOOD LUCK CORNBREAD SKILLET

serves 8

Filling:

1   pound smoked sausage
½   cup chopped onion
1   to 2 garlic cloves, minced
2   (15-ounce) cans black-eyed peas, drained
1   (14½-ounce) can reduced-sodium fat-free chicken broth
1   (10-ounce) package frozen chopped collard or turnip greens, thawed and squeezed dry
½   teaspoon hot pepper sauce

Topping:

1   cup Martha White Self-Rising White Corn Meal Mix

2   teaspoons sugar
¾   cup buttermilk
¼   cup vegetable oil
1   large egg, lightly beaten
1   cup (4 ounces) shredded Cheddar cheese
¼   cup finely chopped fresh parsley or cilantro

Garnishes (optional):

Sour cream, pickled jalapeño chile slices, and/or fresh parsley or cilantro leaves

1. Preheat the oven to 400°.

2. Making the filling: Cut the sausage in half lengthwise; cut crosswise into ¼-inch-thick slices. Combine the sausage, onion, and garlic in a 12-inch cast iron skillet; cook over medium-high heat until the sausage is browned and the onion is softened, stirring occasionally. Add the black-eyed peas, broth, greens, and hot pepper sauce; mix well. Bring to a boil. Reduce the heat to low and simmer 10 minutes.

3. Make the topping: Combine the topping ingredients in a large bowl, stirring until blended. Pour the batter just around the edge of the sausage mixture in the skillet. Bake until the topping is golden brown, 30 to 35 minutes.

4. Serve with desired garnishes.

Valerie Watts Holt of Euharlee, Georgia, won first-place honors at the National Cornbread Cook-off in 2004 with this skillet full of Southern comfort.

THE CRESCENT CITY SKILLET

serves 6

1 tablespoon vegetable oil
½ pound bulk ground hot pork sausage
1 cup chopped sweet onion
½ cup chicken broth
1 cup heavy cream
½ teaspoon minced garlic
⅔ cup (2½ ounces) shredded Monterey Jack cheese
¼ cup grated Parmesan cheese
15 medium shrimp, peeled, deveined, and tails removed

1 (6-ounce) package Martha White Buttermilk Cornbread Mix
⅔ cup milk

Toppings (optional):
Sour cream, chopped fresh cilantro and parsley, and seeded and chopped tomatoes

1. Preheat the oven to 425°.

2. Heat the oil in a 10-inch cast iron skillet over medium heat. Cook the sausage and onion, stirring occasionally, until the sausage crumbles and is no longer pink, 5 to 7 minutes. Drain the mixture on paper towels and return to the skillet. Do not wipe the skillet clean.

3. Add the broth, cream, garlic, and both cheeses to the skillet. Reduce the heat to medium-low (do not allow the mixture to boil). Stir until the cheeses are melted. Add the shrimp, spreading them evenly over the mixture.

4. Stir together the cornbread mix and milk in a small bowl until blended. Pour the batter evenly over the mixture in the skillet (the crust will rise to the top as it bakes). Bake until the cornbread is light golden brown, 18 to 20 minutes.

5. Serve with desired toppings.

ANCHO SHRIMP ON SMOKED GOUDA CORNCAKES

serves 6

Smoked Gouda Corncakes:

1 tablespoon butter

⅓ cup sliced green onions

1 cup fresh or frozen corn kernels

1 large egg

1 cup buttermilk

3 tablespoons sour cream

1⅓ cups Martha White Self-Rising Yellow Corn Meal Mix

1½ cups (6 ounces) shredded smoked Gouda cheese

½ cup canola oil

Ancho Shrimp:

¼ cup (½ stick) butter

2 large ancho chiles, split in half and seeded

1 tablespoon minced garlic

1 pound shrimp, peeled and deveined

Salt and freshly ground black pepper

1 cup canned petite diced tomatoes, undrained

Sliced green onions (green part only)

Lori Stephens of Hendersonville, Tennessee, won first-place honors at the National Cornbread Cook-off in 2008 with this delicious combination of spicy shrimp served over cheesy, crispy corncakes.

ancho chiles

The ancho chile, which is a dried poblano, is a red, heart-shaped pod and has a mild, earthy flavor. If the dried chiles are unavailable, add 1 teaspoon ground ancho chile powder (available in the spice section) with the salt and pepper.

1. Make the smoked gouda corncakes: Melt the butter in a 10-inch cast iron skillet over medium heat. Add the green onions; cook 1 minute. Add the corn; cook 2 minutes.

2. In a large bowl, whisk the egg. Add the buttermilk, sour cream, and corn meal mix, whisking until blended. Stir in the cheese and onion mixture.

3. Wipe out the skillet with a paper towel. Add ¼ cup oil; heat over medium-high heat. Spoon the batter by ¼ cupfuls into the hot oil. Cook until golden brown; turn and brown the other side. Remove the cakes to drain on paper towels. Cook, in batches, adding more of the remaining oil as needed. Wipe the skillet clean.

4. Make the ancho shrimp: Melt the butter in the skillet over medium-high heat. Add the chiles; cook 3 minutes. Add the garlic; cook 1 minute. Add the shrimp; season with salt and pepper to taste. Cook, stirring occasionally, just until the shrimp turn pink. Stir in the tomatoes; cook just until hot. Remove the chiles.

5. To serve, place 2 corncakes slightly overlapping on each plate. Top with shrimp and sauce; sprinkle with sliced green onions.

Kay Gay and Helen Hollansworth, both of Gulf Shores, Alabama, served up a first-place winner at the National Cornbread Cook-off in 2000 with this hearty combination of shrimp, bacon, spinach, and Cheddar cheese.

CORNBREAD SUPREME WITH SHRIMP

serves 8

3 thick bacon slices
4 large eggs
¼ cup milk
½ cup (1 stick) butter, melted and cooled
1 (6-ounce) package Martha White Buttermilk or Cotton Country Cornbread Mix
6 dashes of hot pepper sauce
1 medium onion, chopped
1 (10-ounce) package frozen chopped spinach or chopped broccoli, thawed and drained well

1 pound shrimp, peeled, deveined, and coarsely chopped
2 cups (8 ounces) finely shredded sharp Cheddar cheese
Chopped fresh parsley for garnish

1. Preheat the oven to 375°. Cook the bacon in a 10½-inch cast iron skillet over medium-high heat until crisp. Remove to paper towels to drain; crumble and set aside.

2. Transfer 1 tablespoon of the bacon drippings to a small bowl. Drain off the remaining drippings from the skillet and discard. Wipe the skillet clean, then return the reserved drippings to the skillet. Place in the oven to heat.

3. Beat the eggs in a large bowl. Add the milk, melted butter, cornbread mix, and hot pepper sauce, stirring until blended. Stir in the onion, spinach, shrimp, and 1½ cups cheese. Carefully remove the skillet from the oven. Pour the batter into the hot skillet. Sprinkle the remaining ½ cup cheese over the top.

4. Bake until set and golden brown, 30 to 35 minutes. Remove from the oven and let rest 5 to 10 minutes in the skillet on a wire rack. Sprinkle with the bacon and parsley, if desired; cut into wedges and serve.

DESSERTS, BISCUITS & BREADS

Dessert in cast iron? You bet! It cooks cakes and pies into crisp, caramelized goodness. And biscuits, rolls and breads develop a golden brown crust that just can't be beat.

Lifestyle expert Ross Sveback developed this recipe especially for use with the Lodge Drop Biscuit Pan. "I love the combination of lemon and lavender," Ross says. He suggests splitting the pound cakes open, filling them with fresh berries, and topping with lightly whipped cream, as you would shortcakes. If you don't grow your own lavender, you can purchase culinary lavender from Dean & Deluca at *deandeluca.com*.

LEMON-LAVENDER POUND CAKES

makes 7 individual pound cakes

2 lemons	½ cup (1 stick) unsalted butter, at room temperature
1½ cups sugar, preferably superfine	3 large eggs
1½ cups cake flour (whisk it first before measuring to "sift" it)	½ cup sour cream (regular, not light), at room temperature
¼ teaspoon baking soda	1 teaspoon lemon extract (not lemon oil)
¼ teaspoon salt	
2 tablespoons dried lavender buds	Lavender sprigs for garnish

1. Preheat the oven to 325°. Prepare a Lodge Drop Biscuit Pan by coating it with cooking spray and lightly flouring it (Ross uses Bak-klene, a nonstick spray that contains starch, so you can skip the flouring part).

2. Zest the lemons and place zest in a large bowl with the sugar. Juice the lemons into a liquid measuring cup.

3. Combine the flour, baking soda, salt, and lavender buds in a medium bowl.

4. Add the butter to the sugar. Using an electric mixer on medium speed, cream them together, making sure to scrape down the bowl so that it is fully combined. Add the eggs, one at a time, beating well after each addition. Reduce speed to low and add the dry ingredients all at once, beating until well blended. Add the sour cream, lemon extract, and lemon juice, beating until blended.

5. Divide the batter between the wells of the prepared biscuit pan and bake until a wooden pick inserted in the center of each comes out clean, 20 to 25 minutes. Let the cakes cool in the pan on a wire rack for 5 minutes. Remove the cakes from the pan, and place on the rack until you are ready to serve. Garnish with lavender, if you like.

PINEAPPLE UPSIDE-DOWN CAKES ONE BY ONE

serves 7   *(pictured on page 252)*

Pineapple upside-down cake is a sentimental favorite for many people. Although it's possible to use fresh pineapple and cherries, there is something comforting and familiar about using canned pineapple and bright red maraschino cherries from a jar, just like Mom used to.

Upside-down cake is a classic use of a trusty cast iron skillet, but in this recipe food writer and cooking teacher Sheri Castle uses the Lodge Drop Biscuit Pan to create small, individual cakes that will make each guest feel special. The small cakes also ensure plenty of the buttery sweet topping and pineapple in each bite.

Topping:

3½ tablespoons butter

14 tablespoons light brown sugar

7 canned pineapple slices, drained (from a 20-ounce can)

7 maraschino cherries, drained

Cake:

¼ cup all-purpose flour

1 teaspoon baking powder

⅛ teaspoon salt

¼ teaspoon ground cardamom

¼ teaspoon ground cinnamon

¼ cup whole milk

½ teaspoon vanilla extract

1 tablespoon dark rum or additional milk

2 tablespoons butter, at room temperature

⅓ cup granulated sugar

1 large egg

1. Preheat the oven to 350°.

2. Make the topping: Place ½ tablespoon butter in each cup of a Lodge Drop Biscuit Pan. Place in the oven to melt. Once melted, sprinkle 2 tablespoons brown sugar in the bottom of each cup. Place a pineapple ring in each cup and a cherry in the center of each ring. Set aside.

3. Make the cake batter: Whisk together the flour, baking powder, salt, cardamom, and cinnamon in a small bowl.

4. Whisk together the milk, vanilla, and rum in a small bowl.

5. In a large bowl, using an electric mixer on high speed, beat the butter until creamy. Reduce speed to low and gradually add the granulated sugar. Increase the speed to high and beat until the mixture is light and fluffy, about 5 minutes. Add the egg and beat well. Add half the flour mixture and beat at low speed until blended. Add the milk mixture and beat until smooth. Add the remaining flour mixture and beat until smooth. Increase the speed to high and beat for 1 minute, stopping once to scrape down the side of the bowl with a rubber spatula.

6. Gently spoon the batter into the cups of the pan, taking care to keep the pineapple rings centered. Bake until the cakes are golden brown and spring back when touched lightly in the center, 20 to 25 minutes.

7. Place the pan on a wire rack to cool for 5 minutes. Run a thin knife around the edge of each cup to loosen. Carefully invert the pan onto a large plate. (Place the plate over the pan, hold them tightly together, flip them over together, and lift off the pan.) Replace any bits of the sticky glaze that might stick to the pan. Serve warm or at room temperature.

a cast iron memory

Some people are born with a silver spoon in their mouths. I was born with a cast iron skillet in my hand.

Daily reliance on a steadfast black skillet is among the very few practices that involve both of my grandmothers—the one I know only through other people's reminiscences and the one who mostly raised me.

The one I never got to know raised 11 children on a hardscrabble farm that straddled the banks of the New River high in the Blue Ridge Mountains of western North Carolina. Each time one of her children married, whether son or daughter, she sent them off with a cast iron skillet that she had seasoned into a gleaming ebony showpiece by using it daily until it was just right. The day after one wedding, she took on the skillet intended for the next.

My other grandmother was my best friend, and we were foolish over each other, sharing a love of cooking, reading, and laughing. For the most part, I did no wrong in her eyes. Except for the day that I (with the best of intentions) ran her good skillet through the new dishwasher we had installed in her kitchen. That did neither the skillet nor me any favors. She just stared at it. After an extended, tedious silence, she set the pitiful skillet on the counter and went outside onto the porch and fanned her face with her apron. When she came back inside, all she said was, "That didn't work. Don't do that again. Ever." Once she restored the skillet to serviceability, we resumed washing it by hand along with the other special dishes.

Over the years I have amassed upwards of 50 pieces of cast iron. Some are task-specific, such as the cornbread skillet I inherited from my Aunt Jean that has never been used for anything else. (She left me two things: a fancy ring and a good skillet. I've since learned that the ring is not genuine. The skillet is.)

Cast iron asks only to be used regularly and well. In exchange, it will hang on for generations and do what it's meant to do—make a meal or a memory worth sharing.   —Sheri Castle

BLUEBERRY-GINGER-PEACH UPSIDE-DOWN CAKE WITH GINGER WHIPPED CREAM

makes one 10-inch cake; serves 8 to 10

Prizewinning cookbook author of *A Piece of Cake, The Perfect Cake,* and *Pie in the Sky*, Susan G. Purdy has never forgotten the thrill she felt as a child watching her mother invert an upside-down cake to show its dramatic "face."

Upside-down cake is traditionally prepared in a cast iron skillet so the fruit-topping glaze can be started on the stove before the cake batter is added and the whole thing placed in the oven to bake. Your family and friends will love the drama as well as the bright ginger flavor of this easy-to-make home-style dessert; serve it at room temperature or slightly warm, with the Ginger Whipped Cream or a dollop of vanilla ice cream or yogurt.

Fruit Topping:

⅓ cup unsalted butter, cut up

⅛ teaspoon salt

1 cup firmly packed light or dark brown sugar (see Note on page 259)

½ teaspoon ground nutmeg

¼ teaspoon ground ginger

¼ teaspoon grated peeled fresh ginger (or more to taste)

4 to 5 medium to large peaches (about 4 ounces each), peeled, halved, and pitted

1 cup fresh or frozen blueberries, picked over for stems (fresh berries should be rinsed and patted dry on paper towels)

Cake:

1½ cups sifted all-purpose flour

1 teaspoon baking powder

¼ teaspoon baking soda

⅛ teaspoon salt

½ teaspoon ground cinnamon

½ teaspoon ground nutmeg

¼ teaspoon ground ginger

⅓ cup unsalted butter, at room temperature

½ cup granulated sugar

¼ cup honey or pure maple syrup

½ teaspoon grated peeled fresh ginger

1 teaspoon vanilla extract

2 large eggs, at room temperature

⅓ cup milk

Ginger Whipped Cream *(optional)*:

1 cup heavy cream, chilled

2 tablespoons granulated sugar

½ teaspoon vanilla extract

½ teaspoon ground ginger

2 tablespoons finely minced crystallized candied ginger *(optional)*

1. Position a rack in the center of the oven and preheat to 350°.

2. Make the fruit topping: Place a 10-inch cast iron skillet over medium-low heat and, with a wooden spoon, stir together the butter, salt, brown sugar, nutmeg, ground ginger, and fresh ginger. Allow the mixture to melt together until creamy and bubbling lightly, 3 to 4 minutes; remove the pan from the heat.

3. While the glaze cooks and cools, cut each peach half into 4 to 6 wedges, depending on its size. Arrange the slices in the pan, placing them side by side in a ring around the outer edge of the pan; the sides of the slices should touch each other, with the tips pointed to the center of the pan. In the middle, make a ring with 5 or 6 peach slices placed end to end. Fill the space in the middle of this ring with about two-thirds of the blueberries, piled up (like the center of a flower). Use the remaining berries to make a ring around the outer edge of the pan, just at the tips of the peach slices; scatter any remaining berries between the tips of the peach slices all over. Gently push the berries down through the glaze so they touch the pan bottom. Remember that the "face" of your cake is on the bottom of the pan, and what you're looking at now will be covered with cake batter.

4. Make the cake batter: Whisk together the sifted flour, baking powder, baking soda, salt, cinnamon, nutmeg, and ground ginger. In a large bowl, using an electric mixer, cream together the butter and granulated sugar, then beat in the honey, fresh ginger, and vanilla. Add the eggs, one at a time, beating well after each addition. Reduce speed to low and add the flour mixture alternately with the milk, beginning and ending with flour mixture; scrape down the side of the bowl and beat until well blended.

5. Spoon the batter over the fruit in the skillet, taking care not to disturb the arrangement; spread the batter more or less flat to the edge of the pan. Place the skillet in the oven and bake until the top of the cake is a rich golden color and springy to the touch and a wooden pick inserted in the center comes out clean, 35 to 40 minutes. Cool the cake on a wire rack until the glaze stops bubbling but is still warm, 3 to 4 minutes.

6. Top the skillet with a serving platter and, holding them together with potholders (the pan will still be hot), invert. Lift off the skillet. Reposition any bits of fruit that may have stuck to the skillet. Serve the cake while still warm so the glaze will be soft and slightly runny, or serve at room temperature.

7. If desired, prepare the ginger whipped cream: In a chilled bowl using chilled beaters, whip the cream until soft peaks begin to form. Add the granulated sugar, vanilla, and ground ginger, and whip just a little longer until stiff peaks begin to form; fold in the candied ginger, if desired. Serve.

note

Light brown sugar results in a lighter colored topping; dark brown sugar will taste equally good but will darken the color of the cake top. Also, you can substitute fresh or frozen whole raspberries or other berries for the blueberries, and apricots or nectarines for the peaches.

Bri Malaspino, Creative Manager at Lodge, submitted this recipe on behalf of her mother, Linda Egeto. Linda, an RN from Murfreesboro, Tennessee, created this recipe to avert a Thanksgiving-near-tragedy.

a cast iron memory

I started making this pie years ago. It was the night before Thanksgiving, and we had invited people over for Thanksgiving dinner. I underestimated the number of apples needed to make the pie. At the time, we lived on Cape Cod, and back then everything closed early. So running out to the store the night before Thanksgiving for more apples was not an option. I remember thinking, "what else could go wrong?" So I did what my mom always did–I made a cup of tea. While drinking my tea, I remembered a neighbor had brought me some cranberry apple salad, and thought about how good it was. Cranberries are a major local crop of Cape Cod so I made a point to stock up on cranberries and freeze them to enjoy throughout the year. I had plenty on hand, so I decided to add some cranberries to the apple pie. Everyone loved it so much— and that's how a tradition began.

—Linda Egeto

CRANBERRY APPLE PIE

serves 8

1 tablespoon butter	1 cup sugar (more or less, depending on apple sweetness)
½ teaspoon grated orange zest	
½ teaspoon ground cinnamon	
¼ teaspoon ground nutmeg	5 to 6 tablespoons coarsely chopped pecans
3 pounds Granny Smith or other tart apples, peeled, cored, and thinly sliced	3 to 4 tablespoons all-purpose flour
1½ cups frozen cranberries	Nana Hirl's Pie Crust (see recipe)

1. Preheat the oven to 425°.

2. Melt the butter in a 10-inch cast iron skillet over medium heat. Add the orange zest, cinnamon, and nutmeg; mix well with a wooden spoon. Add the apples and cranberries, stirring to combine.

3. Combine sugar, pecans, and flour; add to apple mixture, stirring to combine. Spoon apple mixture into Nana Hirl's pie crust (in a 10-inch cast iron skillet), packing tightly and mounding in center. Roll out remaining disk to ⅛-inch thickness and gently place over filling; fold edges under and crimp, sealing to bottom crust. Place pie on a jelly-roll pan. Cut 4 or 5 slits in top of pie for steam to escape.

4. Bake at 425° for 15 minutes; reduce oven temperature to 350° and bake until crust is golden, 45 to 55 minutes. Transfer to a wire rack and cool 1½ to 2 hours before serving.

NANA HIRL'S PIE CRUST

makes 1 double pie crust

4 cups all-purpose flour	1 cup (2 sticks) cold unsalted butter, cut in ¼-inch pieces
2 cups cake flour	
2 tablespoons sugar	2 teaspoons white vinegar
2 teaspoons salt	1 cup ice water (use only 12 to 14 tablespoons water)
1 cup cold lard or vegetable shortening	

1. Process both flours, sugar, and salt in a food processor until combined. Add lard and pulse until mixture resembles coarse cornmeal, 5 to 6 times. Add butter and pulse 5 to 6 times, until it's pea-size. Place in a bowl, cover with plastic wrap, and chill 1 to 2 hours.

2. Remove mixture from refrigerator. Gently toss mixture with a fork. Add the vinegar, then the water, a tablespoon at a time; mix just until dry ingredients are moistened and the dough comes together and forms a ball. Gently gather dough into 2 disks and wrap in plastic wrap. Chill 1 to 2 hours.

3. On a floured surface, using a floured rolling pin, roll 1 dough disk to ⅛-inch thickness (about 11 inches wide). Gently press dough into a 10-inch cast iron skillet, allowing excess pastry to hang over edges. (Do not stretch dough or it will shrink during baking.) Proceed with recipe in step 3 as directed on page 260.

BLUEBERRY-PEACH SKILLET PIE

serves 6

Cookbook author and baking expert Julie Hasson loves using her cast iron skillet to bake pie—there's something satisfyingly old-fashioned about it. This pie has no bottom crust, which makes it quick to prepare, perfect for a last-minute dessert. Try it topped with a scoop of ice cream.

Filling:

5 cups frozen blueberries (don't thaw)
⅔ cup granulated sugar
¼ cup plus ⅔ cup water
¼ cup cornstarch
Grated zest from 1 lemon
2 ripe medium peaches, peeled, pitted, and sliced

Topping:

¼ cup unbleached all-purpose flour
½ cup old-fashioned rolled oats (don't use quick cooking)
½ cup firmly packed light brown sugar
1 teaspoon freshly grated nutmeg
¼ cup nonhydrogenated margarine (such as Earth Balance), melted
Ice cream for serving (optional)

1. Preheat the oven to 400°. Lightly grease a 10-inch cast iron skillet with a little shortening.

2. Make the filling: In a large saucepan, combine the blueberries, granulated sugar, and ¼ cup water. Bring to a simmer over medium heat, stirring occasionally.

3. Whisk together the cornstarch and remaining ⅔ cup water in a small bowl until smooth. Stir the cornstarch mixture into the hot berries. Gently stir in the lemon zest and peaches, being careful not to mash the peaches. Reduce the heat to low and continue simmering the fruit, gently stirring, until the juices have thickened and the mixture is clear. Remove the saucepan from the heat and scoop the mixture into the prepared skillet.

4. Make the topping: Stir together the flour, oats, brown sugar, and nutmeg in a small bowl. Add the melted margarine, stirring until incorporated. Using your fingertips, work the margarine into the flour mixture, squeezing until nice and crumbly. Sprinkle the topping over the blueberry filling.

5. Bake the pie just until the topping is nicely browned, 30 to 40 minutes. Serve with ice cream, if you like.

Variation: For an all-blueberry version, omit the peaches and increase the blueberries to 6 cups.

You need to set aside some time to make this classic French upside-down tart, but food editor and cookbook author Martha Holmberg assures you that your efforts will be rewarded with a stunning dessert that's at once homey and elegant—and very much like what you would find in a traditional Parisian bistro.

WORTH-THE-EFFORT TARTE TATIN

serves 8 to 10

Pâte Brisée:

1½ cups unbleached all-purpose flour

3 tablespoons sugar

½ teaspoon kosher salt

5 tablespoons cold unsalted butter, cut into small cubes

1 large egg yolk

½ teaspoon vanilla extract

2 to 3 tablespoons ice water

Filling:

7 tablespoons unsalted butter

¾ cup sugar

⅛ teaspoon kosher salt

5 to 6 pounds tart apples, peeled, cored, and halved (Braeburn and Jonagold work well)

Crème fraîche or vanilla ice cream for serving

1. Make the pâte brisée: Pulse the flour, sugar, and salt in a food processor until blended. Add the butter and pulse until the mixture looks like fine meal. Whisk together the egg yolk, vanilla, and 2 tablespoons water in a small bowl. Pour over the flour mixture and pulse for a few seconds until the dough pulls together; add a little more water, if needed. Turn the dough out onto a lightly floured surface and knead it with the heel of your hand, pushing it away from you and then gathering it up with a dough scraper until the dough is very pliable. Press the dough into a ball, cover with plastic wrap, and chill until firm, 15 to 30 minutes.

2. Make the filling: Place the butter, sugar, and salt in a 10-inch cast iron skillet over medium heat. Cook until the butter melts and the sugar begins to melt around the edges. Stir gently with a wooden spoon to help the sugar melt completely. Reduce heat to medium-low; leave the mixture alone until it reaches a deep mahogany-colored caramel. Check the doneness of the caramel by lifting out some with a spoon to check the color. (The butter will pool on the top of the caramel, which is fine.) As soon as the caramel is the right color, remove skillet from heat. Set aside.

3. Set aside 4 apple halves and place the remaining halves in the skillet in concentric circles, standing them upright on their narrowest end and packing them in as tightly as possible (they'll shrink as they cook).

4. Place the skillet back on medium heat and increase heat to medium-high as the apples start to give off their juices—the liquid should bubble gently. Rotate the skillet occasionally in case there are any hot spots. If you start to smell burnt sugar, immediately turn down the heat. When the bottom halves of the apples are caramelized and slightly tender, flip each one over with a fork and continue cooking.

5. You'll probably have a lot of juice in the skillet at this point and the apples will have shrunk and be slumping a bit. Carefully take the skillet off the heat and, holding the apples back with a spatula, pour off ½ to 1 cup of caramel and juice into a small saucepan (pour off more if necessary; you should have about an inch of liquid left in the skillet). Return the skillet to the heat and continue cooking. Add the 4 reserved apple halves to the caramel in the saucepan and cook over medium-high heat until they're caramelized, about 10 minutes, turning them as necessary.

6. With a rubber spatula or a wooden spoon, slide the apples in the skillet together, so they're tightly packed and standing up; there will be gaps. Holding them in position, slide a reserved apple half from the saucepan, wider end down, into a gap; repeat with as many apple halves as will fit nicely. Reserve the juice in the saucepan. Continue cooking the apples in the skillet until they're tender and thoroughly caramelized, adding another apple half, if necessary. The total cooking time should take 35 minutes or more.

7. Remove the skillet from the heat and let everything cool to room temperature. If there's more than about ½ inch of liquid remaining in the skillet, carefully pour the excess into the small saucepan.

8. Preheat the oven to 375°. Roll the chilled pastry dough into a round about 1 inch larger than the skillet; the dough should be about ⅛-inch thick. Transfer the dough to the skillet, gently draping it over the apples. Tuck the edge of the dough under to make a rim. Put skillet on a baking sheet to catch any overflowing juices; bake until the crust is a deep golden brown and looks crisp, about 25 minutes.

9. Take the tarte out of the oven and cool for about 15 minutes. Invert a large plate on top of the skillet, flip the skillet and plate over in one quick move, and lift off the skillet. If you like, simmer the reserved caramel and juices until thick and syrupy and spoon over the finished tarte. Serve warm or at room temperature with a dollop of crème fraîche or vanilla ice cream.

crazy for cast iron

When I married my husband, I had quite a lot of good cooking equipment that I had acquired during three years in France, where I had gone to study cooking and had stayed to practice what I had learned. One of the pieces I had brought back was a copper tarte tatin pan, which looked gorgeous on my shelf, but frankly wasn't that practical to use because it didn't have a handle.

My husband had been a long-time bachelor when we got together, so he had some kitchenware, too, including a 10-inch cast iron skillet that he had gotten from a landlady in Raleigh, North Carolina—that seemed to me a pretty good pedigree for a skillet, and an excellent dowry item!

I still love my French wood-handled boning knives and copper saucepans, but the cast iron skillet gets just as much use—and it's definitely the pan I now use for my tarte tatin.   —Martha Holmberg

RUSTIC SPICED PEACH TART WITH ALMOND PASTRY

makes one (10-inch) tart

When peaches are ripe and juicy, this divine tart from Christy Rost, cookbook author and host of the public television series *A Home for Christy Rost*, goes together quickly and looks fabulous in a cast iron skillet—perfect for your next picnic or casual gathering. A dash of Saigon cinnamon in the filling imparts a delicate, spicy flavor to the fruit. Purists may want to peel the peaches first, but leaving the skin on saves preparation time, adds extra nutrition and texture, and provides a homey note to this spectacular dessert.

Pastry:

⅓ cup sliced almonds

1½ cups all-purpose flour

1 tablespoon granulated sugar

¼ teaspoon salt

½ cup (1 stick) cold unsalted butter, cut into 8 pieces

3 to 4 tablespoons ice water

¼ teaspoon almond extract

Filling:

8 to 9 large peaches (about 2¼ pounds), pitted and sliced about ½ inch thick

¾ cup granulated sugar

1½ tablespoons cornstarch

¼ teaspoon ground Saigon cinnamon

1 large egg

1 tablespoon water

1 tablespoon turbinado or granulated sugar for garnish

1. Toast the almonds: Preheat the oven to 300°. Scatter the almonds in a single layer on a baking sheet and bake, stirring occasionally, until golden brown, about 15 minutes. Remove from the oven and cool completely.

2. Make the pastry: Process the almonds in a blender or food processor until finely chopped. Add the flour, granulated sugar, and salt and pulse to combine. Add the butter and pulse until it resembles small peas. Add the ice water, 1 tablespoon at a time, and almond extract, and process just until the dough comes together and forms a ball around the blades. (Do not overprocess.) Remove the dough from the processor, wrap it in plastic wrap, and chill at least 30 minutes or overnight (or freeze up to 2 months).

3. Place a rack in the upper third of the oven and preheat to 375°.

4. Make the filling: Place the peach slices in a large bowl. In a small bowl, stir together the granulated sugar, cornstarch, and cinnamon until well blended. Add the sugar mixture to the peaches, stirring gently.

5. Turn the dough out onto a floured pastry cloth or surface and roll into a 16-inch circle using a floured rolling pin. Fold it in half, transfer to an ungreased 10-inch cast iron skillet, and gently unfold the pastry, fitting it into the bottom of the pan and allowing the excess pastry to hang over the edge. (Don't bother to trim the dough—any unevenness adds to the rustic quality of the tart.)

6. Spoon the peach mixture into the pastry, mounding it in the middle. Gently fold the edges of the pastry up around the filling, overlapping them in soft folds. Take care that the pastry doesn't tear around the edge of the tart or the juices will escape during baking.

7. Whisk together the egg and water in a small bowl. Brush the egg wash over the pastry and sprinkle it with the turbinado sugar. Bake until the pastry is golden brown and the fruit is hot and bubbly, 35 to 40 minutes. Let cool for 1 hour to set the juices and serve warm.

Before the earnest heat of summer sets in, a cold snap happens in Tennessee called blackberry winter; the old timers say the colder the snap, the sweeter the berries. Jane Gaither, who blogs at *Gourmet Gadget Gal*, says "My family homeplace at the edge of the Smoky Mountains is covered with raspberry and blackberry brambles, and we pick, can, freeze, and eat them year-round." Her berry cobbler recipe uses raspberries but you can use any type of berry or peaches. Be sure to serve it warm with vanilla ice cream.

SIMPLE BERRY SKILLET COBBLER

serves 6 to 8

1 (10-ounce) package frozen raspberries or 1 pint fresh berries

1 cup granulated sugar

½ cup firmly packed brown sugar

½ cup plus 2 tablespoons all-purpose flour

2 tablespoons fresh lemon juice

½ teaspoon ground nutmeg

¼ cup (½ stick) butter

¼ teaspoon baking powder

¼ teaspoon salt

½ cup milk

1. Place a 10-inch cast iron skillet in the oven and preheat oven to 350°.

2. Stir together the raspberries, ½ cup granulated sugar, the brown sugar, 2 tablespoons flour, the lemon juice, and nutmeg in a medium bowl.

3. Melt the butter in the skillet in the oven until it starts to brown around the edge and foam. It's important to have the butter sizzling hot!

4. While the butter is melting, stir together the remaining ½ cup flour and granulated sugar, the baking powder, salt, and milk in a large bowl, just until combined. The batter may still have a few lumps, but it should be about the consistency of pancake batter.

5. Pour the batter over the butter in the hot skillet. Do not stir. Immediately spoon the berry mixture on top of the batter. Bake until the crust looks golden and crisp, 30 to 35 minutes.

CHERRY CLAFOUTI

serves 12

The batter for this traditional French dessert is somewhere between that of a cake and a custard; it most resembles a thick crêpe, and it takes no more than 10 minutes to prepare it in the blender. Adapted from a recipe in *You Can Trust a Skinny Cook* by Allison Fishman, this gorgeous dessert can be made, baked, cooled, garnished, and ready to eat in one hour.

1   tablespoon butter
6   large eggs
1¼ cups milk
½   cup granulated sugar
2   tablespoons brandy
1   tablespoon vanilla extract
¼   teaspoon salt

⅔   cup all-purpose flour
1   pint black cherries (2 heaping cups), stemmed, or
    1 (12-ounce) package frozen cherries, thawed
Confectioners' sugar for serving

1. Preheat the oven to 400°. Generously coat a 10-inch cast iron skillet with the butter.
2. Process the eggs and next 5 ingredients in a blender until well blended. Add the flour and process until smooth and well blended.
3. Scatter the cherries in the prepared skillet and pour the batter over them. Bake until puffed and golden, about 30 minutes. Lightly dust with confectioners' sugar before serving, if desired.

NEW ORLEANS PRALINES

makes 24 pralines

Barbara Gonce Clepper recalls, "When we lived in New Orleans in the early seventies, we always enjoyed watching the cooks making pralines in the candy shops."

1½ cups granulated sugar
1½ cups firmly packed brown sugar
1   cup evaporated milk
¼   cup (½ stick) butter

2   cups pecan halves, toasted on a baking sheet in a 350° oven until fragrant (about 8 minutes), then chopped
1 teaspoon vanilla extract

1. In a large cast iron Dutch oven or the fryer of a Lodge Combo Cooker, stir together both sugars and the evaporated milk, and bring to a boil. Reduce the heat to medium and cook, stirring often, until a candy thermometer registers 234° (soft ball stage), about 10 minutes.
2. Remove the pan from the heat. Stir in the butter, pecans, and vanilla. Beat with a wooden spoon until the mixture begins to thicken, about 2 minutes. Quickly drop by heaping tablespoonfuls onto buttered wax paper or a slab of marble. Let the pralines stand until firm, about 20 minutes. Store in an airtight container, separating the layers with wax paper.

Cherry Clafouti

a cast iron memory

When I was growing up, my mom ruled the kitchen. She did the lion's share of the cooking and, since it was a small kitchen, I was usually shooed out of it.

Throughout college and thereafter, she received a lot of "How do I make _____?" phone calls from me. But when I graduated from culinary school, my mom came down with a case of kitchen amnesia. Almost overnight, she forgot how to roast a chicken, make her famous lemon meringue pie, and any time she was invited for a potluck, she turned to me for a recipe. Maybe she was humoring me, or perhaps she just wanted a reason to call; we now lived hundreds of miles apart.

Our "Mom, how do I…" conversations were now going both ways.

One spring, after my mom made the trip up north to visit me, I served clafouti in a cast iron skillet. The moment I set the skillet on the table, she asked for the recipe. When I gave it to her, I gave her my cast iron skillet as well, as the presentation is as memorable as the flavor.

And now, every spring, when fresh cherries arrive in the grocery store, my mom and I make this French dessert in our American cast iron skillets. This family tradition was handed up a generation, which gives us a chance to enjoy it together, though we're hundreds of miles apart. —Allison Fishman

Patsy, the wife of former South Pittsburg, Tennessee, mayor Robert Sherrill, makes this fudge every Christmas from a recipe given to her by her favorite aunt, Nadine Gibson Mayfield. Nadine had always been special to Patsy, and after the death of Patsy's mother, she helped her with all her cooking questions.

PEANUT BUTTER FUDGE

makes 20 to 30 pieces

3 cups sugar	Dash of salt
3 tablespoons light corn syrup	3 tablespoons peanut butter
1 cup evaporated milk	1 teaspoon vanilla extract
½ cup (1 stick) butter or	
margarine	

1. Stir together the sugar, corn syrup, evaporated milk, butter, salt, and peanut butter in a medium cast iron Dutch oven or in the fryer of a Lodge Combo Cooker. Cook over medium heat, stirring often, until the sugar dissolves.

2. Increase the heat to medium-high and bring to a boil. Boil until a candy thermometer registers 234° (soft ball stage).

3. Add the vanilla and beat vigorously with an electric mixer until the gloss is gone. Pour into 2 buttered 8-inch square glass baking dishes. Let the fudge sit at room temperature for about 1 hour before cutting into pieces.

Barbara Raulston Russell used to make this brittle from peanuts she and her husband grew on their farm in Anderson, Tennessee, from 1907 through the 1950s.

DIXIE PEANUT BRITTLE

makes about 1½ pounds brittle

2 cups sugar	3 cups shelled raw peanuts
1 cup light corn syrup	with skins (about 1 pound)
½ cup water	2 tablespoons butter
½ teaspoon salt	2 teaspoons baking soda

1. Bring the sugar, corn syrup, water, and salt to a rolling boil in a medium cast iron Dutch oven or the fryer of a Lodge Combo Cooker. Add the peanuts. Reduce the heat to medium and, stirring constantly, cook until a candy thermometer registers 293°.

2. Remove the pan from the heat. Add the butter and baking soda. Beat the mixture rapidly, then pour it out onto a buttered surface, spreading it to ¼-inch thickness. Let cool completely; break into pieces. Store in an airtight container.

This recipe, a variation of one in her book *Batter Up Kids Delicious Desserts* cookbook, is from best-selling cookbook author and kids' cooking expert Barbara Beery, the founder of Batter Up Kids, Inc. "Kids adore giant cookie 'cakes' for birthday and team sport parties," says Barbara. Baking it in a cast iron pan is an easy way to keep the cookie perfectly round.

GIANT COOKIE-IN-A-PAN

makes 1 giant cookie; 16 slices

1 cup firmly packed light brown sugar	2 large eggs
½ cup granulated sugar	2½ cups all-purpose flour
1 cup (2 sticks) unsalted butter, softened	1 teaspoon baking soda
	1 teaspoon salt
1 teaspoon vanilla extract	2 cups chocolate chips
	Assorted M&M's or sprinkles

1. Preheat the oven to 375°.

2. In a large bowl, using an electric mixer, beat both sugars and the butter until smooth. Beat in the vanilla. Add the eggs, one at a time, beating well after each addition. Add the flour, baking soda, and salt. Stir well with a wooden spoon. The dough will be stiff. Stir in the chocolate chips.

3. Spray a 10-inch cast iron skillet with cooking spray. Pat the cookie dough evenly into the skillet and decorate the surface with M&M's or sprinkles. Bake until the edges are lightly browned, about 30 minutes.

4. Remove the skillet from the oven and let cool on a wire rack for 15 minutes. Cut the cookie into 16 wedges and serve it directly from the skillet using a pie server.

Buttermilk Drop Biscuits

BUTTERMILK DROP BISCUITS

makes 7 biscuits

2 cups all-purpose flour	¼ teaspoon baking soda
1 tablespoon baking powder	½ cup butter, margarine, or
2 teaspoons sugar	vegetable shortening
½ teaspoon cream of tartar	1¼ cups buttermilk
¼ teaspoon salt	

1. Preheat the oven to 450°. Grease the wells of a Lodge Drop Biscuit Pan with shortening.

2. Stir together the dry ingredients in a medium bowl. Cut in the butter with a pastry blender or fork until the mixture resembles coarse crumbs. Add the buttermilk and stir just until blended.

3. Drop the dough into the prepared biscuit pan. (The wells will be quite full.) Bake until browned on top, about 20 minutes.

Variation: Add 2 tablespoons finely shredded carrots, 1 tablespoon chopped fresh parsley, and/or 1 tablespoon chopped green onions when you add the buttermilk.

This very simple, old-fashioned recipe from Marilyn Geraldson works only with cast iron and is for all Southerners who love their biscuits. In the 1990s, Marilyn assisted in the selection of recipes to be included with Lodge bakeware.

BLUSHING DROP BISCUITS

makes 7 biscuits

2 cups sifted all-purpose flour	⅓ cup vegetable shortening
2½ teaspoons baking powder	1 cup tomato juice
1 teaspoon salt	

1. Place a Lodge Drop Biscuit Pan in the oven as it preheats to 450°.

2. Sift together the flour, baking powder, and salt into a medium bowl. Add the shortening and cut it in with a pastry blender or fork until the mixture resembles cornmeal. Stir in the tomato juice.

3. Spray the wells with cooking spray before filling. Drop the dough (about ⅓ cup per well) into the hot biscuit pan. Bake until browned, 15 to 17 minutes.

Bacon Biscuits: Add crumbled crisp-cooked bacon to the biscuit dough.

Curried Biscuits: Add ½ teaspoon curry powder to the sifted dry ingredients.

According to Youngie Plaster, who got this recipe from a friend, these biscuits are good with a slice of roast beef in the middle.

This recipe is from Anna Blackmon Dean, by way of Helen Clay, who got it from her mother, Fanny Clay. Mrs. Dean made these rolls for Helen's brother, Fredrick, who loved them so much that he asked for the recipe for his mother. The original recipe called for the rolls to be baked in a wood stove.

QUICK ROLLS

makes about 14 rolls

3 cups all-purpose flour, plus more as needed
1 teaspoon salt
2 teaspoons sugar
2 teaspoons baking powder
½ teaspoon baking soda
1 cup buttermilk

1 (¼-ounce) envelope active dry yeast, dissolved in ½ cup warm (110° to 115°) water
2 tablespoons vegetable shortening, melted and cooled

1. Generously grease a 10-inch cast iron skillet. Combine the first 5 ingredients in a large bowl. Add the buttermilk, dissolved yeast, and melted shortening and mix well. Add more flour if you'd like a stiffer dough.

2. Turn the dough onto a lightly floured surface and knead lightly, just until the dough no longer feels sticky. Roll the dough into a rectangle of your desired thickness. With a biscuit cutter, cut the dough as closely together as possible; be sure not to twist the cutter as you cut down, as those rolls won't rise as high. Pat the scraps together and repeat. Place the rolls in the greased skillet and cover with a lightly greased sheet of wax paper. Let rise in a warm room for 1 hour.

3. Preheat the oven to 425°. Bake the rolls until browned on top, 12 to 15 minutes. Serve immediately.

SPOON ROLLS

makes about 14 rolls

1 (¼-ounce) envelope active
  dry yeast
2 cups warm (110° to115°)
  water
¼ cup sugar

1 large egg, beaten
¼ cup (1½ sticks) margarine
  or butter, melted
4 cups self-rising flour

1. Preheat the oven to 400°. Grease 2 Lodge Drop Biscuit pans or
cast iron muffin pans.

2. In a large bowl, dissolve the yeast in the warm water and let it sit
until it swells. Stir in the remaining ingredients. Spoon the batter
into the prepared pans, filling the wells half to two-thirds full. Bake
until browned, about 20 minutes. Serve immediately.

a cast iron memory

Sarah A. Lodge contributes this
recipe from her mother, Sarah
Kirkwood "Pat" Lodge, with this
remembrance: Mother showed her
love through cooking, as do many
women (especially Southern ones, I
think). She was neither a 'gourmet'
cook nor a 'foodie.' Rather, cooking was a natural extension of her
most gracious hospitality—whether
cooking for her children and
grandchildren or for a house full
of church folks. I imagine she got
tired of making Daddy's sandwiches
(although she would never admit
it), but otherwise she was happiest
in the kitchen and dining room
preparing for the next meal or cel-
ebration. This was simply her way,
and she did it with love and grace.

Brother Anselm Clark was a monk with a baking background, trained at the Culinary Institute of America in New Haven, Connecticut. He resided at the Marion Mission for several years across the Tennessee River from South Pittsburg, hometown of Lodge. His bread baking came to be greatly anticipated by all.

BROTHER ANSELM'S POPOVERS

makes 12 popovers

1 cup sifted all-purpose flour	1 cup milk
¼ teaspoon salt	1 tablespoon butter, melted
2 large eggs	

1. Preheat oven to 425°. Grease 2 (6-cup) cast iron muffin pans with shortening and place them in the oven for 10 minutes as it preheats.

2. Combine the flour and salt in a medium bowl. In a small bowl, beat the eggs until foamy; add milk, stirring to combine. Gradually add the milk mixture to flour mixture, stirring just until blended. Stir in the melted butter.

3. Fill the wells of the prepared muffin pans two-thirds full with batter. Bake until browned, 32 to 35 minutes. They should have hollow centers when they come out of the oven. Turn them over and make a split in the bottom. At the table, fill the centers with gravy or jelly, depending on the meal. (Or you can simply dollop the gravy or jelly on top.)

Popovers with Horseradish Sauce: Prepare popovers as directed, adding a dash of Worcestershire sauce and a pinch of dillweed to the batter. When they come out of the oven, slit them on the bottom and fill them with Horseradish Sauce: Combine *1 cup sour cream, 2 tablespoons prepared horseradish, 1 chopped green onion, ¼ teaspoon Texas Pete hot sauce, ¼ teaspoon salt,* and *¼ teaspoon freshly ground black pepper* in a small bowl. Refrigerate sauce until ready to serve.

CRUSTY WHITE PEASANT-STYLE POT BREAD

makes 1 large loaf; 12 to 14 slices

This hearty white boule (and its rosemary- and olive-flavored variation on page 281) is one of Nancy Baggett's favorites, adapted from her cookbook *Kneadlessly Simple: Fabulous, Fuss-Free, No-Knead Breads*. It has a beautiful crusty top, a slightly holey, creamy-soft interior, and deep, sweet yeast taste and aroma. Be sure to use fast-rising, instant, or bread machine yeast; regular active dry yeast doesn't perform well when combined with cold water. (Using cold water improves the flavor and texture of the finished bread.)

4	cups (20 ounces) unbleached all-purpose flour or white bread flour, plus more as needed
1	teaspoon sugar
2	teaspoons salt

¾	teaspoon instant, fast-rising, or bread-machine yeast
2	cups ice water, plus more if needed
	Corn oil or canola oil cooking spray

1. Stir together the flour, sugar, salt, and yeast in a large bowl. Vigorously stir the water into the bowl, scraping down the side and mixing until the ingredients are thoroughly blended. If the mixture is too dry to incorporate all the flour, stir in more water, a little bit at a time—just enough to blend the ingredients. Don't overmoisten; the dough should be stiff enough so that it holds its shape but does not look dry. If necessary, stir in enough additional flour to yield a stiffer, hard-to-stir but not dry dough. Brush or spray the top with oil. Cover the bowl with plastic wrap. If desired, for best flavor or for convenience, you can refrigerate the dough for 3 to 10 hours; this is entirely optional. Let rise at cool room temperature for 18 to 24 hours; this is required. If convenient, vigorously stir the dough once about halfway through the rise.

2. Using an oiled rubber spatula, gently lift and fold the dough in toward the center, all the way around, until mostly deflated; don't stir. Brush or spray the surface with oil. Cover the bowl with plastic wrap coated with cooking spray. Let rise using any of these methods: for a 1½- to 2½-hour regular rise, let stand at warm room temperature; for a 1- to 2-hour accelerated rise, let stand in a turned-off microwave oven along with 1 cup of boiling-hot water; or, for an extended rise, refrigerate, covered, for 4 to 24 hours, then set out at room temperature. Continue the rise until the dough doubles in size from the deflated size; remove the plastic if the dough nears it.

3. Twenty minutes before baking time, put a rack in the lower third of the oven; preheat oven to 450°. Heat a 3½- to 4-quart (or larger) cast iron Dutch oven or similar pot in the oven until sizzling hot (test with a few drops of water), then remove it, using heavy mitts. Spritz the pot interior with cooking spray. Taking care not to deflate the dough (or burn yourself), loosen the dough from the side of the bowl with an oiled rubber spatula and gently invert it into the pot. Don't worry if it's lopsided and ragged-looking; it will even out during baking. Generously spritz or brush the top with water. Immediately top with the lid. Shake the pot back and forth to center the dough.

4. Reduce the oven temperature to 425°. Bake on the lower rack for 55 minutes. Remove the lid. Bake until the top is well browned and a wooden skewer inserted into the thickest portion comes out with just a few crumbs on the tip (or until the center registers 209° to 212° on an instant-read thermometer), another 15 to 20 minutes. When it seems done, bake 5 minutes longer to ensure the center is baked through. Cool in the pan on a wire rack for 10 to 15 minutes. Remove the loaf to the rack and cool thoroughly; run a table knife around the edge, if necessary, to loosen.

5. Cut or tear the loaf into portions; it tastes good warm but will cut much better when cool. Cool completely before storing. To maintain the crisp crust, store draped with a clean tea towel or in a heavy paper bag. Or store in an airtight plastic bag or wrapped in aluminum foil: The crust will soften, but can be crisped by heating the loaf, uncovered, in a 400° oven for a few minutes. The bread will keep at room temperature for 3 days, and may be frozen, airtight, for up to 2 months.

Crusty Black Olive and Rosemary Peasant-Style Pot Bread:
This recipe is made exactly the same way, except it calls for kalamata olives and rosemary. In step 1, when you add the water, also add *1 cup well-drained, coarsely chopped, pitted kalamata olives* and *3 tablespoons finely chopped fresh (not dried) rosemary.* Note that you need fresh, not dried, rosemary—the fresh not only has more vibrant flavor, but its texture is more tender and succulent. Also, be sure to use the very flavorful imported kalamata olives and not the milder, more readily available ones. Proceed with the recipe as directed above. Due to the olives and herbs, this loaf seems slightly moister and more substantial than the white loaf. It's also a bit larger and heavier, though not at all dense. Enjoy it with any hearty soup or an Italian-style meal. See photograph on page 282.

 tip

This dough usually doesn't stick to a seasoned plain or enameled cast iron pan, but if you aren't sure about yours and don't want to take any chances, spritz the interior with a little corn oil or canola oil cooking spray *immediately* before you turn out the dough into it.

the joy of kneadless "pot breads"

Nancy Baggett, *baking expert and author of* Kneadlessly Simple: Fabulous, Fuss-Free, No-Knead Breads, *gives us the inside scoop on how knead-free breads work and why they taste so good.*

Crusty, peasant-style yeast loaves called "pot breads" are the rage—and no wonder! With just a plain or enameled cast iron pot and a simple yeast dough that you don't even have to knead or shape, you can make fragrant, wonderfully crisp-crusted round loaves that are infinitely better than most store-bought ones.

Crusty Black Olive and Rosemary Peasant-Style Pot Bread, page 281

How are these amazingly good yet "kneadless" yeast breads possible? Kneading can be bypassed because the natural bubbling action of the yeast during a long, cool rise actually does the kneading for you. The gas bubbles created by the yeast move the dough around, slowly "kneading" it on the molecular level in much the same way as the traditional pulling and pushing action does more quickly. Besides eliminating the countertop muss and fuss of kneading, the long, slow rise also allows time for the dough to develop a rich, soul-satisfying aroma and complex flavor that can't be achieved with the usual quicker rise.

Having a heavy, good-quality 3½- to 4-quart cast iron Dutch oven or similarly shaped pot is the other secret to these remarkable breads. (Both the Lodge Logic Combo Cooker and 4-quart L-Series enameled Dutch ovens are the perfect size, because they form an attractive, homey-looking, domed loaf. In larger pots, the loaves tend to flatten out too much.) Even more important, this type of pot distributes heat evenly and traps steam inside during baking, which produces the prettiest, crustiest, crispest top possible without having access to a powerful steam-jetted commercial bread oven and a baker's dough-shaping skills. It's no wonder that pot breads are so wildly popular.

So, grab that pot, and use the recipes on pages 280-281 to turn out what will likely be both the best and the easiest yeast breads you've ever made!

Maggie Doherty was cookbook author Peggy Fallon's mother, who swore by cast iron when it came to her soda bread (see Peggy's A Cast Iron Memory, at right).

MAGGIE DOHERTY'S IRISH SODA BREAD

makes one (9-inch) round loaf

4	cups all-purpose flour	2	cups raisins (preferably 1 cup each golden and dark raisins)
3	tablespoons sugar		
1	teaspoon baking soda	2	cups buttermilk
1	teaspoon salt	1	large egg, lightly beaten

1. Preheat the oven to 375°. Generously grease a 9-inch cast iron skillet with vegetable shortening.

2. Combine the flour, sugar, baking soda, and salt in a large bowl; whisk gently to blend. Stir in the raisins to coat with the flour mixture. Make a well in the center and add the buttermilk and egg; stir until a stiff dough forms. (Use a wooden spoon if you must, but the most efficient way to mix this soft, sticky dough is with floured hands. Alternatively, the dough can be mixed in a heavy-duty stand mixer fitted with the dough hook.)

3. Remove the dough from the bowl and mound it into the prepared skillet, roughly forming a round loaf. (Don't be concerned that it won't hold its shape; it will be corrected during baking.) Lightly moisten your hands with water to smooth the top. Using a serrated knife dipped in flour, score the top with a large X, about ½-inch deep. (This will ensure even baking, and it will also scare away the devil, according to Peggy's mother.) Bake until the loaf is golden brown with a firm crust and the bottom sounds hollow when tapped with a knife, about 1 hour.

4. Remove the bread from the skillet and let cool on a wire rack at least 30 minutes before cutting into ½-inch-thick slices. Serve warm, at room temperature, or toasted, with or without butter.

a cast iron memory

When my mother emigrated from Ireland to the U.S. in 1929, she brought along her family's recipe for Irish soda bread. Over the years, she tweaked the recipe a bit, as cooks often do, but one thing remained the same: She always baked it in a cast iron skillet.

I remember a family member once gave her a professional-quality cake pan, implying that my mother should catch up with the times. Those anemic soda breads lacked soul (not to mention the crispy crust), and she soon reverted to her beloved skillet.

My mother has passed on, but her soda bread is still part of every family gathering. And to this day, I bake her recipe in a cast iron skillet. —Peggy Fallon

CARING FOR CAST IRON

All of the cast iron that Lodge sells (not including their enameled line, of course) is preseasoned at the foundry, using vegetable oil. As a result, seasoning the pan, the traditional first step in cast iron cookware ownership, is now not necessary. But your preseasoned cookware still benefits from correct care. Here's what to do:

1. Rinse your cast iron cookware with hot water. If there is any stuck-on food, use a stiff brush to remove it. Do not use soap, as any type of detergent will break down the oil-based seasoning.

2. After rinsing, dry the cookware immediately inside and out. If water remains on the surface, rusting can occur, even with a seasoned piece.

3. While the piece is still warm from being washed, use cooking spray or a paper towel soaked with melted vegetable shortening to give the interior and exterior surfaces of the pan (including the underside of the lid if the piece has one) a light coating of oil.

4. Store in a cool, dry place. If the piece has a lid, folded paper towels should be placed between the lid and pot to allow air to circulate.

WHEN YOU NEED TO RE-SEASON A PAN

It happens sometimes—a friend helpfully puts your cast iron skillet in the dishwasher without you knowing it or takes a Brillo pad to it, stripping the seasoning from its surface. Or you inherit or acquire an older piece of cast iron that needs refurbishing. Here's how to do it:

1. Preheat the oven to 350°. If you have three racks in the oven, remove one and move the others so they are in the two lowest positions.

2. Prepare the piece for re-seasoning by washing it in hot, soapy water, using a stiff brush to remove any stuck-on food. If the pan has surface rust, remove it using fine steel wool or an abrasive soap pad such as Brillo or S.O.S. (If a piece is severely rusted, you'll need to take it to a local machine shop to have it sandblasted. It will then need to be re-seasoned IMMEDIATELY.) Rinse and towel-dry the pan immediately and thoroughly.

3. Coat the piece with oil as instructed in step 3 above, making sure to also include the handle.

4. Place a large sheet of aluminum foil on the lowest oven rack. Set the pan upside down on the rack above it. Bake for 1 hour.

5. If the piece has a lid, set it beside the pan. Close the oven door, turn off the oven, and leave until the pieces cool off. Store as directed above.

METRIC EQUIVALENTS

The recipes that appear in this cookbook use the standard United States method for measuring liquid and dry or solid ingredients (teaspoons, tablespoons, and cups). The information on this chart is provided to help cooks outside the U.S. successfully use these recipes. All equivalents are approximate.

Metric Equivalents for Different Types of Ingredients

A standard cup measure of a dry or solid ingredient will vary in weight depending on the type of ingredient. A standard cup of liquid is the same volume for any type of liquid. Use the following chart when converting standard cup measures to grams (weight) or milliliters (volume).

Standard Cup	Fine Powder (ex. flour)	Grain (ex. rice)	Granular (ex. sugar)	Liquid Solids (ex. butter)	Liquid (ex. milk)
1	140 g	150 g	190 g	200 g	240 ml
¾	105 g	113 g	143 g	150 g	180 ml
⅔	93 g	100 g	125 g	133 g	160 ml
½	70 g	75 g	95 g	100 g	120 ml
⅓	47 g	50 g	63 g	67 g	80 ml
¼	35 g	38 g	48 g	50 g	60 ml
⅛	18 g	19 g	24 g	25 g	30 ml

Useful Equivalents for Liquid Ingredients by Volume

¼ tsp					=	1 ml	
½ tsp					=	2 ml	
1 tsp					=	5 ml	
3 tsp	=	1 Tbsp		=	½ fl oz =	15 ml	
		2 Tbsp	=	⅛ cup	= 1 fl oz =	30 ml	
		4 Tbsp	=	¼ cup	= 2 fl oz =	60 ml	
		5⅓ Tbsp	=	⅓ cup	= 3 fl oz =	80 ml	
		8 Tbsp	=	½ cup	= 4 fl oz =	120 ml	
		10⅔ Tbsp	=	⅔ cup	= 5 fl oz =	160 ml	
		12 Tbsp	=	¾ cup	= 6 fl oz =	180 ml	
		16 Tbsp	=	1 cup	= 8 fl oz =	240 ml	
		1 pt	=	2 cups	= 16 fl oz =	480 ml	
		1 qt	=	4 cups	= 32 fl oz =	960 ml	
					33 fl oz =	1000 ml	= 1 l

Useful Equivalents for Dry Ingredients by Weight

(To convert ounces to grams, multiply the number of ounces by 30.)

1 oz	=	1/16 lb	=	30 g
4 oz	=	¼ lb	=	120 g
8 oz	=	½ lb	=	240 g
12 oz	=	¾ lb	=	360 g
16 oz	=	1 lb	=	480 g

Useful Equivalents for Length

(To convert inches to centimeters, multiply the number of inches by 2.5.)

1 in				=	2.5 cm	
6 in	=	½ ft		=	15 cm	
12 in	=	1 ft		=	30 cm	
36 in	=	3 ft	= 1 yd	=	90 cm	
40 in				=	100 cm	= 1 m

Useful Equivalents for Cooking/Oven Temperatures

	Fahrenheit	Celsius	Gas Mark
Freeze water	32° F	0° C	
Room temperature	68° F	20° C	
Boil water	212° F	100° C	
Bake	325° F	160° C	3
	350° F	180° C	4
	375° F	190° C	5
	400° F	200° C	6
	425° F	220° C	7
	450° F	230° C	8
Broil			Grill

INDEX